# Crossings

*Self-portrait of Leo Saal, 1957.*

# Crossings

## A LIFE IN RUSSIA & GERMANY
## IN THE FIRST HALF
## OF THE 20TH CENTURY

*Leo R. Saal*

*with Marilyn H. Heilprin*

Chronos Press
Washington, D.C.

Printed in the United States of America.

Paintings and drawings by Leo Saal.
Book design by Sandy Harpe.

Excerpts from *Crossings* were published in *The Journal of Contemporary History*, October 1993.

Published by Chronos Press
Washington, D.C.

Distributed by Dryad Press
15 Sherman Avenue
Takoma Park, Maryland 20912

Library of Congress Card Catalog Number: 95-083400
ISBN 0-931-848-91-1

*For my children*

*Irene Holmes, Christine Losq, Stefan Saal, and Peter Saal*

*and in memory of their mother*

*Rosemarie Fabian Saal*

# Table of Contents

# CAST OF CHARACTERS

## *Family*

**Eilers, Hermann ("Old Eilers" or "Uncle Hermann"):** author's great grand uncle; b. East Frisia, Germany, in 1830s; hired in 1860 as chief gardener by Prince Yusupov for his St. Petersburg estates; proprietor of the "New World," the renowned nurseries in St. Petersburg; d. 1917 on his estate in Finland. His eight children included Constantin and Erica (first married Eugene Salome and then Captain Nicol)

**Saal, Else:** author's mother; née Seeger, b. 1886 in Soest, Germany; married 1910 in Göttingen; lived in Russia 1910-42; exiled to Kazakhstan 1935-40; d. Bremen in 1965.

**Saal, Hermann:** author's father; b. 1884 in Petersburg; d. 1932 in exile in Alma Ata.

**Saal, Ira:** author's sister; b. 1918 in Petrograd; exiled to Kazakhstan 1935-36 and again 1942-56; resides with son Lev and his family in Yoshkar-Ola, east of the Volga River.

**Saal, Irina:** author's first wife 1936 to 1943; b. 1917 in Krasnoyarsk; mother of Andrey ("Andryusha") Saal, b. July 1938; d. April 1940.

> **Maria Gerasimovna:** Irina's mother.

> **"Papa Misha":** second husband of Maria Gerasimovna; a former Czarist naval officer.

> **"Aunt Zina":** distant relative of Irina's who shared her Moscow room following the arrest of Irina's parents.

> **"Aunt Nina":** sister of Irina's mother; translator of French literature.

**Saal, Rosemarie, née Fabian:** author's second wife; b. 1921 in Berlin; d. 1976 in Baltimore.

**Saal, Jacob:** author's grandfather; b. 1853 in Estonia; assistant and companion to Hermann Eilers; married Johanna Dedeke, Old Eilers' niece, in 1880; emigrated to Estonia in 1921; d. 1936 in Tallin.

**Saal, Vera:** sister of Hermann Saal; b. 1896 in Petersburg; married Rolf Schmiedeberg in 1918; emigrated to Estonia in 1921; resettled to Posen in 1940; d. 1979 in Heidelberg.

**Schmiedeberg, Rolf:** husband of Vera Saal and father of Edith Schmiedeberg; emigrated from Petrograd to Estonia in 1921; d. 1932 in Tallin.

### Family Friends

**Becker, Isadore:** tenor singer and head of engineering translation office in Leningrad; supported Else Saal during her years of exile in Kazakhstan.

**Blumenfeld, Robert:** schoolmate of Hermann Saal and author's godfather; Legal Counsel to the German Consulate 1921-1932.

**Blumenfeld, Alfred:** son of Robert Blumenfeld; author's friend and schoolmate; b. 1912 in Petersburg; left Russia for Berlin 1928; served with Embassy of the Federal Republic of Germany in Moscow and was Consul-General in Leningrad in the 1960s and 70s.

**Holl, Albrecht:** b. in Bavaria; businessman in Russia 1910-1932; married Martha Schotte in 1918; killed in Berlin May 1945.

**Holl, Martha (née Schotte):** friend of author's mother; mother of Ernst, Gudrun, and Roderick; left Leningrad for Germany in 1932; d. in Berlin in 1970s.

**Schotte, Fritz:** schoolmate of Hermann Saal; proprietor, with British-born wife, Rhoda, of the Grand Hotel and Hotel d'Angleterre in St. Petersburg.

**Wegerer, Eugene:** German businessman in Russia 1910-1930s; lived in Saal apartment 1926-32.

### Childhood Friends

**Aleka:** graduated with author from Petri School in Petersburg in 1928.

**Andrey (Andrey Behrens):** filmmaker; arrested and exiled 1933; fate unknown.

**Harry (Harry Pufahl):** son of Elizabeth née "Lieschen" Schotte; sister of Martha Schotte; graduated from Petri School 1929; arrested and exiled in 1933; fate unknown.

**Kolya (Nikolai Kruger):** fellow Bamlag (Baikal-Amur Labor Camp) inmate with author, artist; d. 1938 in Tashkent.

**Orest (Orest Vereyskiy):** b. 1915; close friend and well-known Soviet graphic artist; d. 1994 in Moscow.

**Volik (Vladimir Fesenko):** author's best friend; b. 1911 in Kronstadt, Russia; arrested 1933 and perished 1938 in Gulag Archipelago; son of Iosif Ivanovich Fesenko and Dagmara Ernestovna née Hilbich.

**Vronskiy, William:** fellow Bamlag inmate; news reporter and former petty criminal with whom author stayed in Kalinin following prison discharge.

**Werner (Werner Christiani):** author's friend and mentor; husband of Aleka 1929-31; secret police informer.

### Others

**Belskiy:** Chief of Bamlag Culture and Education Department.

**Berman, Matvey:** Chief of Gulag.

**Dikiy:** Chief of Bamlag Third Department.

**Frankel, Naftaliy A.:** Chief of the BAM (Baikal-Amur Mainline) Project.

**Goldin, Oscar and Nadya:** shared Saal apartment 1926-1934; remained there until 1941.

**Levit, Captain:** Chief of Bamlag Skovorodino Project.

**Savenko, Saveliy and Maria:** Gulag filmmakers assigned to BAM Project.

**Schaak, Wilhelm Adolfovich:** author's next-door neighbor in Petersburg; dean of surgery at the Leningrad Medical School; befriended Ira Saal during her mother's exile 1936-41; evacuated with the Medical School in 1942 to North Caucasus and, upon occupation of the area by German Army, to Berlin; returned to Leningrad in 1946; d. in Leningrad some years later; daughters Tatiana and Michaela were best friends of Ira Saal.

**Weinschrot:** Austrian-born Chief of the Special Department of the Leningrad OGPU.

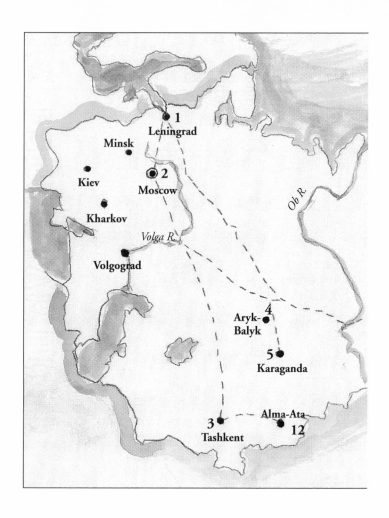

## MAP OF USSR

1 Leningrad (St. Petersburg) – author's home-town
2 Moscow – where author resided 1937-1941
3 Tashkent – where author stayed during summer of 1936
4 Aryk-Balyk – where author's mother was exiled 1935-1940
5 Karaganda – where author's sister Ira was exiled 1943-1956
6 Urulga – beginning of Bamlag
7 Tynda – northernmost point of Bamlag

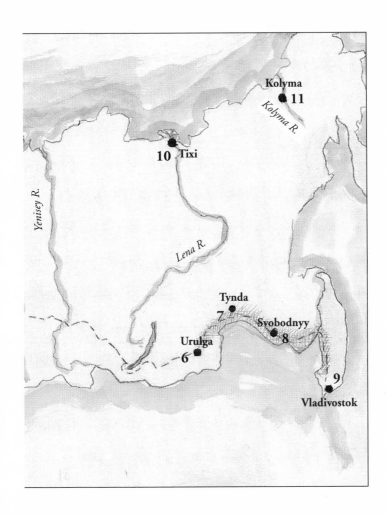

8  Svobodnyy – headquarters of Bamlag
9  Vladivostock – where film was developed
10 Tixi – where Rosanovs went in 1939 and wanted the
   author to join them
11 Kolyma – where Volik probably perished
12 Alma-Ata – where author's father died in exile

*Shaded area* – extent of Bamlag

*"Wartime," pen and ink drawing by the author, 1943.*

# Preface

"I only want to set down what I know of my own knowledge."

W. Somerset Maugham
*The Razor's Edge*

Russian writing during the years preceding World War II was mainly of two kinds: works which appeared in the West that were written by Russian émigrés who had left the country after the 1917 October Revolution, and works directed by Soviet government agencies and controlled by strict censorship. Many books have been written about Russia in recent years, but mostly by authors of the post-World War II generation. My own generation, which experienced both world wars in Russia, is fast disappearing; first-hand accounts of these times — the grains of history on which future historians can draw their observations and conclusions — will only remain in the common memory if committed to paper.

My main purpose is to record a piece of ordinary personal Russian history between 1917 and the 1940s on which relatively little authentic material is available, Nadezhda Mandelstam's books being a rare exception. The true story of this period was largely obscured by Soviet propaganda or reports by fellow travelers, i.e., Western intellectuals who visited the Soviet Union and filed glowing reports about the "land of the future." My account is based on memories of events and personal experiences; I have tried to describe events from the perspective of what I knew at the time they occurred and to avoid retrospective judgments. At the same time I have endeavored to provide some historical context for the reader.

The first part of the story is one of personal "roots" as well as a social history of the time. St. Petersburg in the early part of the century was an international center probably comparable only to New York. To have German or Swedish or Estonian or any other foreign roots did not prevent people from being Russians. After all, the Imperial Romanov family had no Russian ancestors since the late 18th century. Old photos of Petersburg's main avenue, the Nevskiy Prospekt, show business signs with names like Freundlich, Lutterman, Orenstein, Koppel, Pollack, Thonet, Lorens, Adolphe, Busch, Mandel, Blooker, Winter, Mellier, Singer, Konradi, Treuman, Albert, Shapiro. The roster of foreign names among the builders of the city and officers of the Russian army is equally extensive.

After the revolution, the 1920s and 1930s were years of "internationalism" and of the Comintern, later the Popular Front. Russian nationalism or patriotism, so strongly emphasized in contemporary writing, was born essentially in 1942 as a result of Hitler's policies. The three million Soviet prisoners taken in 1941 were not so much the result of German military proficiency as of the disinclination to fight by Soviet soldiers stationed in occupied Poland and the Baltic countries and by their officers who remembered the purges of 1938. Some of the more personal relationships described in the narrative illustrate the penetration of private lives by the Russian secret police.

My accounts of the Gulag, World War II, and postwar military intelligence are largely limited to my own experience. It would be futile to attempt to improve on Solzhenitsyn's *Gulag Archipelago*, Lev Kopelev's *To Be Kept Forever*, Paul Fussell's *Wartime*, or existing accounts of German-American postwar intelligence. Nor did I have the advantage of having kept a diary as did Jakob Walter in *The Diary of a Napoleonic Foot Soldier* or Marie Vassiltchikov in *Berlin Diaries 1940-1945.* Whatever letters, notes, sketches and drawings I possessed were lost in the last days of the war.

For the majority of soldiers in various support functions, the days of World War II were mostly days of tedious work and boredom. Civilians on the German home front were subjected to more "combat," i.e., bombings, than soldiers serving in the army's rear echelons. Wartime intelligence activities consisted primarily of the collection and collation of minute data on a need-to-know basis in a highly compartmentalized structure. Daily wartime intelligence came from the interrogation of prisoners and analysis of their documents, from aerial surveillance, and from listening to and decoding radio communications. The recruiting or selection of agents, their training and equipment, their assignments and deployment, their communication and its analysis, the debriefing in cases of their return, were all compartmentalized activities performed by individual staffs. While intelligence was a useful tool on the tactical level, it is common knowledge that important strategic conclusions were too often discounted by the supreme political authorities.

This writing would not have been possible without the encouragement and help of Marilyn Heilprin, Walter Laqueur, Katya Martinoff, Remi Clignet and Jeanne O'Connell. I also have appreciated the comments received from those who read earlier versions of the manuscript: Frederica Bunge, Warren Frank and Klemens v. Klemperer. Merrill Leffler and Sandy Harpe prepared the manuscript for publication.

# Foreword

I first met Leo Saal around 1980 and over the years he told me about his origins and his life. I was among those who encouraged him to put his remarkable story on paper. Saal was born in St. Petersburg in 1912 to a Russian-German family whose German branch came to Russia in the 1860s. His story is in many ways extraordinary, even against the background of a century abounding with uncommon and strange individual histories. In some ways it reminds the student of literature of Grimmelshausen's *Simplizissmus* (1669) about a child growing up during the Thirty Years War, uprooted, passing mostly by accident from one camp to another warring faction, German and French, Swedish and Croat. He describes in loving detail his childhood and adolescence in St. Petersburg. In view of his bourgeois background, he could not study at a university, but learned photography and filmmaking.

He was arrested for the first time in 1930 and again in 1933. He was sent to the Gulag where he worked as photographer for Naftaliy A. Frenkel, then head of BAM (Baikalo-Amurskaya Magistral). (Readers will find much detail about Frenkel and his ambitious projects in Solzhenitsyn's *Gulag Archipelago*.) Released on the eve of the great purges, he lived and worked illegally in Moscow, married and became a father. During this period, he was a construction supervisor on the Moscow-Volga Canal and an assistant to the architect Aleksander Pasternak. He became more and more interested in drawing and painting but could not follow his avocation at the time.

A brief stint in the Polish campaign of September 1939 was followed by mobilization as a civilian construction worker. In October 1941, near Vyazma, he found himself behind German lines and surrendered. When the Germans discovered that he was equally at home in Russian and German, he was eventually enlisted by *Fremde Heere Ost*, German military intelligence, in a technical capacity. At the end of the war, he and his German-born mother were reunited in Germany. Still later, he went to the United States and was employed by the intelligence community for twenty years. Upon his retirement, he realized at long last the dream of his youth — to devote his time to painting.

This is a story not of moods and introspection, not an analytical appraisal of world affairs in the twentieth century. It is a dispassionate account, written without embellishment and self-pity, by a survivor who happened to witness some of the most dramatic events of this century in Europe. As such I found it of absorbing interest and I am sure it will get a wide readership.

Walter Laqueur
Washington, October 1995

*View of Moscow courtyard from Saal apartment, 1939.*

# 1

# St. Petersburg

## CHILDHOOD

I was born a Russian national in the German Hospital on St. Petersburg's Vasiliy Island on May 7, 1912. My father, Hermann Vladimir Saal, was also born in St. Petersburg. My grandfather, Jacob Saal, was a Russian subject from Estonia. He was born in 1853 on the shores of the Baltic Sea which once belonged to the Swedes, then were conquered by Russia's Peter the Great when he defeated Charles of Sweden at the Battle of Poltava. Today these shores are called again Estonia.

I was told that Jacob was a descendent of fishermen who roamed the Baltic Sea for fish and bounty from stranded merchant ships. His forebears must have been poor since, as a child, Jacob was given to the family of a German teacher in the port city of Pernau, or Pernov, or Pyarnu, depending on the language used. There he learned the three Rs, the German language, and the trade of a gardener. He grew up trilingual: Estonian being the language of the land, Russian the language of the realm, and German the language spoken commonly in Baltic urban settlements whose skylines of predominantly Gothic spires, fortress towers, and steep gables bore witness to their Hanseatic origins. As a teenager, having learned his trade,

1

Jacob went East, first to a grand estate near Voronezh, later to Moscow, and then to St. Petersburg. In 1877, he was hired by Hermann Eilers who owned a nursery business. Jacob was then 24 years old; in 1880 he married Eilers' niece Johanna whom Eilers had brought from Germany to help in his business.

Eilers himself came to St. Petersburg from Germany on August 2, 1860. He was born in the 1830s near the Dutch border in a land called East Frisia. In a letter, which is in my possession, he remembered the famines of 1847-48 and 1854-55, the first one caused by a potato plague, the second because no ships with Russian rye from Odessa could reach Holland due to the Crimean War. He went to school at age six, but always preferred working in his mother's garden; already as a preschool boy he loved to dig and plant and sow and later even to propagate and cross-pollinate plant stock. At the age of 14 he was sent away from home to learn the nursery trade and, while working in Dresden in 1859, he was hired by the Russian Prince Yusupov to be a gardener at his estate in St. Petersburg. He arrived by ship from Stettin at Petersburg's Vasiliy Island in 1860 with forty kopeks left in his pocket after he had paid for drinks and tips on board the ship. Kalaush, the major domo of the Yusupov Palace, paid eighty kopeks for the *izvozchik* which brought young Hermann and his luggage to the palace. This was before the serfs were freed by Czar Alexander II in 1862.

In 1867, while still in Yusupov's employ, Eilers started his own business. With Gradke, another Petersburg nurseryman, he traveled to Germany, Holland, Belgium, and France to purchase nursery stock. He leased a store on fashionable Morskaya Street from Consoir, the pastry maker; he also rented a plot in the Prince's garden on Sadovaya Street to start a small nursery.

By 1879 Eilers had made his first 100,000 rubles. He bought the Stegeman nursery on Stone Island Prospekt and properties adjacent to it on Litseyskaya Street for 85,000 rubles. Here in 1887-88 he built his house and nurseries and called them "The New World." Twenty-five years later he sold the nurseries to the Rossiya Insurance Company for 1,470,000 rubles. On seventy-five acres, at the Vyborg Side, he built another "New World." It was the biggest nursery in Petersburg; a narrow-gauge rail line ran through half a mile of hothouses. He built a cold storage house — the first of its kind in Russia — to keep his beloved camellias, azaleas, and rhododendrons when they were dormant. He raised 50,000 roses. From Germany, Belgium, Holland, and Japan he imported flowers in great numbers, including 70,000 hyacinths, 35,000 tulips, and 5,000 white lilies annually. At his peak, he employed a staff of 200.

In 1873, Hermann Eilers had married Emma Osterthun, then 23 years old. She bore him eight children: August, Helen, Hermann, Margaret, Hajo, Emma, Constantin, and Erica. In 1910 old Eilers wrote to his youngest son Constantin:

> My business can give sustenance to many families for many generations to come and, although gardening and the nursery business are hard work, it is an activity [sic] where healthy people are in contact with beautiful nature, the observation of which induces people to work happily and to find satisfaction.... Russia is a country with a great future, and flowers and the nursery business have here a great future too.... And don't forget that your childrens' hearts and dreams do not look back towards Germany. Probably they feel more at home in Russia and will consider Russia to be their fatherland. And why not?

However, only his daughter Helen who married a Russian officer remained in Russia. His other descendents all left Russia either before or after World War I for Finland, Sweden, Germany, Africa, and Canada.

I remember my grandfather Jacob amid exotic plants behind the glittering plate glass window of the flower store, situated in the sedate elegance of fashionable Morskaya Street. The shop was only a short walk from Rossi's triumphal arches and the vast plaza of the Winter Palace where in its midst an angel stands on the 150-foot granite column, brought in one piece from distant Karelia.

His association with the firm of H.F. Eilers made my grandfather a member of the German colony of St. Petersburg. His four children all attended the German St. Petri School founded in 1712 by Admiral Cornelius Cruis to educate the children of shipbuilders and sailors whom Peter the Great had hired abroad; all subjects were taught in German. The students all studied Latin and Greek and became fluent in Russian, German, French, and English.

At the beginning of the twentieth century about 100,000 German nationals lived in St. Petersburg, of whom 12,000 were German citizens. The German colony maintained five Protestant and two Catholic churches, four schools, two hospitals, a home for the aged, and various associations. After World War I, the colony was reduced to about five thousand, among them four hundred German citizens.[1] In 1920 the Petri School was the only German language school still in existence.

After graduation from the Petri School, my father studied oriental languages both at the University of Petersburg and abroad. He met my mother on the occasion of a visit to his maternal relatives while taking a semester at the University of Göttingen, my mother's home town.

A 1908 photograph of the Saal family was taken during my mother's first visit to St. Petersburg. My parents married in

---

[1] *Osteuropa: Zeitschrift für Gegenwartsfragen des Ostens, Sonderdruck.* Stuttgart: Deutscher Verlag, 1990.

1910 in Göttingen. They made their home in St. Petersburg, "The Palmyra of the North," which promised the young couple the splendors of a brilliant capital enhanced by the expectations of a new century.

It is not uncommon on the long train rides in Russia to make new friends. The comforts of the Compagnie International de Wagons Lit, as well as the monotony of the Russian landscape, are conducive to friendly visits and long conversations. It was on this 1910 train ride that my parents met Albrecht Holl who became a lifelong family friend. He was a forester, a native of Bavaria, then on the way to Russia to engage in the lumber trade. Their common admiration for Wagner operas and Viennese operetta, among other things, sealed their friendship by the time the train reached St. Petersburg's Warsaw Station.

As a first pied-a-terre for the newcomer, father recommended the Grand Hotel, owned by the Schotte family. Fritz Schotte, a German national, was father's friend from school days and his British-born wife, Rhoda, was the proprietor of the adjacent Hotel d'Angleterre. Albrecht Holl followed father's suggestion. After World War I and his wartime internment in Siberia, he returned to the Grand Hotel to marry Martha Schotte. The family friendship continued through many tragic events, including my father's death in exile in 1932 and Albrecht Holl's death in a Berlin bunker in 1945.

\* \* \*

Goethe said in *Dichtung und Warheit:* "When someone tries to remember his earliest childhood experience he may easily confuse his own real recollection with what he has heard from others." I remember my first encounter with the Russian Secret Police in Petrograd in 1916 when I was four years old. The Schotte family, friends of my family and proprietors of the Grand Hotel and Hotel d'Angleterre, were interned with other German citizens at Kamyshlov in Western Siberia. For this reason, in 1914, they asked my parents to move into the hotel during their absence. While father worked at the headquarters of the Manchurian Railroad, mother took over the business of running the hotel.

It is wintertime, probably 1916. In front of the Grand Hotel stands the costumed doorman. Along the streets the snow is piled high like haystacks. Across the plaza in St. Isaak's Cathedral it is dark despite the hundreds of candles at the altar. Our maid Nastya and I kneel there among the crowd; we bow our heads and make the sign of the cross. It is wartime, World War I, and the crowd prays for their loved ones at the front.

In our apartment at the hotel a man sits with my parents at the dining table; as we come in, the man asks me something which I don't understand. He speaks German and I don't yet speak this language. Then he asks in Russian where I have come from. I tell him as I kneel, bow, and cross myself.

He had been sent from the Okhrana, the czarist secret police, to investigate a denunciation of my mother by some hotel employees. They knew that my mother was German-born and wanted her removed, perhaps to partake of some of the enemy's property, and accused her of spreading enemy propaganda. The investigator, however, dropped the case. My mother was a Russian citizen by marriage and I didn't even understand German.

We soon left the hotel to go back to our fifth-floor flat across the river on Nobility Lane. Around the corner was the Kshessinskaya Villa; Kshessinskaya, the ballerina, was a favorite of the Czar. In 1917, after the Bolshevik Revolution, the villa became headquarters for the Bolshevik Party and Nobility Lane was renamed "Lane of the Village Poor." From the high gazebo at the corner, Lenin would speak to the crowd assembled in Alexander Park.

## NOBILITY LANE

Nobility Lane No. 7, was a five-story apartment house. The building, facing the street, had a marble lobby, doorman, and elevator. We lived in the rear building, apartment No. 49, a walkup on the fifth floor, in three rooms with a toilet and kitchen. Although my father had been working at the Petersburg headquarters of the Chinese Eastern Railroad, a Russian railroad which crossed Manchuria and was a short-cut to Vladivostok, he augmented his income by giving private lessons in foreign languages.

There were two flats on our floor. On our door was a polished brass nameplate and next to it a bell which said "Please Turn." When turned, the bell sounded like a bicycle bell. Upon entering one was in a small hall with a wardrobe, a full length mirror, and a stand for umbrellas and galoshes. There were four more doors: one to the right leading to a toilet, the one straight ahead going to the kitchen; a big door opening to the drawing room, and the one to the left leading to a dark corridor through which one could reach the dining room and the bedroom. In the dark corridor was a niche where my nurse, Nastya, slept behind a curtain. Between the three rooms were two round tiled stoves built into the walls. Each winter day the janitor brought a bundle of birch wood for the stoves which were lit before noon. In the afternoon the chimneys were shut tight and warmth radiated from round columns until morning.

On the fifth floor at Nobility Lane the sky stretched across the window, an ever-changing glittering mother-of-pearl. Fluttering specks rising and falling criss-crossed the spacious emptiness beyond the window panes; crows and doves, sparrows and rooks. When a bird landed on the window-sill behind the double window panes — a fluttering splash of wings, a grasping gesture of the claws, a startled blinking of the eyes — excitement and melancholy filled my heart.

Under the window in the dining room stood a small table and a chair, both varnished yellow, with a big drawing pad bound in linen for me to draw on. I drew mostly horses with big nostrils and curved necks, their manes and tails flying. Sometimes soldiers rode them or circus girls stood upright on their backs; or they pulled sleighs or carriages on thick rubber tires like those standing in front of the white mansion facing Trinity Plaza.

If one knelt on this little table or stood on tiptoe next to the window, one could see the landscape beneath the sky: walls, chimneys, roofs, rusty color of brick and painted sheet iron. To the right there were five rows of windows. Some windows had green boxes hanging outside with round holes like Swiss cheese. These were the kitchen windows; food was stored in these window boxes to keep it fresh. When one looked left towards the river, a red brick tower protruded into the sky. It had a lookout on top and a mast with wire riggings like a castle tower or a battleship sailing through the sky. It was the tower of a firehouse and, when I went down with Nastya for a walk to the river, we often stopped at the firehouse. She had a friend there, a fireman with a golden helmet. Sometimes we went inside and had a look at the shining black horses in their wooden stalls. They had fierce eyes, stamped their hooves, and let their long tails swish through the air with a hissing sound. And, of course, there were the red sparkling fire engines. The tower of the firehouse overlooked Hare Island and Birch Island, where the city was founded.

Above the fake horizon of rusty roofs and patches of green, one could see the golden needle with an angel glistening gaily in the sky. It is still the landmark of the city, the Archangel Cathedral standing amid the six bastions of Peter Paul's Fortress built by Peter the Great in 1703. After Peter took Noteburg, the Swedish fortress at the head of the Neva River, and renamed it Shluesselburg (Key Fortress), he decided to build a new Russian capital there in the delta of the river. Saint Petersburg was dug out of the swamp by soldiers who often worked with their bare hands. To build the new city, his new capital, forty thousand souls were brought by Peter to these islands, sometimes called "the hundred islands of the Neva delta."

On my walks with Nastya to the river, we usually stopped at the little park next to Peter's Blockhouse which was the Czar's first residence. Peter's boat was also enshrined there. It is said that during a storm Peter rescued drowning sailors from this boat. On this occasion he caught cold, and subsequently died at the age of 53.

In winter, the river was frozen solid. People walked across the ice to the Summer Garden on the southern bank. Farther west the big Trinity Bridge spanned the river. In summer, there was much life on the river bank clad in granite and embellished by two mythological Manchurian lions. There were many barges; the men loading and unloading them walked across bouncing planks. The river was alive with sounds of movement; tugboats moving to and fro, smoke streaming from their chimneys above the river's whitecaps.

I also remember the drawing room of our apartment with its wine-red plush settee and armchairs, its narrow bookcases and bric-a-brac shelves, where ladies in rustling dresses and big hats and gentlemen in dark, long coats and high stiff collars assembled in happy animation. When all of them left, Nastya and I remained alone at home.

Then I would climb on the head piece of the chaise longue; it was my driver's seat, the reins tied to the doorknob, and I drove along cobblestone streets across the river over bridges, along wide wood-paved boulevards, past the hay market to my grandparents' flat on the Catherine Canal. With "Watch out!" or "Out of the way!" I kept pedestrians on guard.

"Where are you going?" asked Nastya. "Still far to go? It's porridge time. Stop for a while."

In the bedroom stood a marble-topped washstand. In front

of it was a tub where I stood naked and sometimes crying, while mother was laughing while she rubbed me down with cold water.

## SPRING

It was usually a sunny day in March when the snow began to melt on the surface. In April the air got warm and moist; the sea wind chased low clouds and whipped up a cold rain. The snow got heavy, gray, and dirty. Muddy waters ran down the culverts of the streets. Heavily-loaded sleighs got stuck on bare cobblestones; their drivers beat the steaming horses mercilessly. Crowds gathered around a fallen horse lying helplessly on its side while cursing drivers tried to free it from its harness.

Bluish lines and blemishes covered the frozen river like veins on a sick body. Someday soon the ice would burst and begin to move; shoving, pushing, cracking, roaring like distant thunder. The word would get around town: "The ice is moving." Groups of bypassers watched the dramatic struggle from the bridges as ice blocks assaulted the bridges. Days passed by; eventually the river cleared itself from its bondage and rolled unchained, disturbed only by winds from the sea.

People still wore their winter attire, even heavier from rain and moisture in the air. Spring was not there yet but suddenly, overnight, the river would be covered by islands of sparkling white ice moving majestically downriver like white clouds in the sky. Some carried passengers — funny-looking seals — from the distant shores of Karelia. The ice from Lake Ladoga was the last sign of waning winter; when it had passed, spring officially began. People changed into lighter overcoats or jackets and summer hats. By the end of April the streets were dried by wind or occasional sun. Only gray heaps of melting snow still remained in dark secluded corners.

The houses opened their windows and paper strips around

windows and cotton layers between the double frames were removed. Then thin air full of noises rushed into our rooms after the silence of the winter. There was a restlessness in the air. It was a time for house cleaning, window washing, and carpet beating in the yards. Winter clothes were packed away in heavy smelly chests. Men in red shirts came with buckets and big brushes to wax the floors; then, barefoot, they stepped on their brushes and polished the floors as if roller skating.

The beginning of summer was marked by the move away from town. Working folk remained in the city while others moved to their *dacha* (summer house) or to "the village" or to the "south." *Dachas* were scattered around the outskirts of the city and were either owned or rented. Peasants came with their horse-drawn carriages to pick up the baskets and trunks packed for the summer months. Some people moved to their own estates. If they went south it was mostly to the Crimea, a three-day journey by train. Our family went north to Finland, to Terijoki where grandfather had his *dacha* and the Eilers family had their estate.

On the morning of departure everybody would be up early, mother watching the clock and urging an early start, father checking his vest pocket watch and trying to convince us that there was ample time and no cause for hurry. Nastya dried an occasional tear with her apron. She would remain in town to care for father; at harvest time she would leave for her native village to help her family.

Eventually somebody would go to the street corner to hire two *izvozchiks*. The janitor would arrive to shoulder the luggage with the same prowess with which in winter he carried the daily loads of wood. Down in the yard the suitcases and baskets would be loaded on one *izvozchik*. The four of us would sit down for a silent moment, then go downstairs, three of us taking seats in the other carriage, and we would drive out of the yard followed by waving Nastya.

As we turned into the street, the small horses fell into a slow trot; we passed the policeman at the corner and turned towards Vyborg Side, passing the familiar signs: "butter, cheese," "bakery" (with a big pretzel), "meats, sausages," "vegetables, fruits." Soon we reached a wooden bridge which spanned an arm of the Neva delta. On the even wooden pavement the carriage rolled smoothly and the clanking sound of hooves was muted.

The Vyborg Side was an industrial district with high red chimneys in the distance; black columns of smoke rose straight into the air. We drove past endless rows of uniform buildings surrounded by trees and iron fences, a big hospital. We crossed a busy intersection full of ringing streetcars, lorries, carriages and people crowding sidewalks, moving through the tumult of busy commerce and across a plaza to stop finally in front of Finland Station. Porters in white aprons hurried by and got busy with our luggage.

Finland Station was the smallest among the five railroad stations of the city; it did not have the official dressiness of the pilastered, palatial buildings of the other stations. Karelian or Finnish peasant women in kerchiefs carried their big milk containers early in the morning, going from place to place, apartment to apartment, to supply the city dwellers with fresh milk.

The Finnish border was less than an hour away by train. Finland was then a Russian province, but there was still a real border where customs officials come through the train to ask questions.

**✳ ✳ ✳**

Terijoki was about two hours by train from Petersburg. We spent three summers there in 1915, 1916, 1917.

Aunt Vera, my father's younger sister, called it Terry and she knew it best; she spent the carefree summers of her youth there. For her it was not just a summer place; it was her Riviera, the Riviera of the *nouvelle bourgeoisie.*

My grandparents' place in Terry was a two-story log house on the road to Tyurisevo, the next half stop after Terijoki. Along the road behind the bushes was grandfather's vegetable garden. In its center was a well where grandpa and I filled our watering cans. On the far end towards the dark pine forest were black current bushes, my favorites.

Opposite my grandparents' dacha was a roadway flanked by dark firs. It led to old Eilers' house, a stone building overgrown with vines; to the left were the stables and the carriage house. On Saturdays we drove by carriage to the station to meet my father who came for the weekend. The name of the horse was Poiga.

Old Eilers' stone house was only the first one of five on the estate. Farther down a path across the brook and past a stand of dark firs was the modern log house on stilts of his youngest son Constantin. Up the brook were tennis courts, a stage, and a gazebo. And along the ridge were dachas belonging to Old Eilers' three daughters: Erica Salome, Aunt Vera's closest friend, and to the Sevigs and Lidval families.

I do not remember Old Eilers — Uncle Hermann — except from photographs; I do remember his funeral and it was for him that my father was called Hermann Vladimir. Old Eilers died in the summer of 1917 before losing all his possessions. A big black crowd gathered in front of his vine-covered house. The cortege assembled there to bring him to the station for burial in Petrograd. We children were not allowed to go to the station and were to remain at home with our Finnish maids. But we were given pieces of Suchard chocolate; in those times this was something special.

Mother and I stayed in Terry also in the winter of 1917-18, the winter after the Russian revolution. We stayed with Constantin's wife Gertrude and their children while he was interned at Olonets near Lake Ladoga. Although Old Eilers had become a Russian citizen, his sons had retained their German citizenship. Then one day at the beginning of 1918 Constantin arrived in Teriyoki. He had not seen his children for three years. Bruno was now seven, the twins six years old; we had a wonderful time with him playing hide and seek both outside in the snow and inside the house where it was warm and cozy, especially around the table in the dining room under the big petroleum lamp when the cook would bring a big tureen filled with steaming stew.

It was decided at this time that, upon our return to Petrograd, we would move to Litseyskaya Street to the house which Constantin had built for himself and his sisters; they wanted to return to Gertrude's home in Luebeck, Germany. The Eilers' properties in Russia had been nationalized by now and they had no wish to return to a country engaged in civil war. By our moving into their apartment, we were able to protect their personal belongings.

# 2

## *Ten Days That Shook the World*[2]

1917 was the year of the February revolution and the October 7 *coup d'état* which overthrew the provisional government of Kerenskiy. We were still living on Nobility Lane, having not yet moved to Litseyskaya Street.

In the front building on Nobility Lane, the one with the doorman and humming elevator, I had a playmate. From the windows of his room on the *bel-étage* one could see all of Nobility Lane and the river to the left. It was winter and the double windows were closed, but one could hear an unusual noise outside — "tack, tack, tack" — like loud handclapping. We looked out the window; there was our policeman running. Why was he running? He was the one who always stood at the street-crossing in his polished boots telling people what to do, turning around on his heels and stroking his long dark moustache which hung down the corners of his mouth. Now he was

---

[2] John Reed. *Ten Days That Shook the World.* New York: Modern Library, 1960.

15

running, holding his sabre with one hand, pistol in the other; sometimes he stopped, turned, and shot the pistol with a "tack, tack." Other dark figures came running too, sailors with ribbons flying at the back of their caps and other men with pistols and rifles; sometimes they were shooting too. One could hear it behind the closed double windows.

The policeman disappeared in the house on the opposite side, the pursuers too. He emerged from an attic window and ran around the chimneys on the red roof. The others came to the roof too and caught the policeman; after a while they came out into the street, the policeman without his cap and over-coat. They proceeded up the street holding the policeman by his belt, pushing him and hitting him over his head once in a while and finally disappearing around the corner.

I remember another time when father and I walked to the street corner where he bought an armful of newspapers. Big trucks rattled down the street jammed with soldiers, sailors, or men with rifles with red arm bands and red flags. Rattling chains turned the rear wheels; the tires were of solid rubber. They drove to and from the corner of Alexander Park where the Kchessinskaya mansion stood, now the Bolshevik Head-quarters.

These are the impressions of a six-year-old of "the days that shook the world." [3]

* * *

On March 18, 1918, the Brest-Litovsk Treaty was signed by Imperial Germany and Bolshevik Russia. The Schotte fami-ly returned from wartime internment to the Grand Hotel

---

[3] Recollections of two adult witnesses whose paths crossed those of my family are included in the appendix.

where a German Consulate was opened. I remember the wedding that year of Albrecht Holl and Martha Schotte at the Grand Hotel, myself sitting with Aunt Rhoda in her elegant drawing room in front of a fireplace protected from its heat by an etched glass screen and with a big engraved portrait of Count Bismarck, the Iron Chancellor, looking down at us.

Fritz and Rhoda Schotte left for Germany in the fall of 1918. In November the Kaiser abdicated and all diplomatic relations were cut off. Revolutionary German Workers and Soldiers Councils were organized by the Bolsheviks to expedite the return of German POWs and promote world revolution.[4]

Uprisings and civil wars held sway over the former imperial territories of Russia, Austro-Hungary, and Germany following the end of the Great War. For five years Red and White Terrors, famine, and cholera ravaged the Russian land. Saint Petersburg, now Petrograd, became depopulated, dilapidated, unheated in winter, and without light most of the time. Through the dark streets, covered in winter by deep snow, only occasional streetcars moved slowly, brightly lit, through the gray winter; bundled up black figures moved along streetcar tracks with snow shovels and brooms, women unaccustomed to such work and mobilized as members of the bourgeoisie. "Those who do not work do not eat" was the slogan of the time. The city seemed dormant; people with sleds carried lumber from torn-down empty frame buildings or stood in long lines waiting for something to be distributed. One heard stories of creatures living in big abandoned buildings in the center of the city who assailed pedestrians; robbers who wore springs on their feet and could jump high and wide at great speed; armies of rats which derailed streetcars while crossing

---

[4] For a personal narrative by Fedor Schotte of these events, see Appendix 2.

tracks on their way to the river. In 1920 a visitor to the city wrote:

> The faces of the population were modeled by starvation, misery, and desperation, no matter whether they were the sorry remnants of the dispossessed classes or representatives of the victorious proletariat. All had but one thought: To obtain a crust of bread. The food obtainable by means of official ration cards meant certain starvation. Not a single shop was open; no public means of conveyance was running; and much of the once famous wooden pavement of St. Petersburg had disappeared: the people had used it to fire their stoves.[5]

Petersburg was renamed Petrograd in 1914 but in 1925, after ten short years, Petrograd became Leningrad by "overwhelming popular demand." When two true natives of the city met they referred to the city by its ancient name of "Peeter," the way I think the Dutch pronounce the name of Peter. Lenin moved his capital to Moscow thus closing Peter's "window to Europe." Lenin's successor bricked the window up and extended an invisible wall around his Eurasian empire long before there was an "Iron Curtain." A border zone of a hundred kilometers in width kept the country — as the saying went — "under lock and key."

## LITSEYSKAYA STREET

We moved to Litseyskaya Street in the summer of 1918 just before my sister Irene was born. It was a quiet street paved

---

[5] Gustav Hilger and Alfred G. Meyer. *The Incompatible Allies: A Memoir-History of German-Soviet Relations 1918-1941.* New York: The Macmillan Co., 1953, p. 31.

with cobblestones and lined with trees. Lyceum Park extended three-quarters of its length on its south side. On the north side was the park-like setting of the Roentgen Institute, our own house and garden, and Old Eilers' abandoned nursery grounds stretching all the way to Prelate Street. Except for two five-story apartment buildings at both ends of the street one could forget that it was in the city.

Old Eilers' first "New World," the villa at the corner of Stone Island Prospekt, stood empty for years until it was torn down for firewood in 1919 or 1920. Many frame buildings bereft of occupants were torn down by those still living in Petrograd. These were the years of civil war in Russia, a war which lasted longer than World War I.

The move from our three-room apartment on Nobility Lane to the six rooms on Litseyskaya Street was not a distant one, just six blocks down Stone Island Prospekt, one of the oldest streets in St. Petersburg and at my time one of the most modern. From its beginning at the fortress, Stone Island Prospekt crossed many streets named after their first occupants: Nobility Street, Crownworks Street, Settler Street, Rifle Street, Coinage Street, Canon Street, Powder Street, Oarsman Street. First it crossed Birch Island and Apothecary Island, usually called the Petrograd Side; next it jumped across two more arms of the Neva River and the tip of Stone Island to end on the northern delta shore at New Village, a place known then for its gypsies.

Litseyskaya 14 was a comfortable house, a modernistic dandy comfortable in its Scandinavian look behind the fancy lattice of its fence. On three sides it was surrounded by a garden; on the fourth side a paved driveway led past the gates to the janitor's house in the rear and the wash house next to it. A photograph recalls the warm exterior of its oiled wood covered with vines, its windows different in every room.

In wintertime one was embraced by the warmth of the

vestibule behind a heavy oak door with its fancy wrought iron grille and shining brass lock and handle. Past a second door — a swinging frame with textured glass — was a hall which could comfortably accommodate bicycles, a perambulator, or a Finnish sleigh. The landing halfway up to the second floor had a big window behind a planter with exotic plants flanked by two wicker chairs.

Ours was the street-front apartment on the second floor. From the kitchen and maid's room windows one looked down on a small chapel in the adjoining lot; it had an onion-domed turret and three tall windows. In this chapel, on a big table, the Roentgen Institute deposited corpses awaiting burial. We could see them from the kitchen window. I do not remember that any of us had qualms about these neighbors.

Next to the kitchen was a pantry leading to the dining room and to a spacious entrance hall with room for big armoires. In the adjoining bathroom, the hot water heater was lit on Saturdays with small birch logs. Its warmth extended throughout the hall. Bathing time lasted from supper until midnight; first my little sister, then myself, were bathed, followed by our household helper, mother, and last of all father. It was a long procedure and fresh hot water had to be heated constantly.

When we moved to Litseyskaya Street only one of the four apartments in the house was occupied. It belonged to Erica, Old Eilers' beautiful youngest daughter. Her lawyer husband, Eugene Salome, hung an Austro-Hungarian flag in front of the house and placed a tablet at the gate reading "Austro-Hungarian Jurisconsulate." Through this device the house remained a refuge from the decline and squalor of the city during the early years of civil war. Father worked first for the German Soldiers' Council, later for the German Care Agency. The downstairs of our house became transit quarters for returning POWs, officers on their way home to Austria and Germany. A Captain

Nicol arrived from Germany to take charge of the shipping arrangements and took up residence in a downstairs apartment. Litseyskaya Street became on occasion a center of international activity. Comrade Weinstock from the Foreign Service parked his silver sports car with a red devil on its radiator next to a Stoever car with the inscription "Germania" on its hood. These were two of the very few cars in Petersburg at the time. The German ship captains, Koenig, Kaiser, and Herzog, supplied beer in barrels from Germany. Herr Wetzel, first violinist from the Mariinskiy Theater and a Viennese by birth, provided music and ballerinas for the parties which spilled over from Captain Nichol's apartment into the garden. I remember Captain Koenig, a strong man, carrying ballerinas on his outstretched arms above his head. A young lady was married with little ceremony to an Austrian officer quartered for a few days in a room downstairs, which made it possible for her to leave the country.

Aunt Vera, father's young sister, married Uncle Rolf Schmiedeberg in our apartment in 1919. Like grandfather, the Schmiedebergs hailed from Estonia. One day Eugene Salome was brought home with a head injury; Erica was not in town and a nurse was hired to take care of him while he was confined to bed. When Erica came back, she found the nurse in bed with her husband. The Salomes were divorced and Erica married Captain Nicol; Eugene married the nurse. In due time they all left the country — the Nicols for Germany, the Salomes for Sweden.

While our house enjoyed its special status under the Austro-Hungarian flag, later — as a tenants' cooperative presided over by my father — it could not escape the vagaries of the times. When coal reserves were exhausted, the wash house in the backyard was torn down and our central heating was maintained for only one more winter. The inhabitants of the house congregated in the basement to saw wood, father instructing the weaker sex on how to handle the big saw. The next winter a *burzhuyka* — a stove made from an iron barrel — was installed in our bedroom next to the bath. Besides the kitchen, it was the only room used during these winter months.

These were the times when I walked with other kindergarten children to the ARA — the American Relief Agency — six blocks away on Bolshoi Prospekt for soft white buns and hot cocoa. Or stood in line, my little sister on a sled, in front of the public mess hall waiting for millet soup and *vobla* — a salted dried fish — and for a *vos'mushka*, the common word for the daily bread ration of one-eighth of a pound.

Father's helpers around the house were mostly women: mother and our household help Frau Beirot, a widow who had seen better times; Erica's distant relative, a lady with a limp; and Malasha, the former janitor's widow and her daughter Nyusha, the only ones who had lived on the property from the time it was built in 1910. Malasha, still a faithful servant while my father managed the property, became in later years — when the house was nationalized — a police informer and assistant housing administrator, advancing in accordance with her proletarian status.

While I can assume that father had welcomed the 1917 revolution having been a student during the heady years at the beginning of the century, I knew that Grandfather, who lost all he had worked for, hated the Bolsheviks. I often heard him cursing them while getting mice out of the traps and flushing their corpses down the toilet while naming Bolshevik victims he knew who had been arrested and executed in the basement of infamous Gorokhovaya 2, the Cheka headquarters.

My grandparents at this time lived with Rolf and Vera Schmiedeberg, the only providers for the big clan: Vera gave private lessons — she spoke four languages fluently — and Rolf designed the "Makhonin Electric Train" in a big studio furnished with drafting tables and shelves filled with blueprints. Makhonin was the Party man in charge of the project meant to serve Lev Trotsky, the Commissar-in-Chief of the Red Army. At this time railroads were barely functioning; the coal mines were in the south where the White Armies were in control.

The electric train — to be run on batteries — was to provide the Commander-in-Chief with reliable transportation. It was indeed built and Uncle Rolf made the first run to Moscow with Trotsky aboard. On the way there were some problems and delays, but they made it in reasonable time to their destination and my uncle received a gold pocket watch from Trotsky. Inside its back cover an engraving recorded the occasion when the watch had been presented to its original pre-revolutionary owner but on what occasion it had been taken away from him remained unknown.

A photograph of my family taken in our garden shows our grandparents and Aunt Vera and Uncle Rolf Schmiedeberg shortly before they emigrated to Estonia. It was 1921 and by then Estonia had become an independent country. They all hoped to start a new life there and left by rail in an unheated boxcar, then the usual means of transportation. Some months later a telegram arrived from Tallinn informing us of grandmother's death. Before they left Aunt Vera had introduced me to Volik to whom she was teaching German so that he could enter St. Petri School. Volik became my best and closest friend, my brother, for eighteen years until he vanished in the Gulag Archipelago.

I grew up in the house at No. 14, Litseyskaya Street. From here I went to school; in this house I suffered through my first love and first sorrows; here I had my dreams of "fame and fortune." In its embrace I was happy until I was taken away forcibly one night by the secret police at the age of twenty. I visited there briefly three years later. In 1942 the house on Litseyskaya St. was destroyed during the siege of Leningrad, torn down for firewood because the inhabitants had either left or perished.

* * *

In the fall of 1920 I entered the second grade of the German Petri School and graduated eight years later from the 41st Unified Labor School. We were taught botany and zoology, Russian, German, French and English, literature and history, geography, physics and chemistry, arithmetic and algebra, geometry and trigonometry. At the tail end, we caught some Marxist political economy. Basketball was my favorite sport; I was poor in gymnastics. The first day I went to school with Alfred Blumenfeld and our mothers. Both our fathers and Fritz Schotte had attended Petri School together.

The school was on Nevskiy Prospekt, the main street across the river and about four kilometers away from home. Either the streetcar took me there or I met Volik and Alfred and we walked to school together, sometimes accompanied by Uncle Robert Blumenfeld who worked at the German Consulate. In winter we took a short cut crossing over the frozen Neva River.

In 1921, when father worked for the German Red Cross, he often took me to school in the official car. Timofeyev, a World War I veteran, was the driver. He disliked the Red Militia who had replaced the former police and, when approaching an intersection with a militiaman standing amidst slush and puddles, Timofeyev steered with the purpose of splashing dirt over the guardian of the new order. Father admonished Timofeyev via the "telephone," a contraption for passengers to talk with the driver up front. During the Volga famine and pestilence in 1921, the German Red Cross supplied food, medical supplies, and personnel to the affected regions, as did Herbert Hoover's American Relief Administration, the Swedish Red

Cross, the Quakers, the Vatican, and Nansen Aid.[6]

There were about two dozen boys and girls in my class: students with Russian names like Nemirovskiy, Belyaev, Rozanova, and Tsigalskiy; German names like Witte, Maar, Ulmann, Goldman, Blumenfeld, Rosenfeld; and Latvian names like Putsep or Urbanek. During class breaks in the hallway, we spoke Russian. At mid-day we went to the big assembly hall which had a stage, very high windows on both sides, and life-size portraits of school principals since Czar Peter's time hung in golden frames between the windows. In the assembly hall stood long tables and benches where we had a hot lunch which, during the famine years, was provided by the German Red Cross.

On the way home from school Alfred and I were often joined by Yura Tsigalskiy, another boy in our class. We walked, having spent our seven kopeks for carfare buying candies or a glass of sunflower seed from women peddlers at the school entrance. We spat out sunflower hulls as we continued along the Catherine Canal past Mars Field — now Field of Revolutionary Victims — to Trinity Bridge, now Bridge of the Revolution. In bad weather we tried to get a free ride across the bridge by hanging on at the exit platform of the streetcar. If the conductor saw us, we were chased off.

We often stopped at Yura's place; he had his own key since his mother worked in some office. A photograph of an officer in an old uniform hung in his sparsely furnished apartment. We never asked whether or not this was his father. Even children knew that one didn't ask about people in old uniforms. In every questionnaire the most critical questions were: did you or any of your relatives serve in the White Armies? did you ever reside in territories occupied by the Whites? There was not much to do at Yura's except talk; there were no toys, only old books, and no yard to play in.

---

[6] Gustav Hilger and Alfred G. Meyer. *Op. cit.*, p. 41.

# 3

# Growing Up

## VOLIK

I have already mentioned Volik twice; now I need to tell more about him, about us, about our time of growing up together: first eighteen years of childhood, adolescence, and early adulthood during the years of civil war, then, under the New Economic Policy (NEP), industrialization, collectivization, and the terror with its tragic consequences. We met in 1920, a cold and hungry year, when Aunt Vera brought Volik to our place.

"Meet Volik Fesenko," said Aunt Vera. "We just had a German lesson. He will also go to the Petri School and you should speak German to him too." At home my parents spoke German and I had learned the language from them after Nastya left us at the end of World War I.

I certainly wanted to make friends with him if only because of the bicycle he was riding, a real two-wheeler for children. I took Volik to the backyard to show him my fortress, the ice cellar behind the janitor's house where, in old times, ice from the river was stored for the summer. From the roof one looked over the big empty lot where Eilers' nurseries once spread all the way to Prelate Street. In the empty lot stood a big barn left over from wartime; a military searchlight unit had been stationed there and left a lot of abandoned equipment: searchlights, broken parts of carriages, wheels, and boxes.

When Volik had to go home, I went with him; he lived just across Stone Island Prospekt opposite our street. Now I could try out his bicycle; he held me steady — I had never been on a two-wheeler before. Approaching Old Eilers' house I saw my foe, the janitor's son at Old Eilers' big apartment house. His name was Nicolai Romanov and the other boys teased him by shouting "Nikolashka," the name disparagingly applied to the murdered Czar as well as to a fifth of vodka. He used to threaten me by throwing stones or "horse apples" (frozen horse dung). I told Volik about the danger and got off the bike. Volik jumped on it and rode at high speed, aiming directly at Nikolashka who fled into the archway and inside the building.

Volik lived in the big Rossiya apartment house which faced three streets and had its own electric power station and central heating plant which, even during this difficult winter, supplied electricity and heat to the complex because Zinovyev lived there. Everyone knew Zinovyev: Lenin, Trotsky and Zinovyev were the big leaders. Lenin and Trotsky now lived in Moscow; Zinovyev was the boss of Petrograd.

At Volik's place I met his mother, Dagmara Ernestovna, a Danish beauty, and his younger brother, Oleg, with whom he shared a room. There they could do whatever they wanted. The big wardrobe had been toppled and laid on its back on the floor. It was being converted into a ship. Tools, nails, and pieces of plywood were everywhere; a captain's bridge, a funnel, and a mast were built. Inside the wardrobe was the engine room. There were battery-operated flashlights. Green and red pieces of glass indicated port and starboard; Volik was very knowledgeable about things maritime.

On the wall hung a big framed photograph of a sailor decorated with a St. George Cross. It was Volik's grandfather who was a lifelong sailor; in olden times sailors were drafted for life. Volik's father, Iosif Ivanovich Fesenko, was a naval officer — or rather he had been one. In the living room under glass was a big model of the cruiser "Oslybia." There were also a diver's helmet and photographs of a gunboat at sea and officers standing on deck with ladies in white dresses and big hats.

"Where is your father?" I asked.

"Presently he sits," said Volik. Everyone knew what that meant: he sits — he has been arrested. Volik's father was to be arrested many times over the years but he always came home; he was a "spets," — a diving specialist. And he was also a sailor's son, he knew how to talk to the rabble, his investigators.

There were big leather fauteuils and a black grand piano in the living room. Volik's mother was vivacious and liked to cuddle and kiss us. Volik hated it. In the hall were prints of pretty ladies in silk dresses and big hats showing a leg, adjusting a garter, or kissing elegant men. His home would come to be my favorite place for the next ten years and where I would go most often.

When, in 1922, my sister Ira was sick with scarlet fever, I had to be quarantined. Father then worked for the German Red Cross and took me to the old people's home which it maintained. After the prescribed period of isolation was over, I went to stay with Volik while my sister recuperated.

Volik's father, Iosif Ivanovich, had by now returned home and was very much in command. He wore his grey hair parted in the middle and combed it in front to both sides which reminded me of a ship cutting through water with two white waves on each side of the bow. I remember him also giving us a belting, pants down, in the bathroom; it was not very painful and didn't diminish our affection for Iosif Ivanovich.

In one corner of our room was the port of Kronstadt, Petrograd's naval base. Volik was born there when his father was Commander of the Imperial Diving School. While Volik built the ships, I drew and cut out all the inhabitants: sailors, captains, and admirals. One of the sailors was my favorite, but Volik decided that he was the one who instigated a mutiny and sentenced him to be hanged despite my protests. This scenario was prompted by the 1921 sailors' mutiny in Kronstadt which was suppressed by Trotsky.

## NEP

The New Economic Policy (NEP), started in 1922, brought the "Nepmen," new entrepreneurs in the consumer industries and retail trade. Now the peasants had not only the land but also the freedom to market what they produced.

In a short span of time, stores opened everywhere. On the Nevskiy Prospekt and Sadovaya Street the mile-long arcades of Gostinyy and Apraksin Dvors again featured dozens of stores. Yeliseyev, the famous giant delicatessen store, offered an endless variety of foods; pyramids of Crimean fruit embellished many store windows. Lohr's bakeries and cafes sprang up everywhere and old name restaurants like "Medved" and "Donon" again opened their doors. The "Aquarium" featured dancing, variety programs, and *chambres séparées.* The Chiniselli Circus opened its doors as did theatres and movie houses.

Many old name merchants had left the country; their former salesmen often became proprietors of the old establishments. Cabbies and *likhachi* waited at street corners for customers. In time a fleet of Lincoln convertibles appeared in the streets; they were owned by Intourist for sightseeing by foreigners. Ford cars painted green and yellow appeared as taxis; they were called "pubs on wheels" because traditional beer hall signs were also painted green and yellow.

The city spruced up. The Winter Palace was now resplendent in emerald green, white, and gold, instead of the former undercoating of dirty red. Rossi's and Kvarengi's neoclassical General Staff building, the Admiralty building, and drama theatre complex again wore their traditional yellow and white dress.

On church holidays — Easter, Pentecost, Trinity — church bells rang again, after having been silenced during the revolution and civil war. On Easter night streets were dotted with moving candlelight; people were bringing their *kulich* — Easter bread wrapped in white napkins — to church to be sanctified. On Easter, as on the name day of Vera, Nadezhda, Lyubov (Faith, Hope, and Charity) and Sofia (Wisdom), it was difficult to get an *izvozchik.* People were making visits; on Easter Sunday and Monday it was open house at many homes. One went from home to home and — even with the host absent — one tasted some *paskha* and *kulich,* had a shot of vodka, a piece of ham or a deviled egg, and hurried to the next place. During *maslenitsa* (Shrovetide) the city was invaded by the horse-drawn sleighs of the *chukhontsy* — the Karelo-Finns -from nearby villages. The troikas — three-horse sleighs decorated with ribbons and bells and covered with straw and bearskins — were the most fashionable and expensive pieces of transportation. One went for bliny and caviar to friends or to restaurants. In our home Christmas was the most important holiday of the year and one of the few times during the year we went to church.

On Stone Island Avenue the "Aquarium," a dance-hall restaurant with *chambres séparées* and an open air stage in the garden opened again. From here the cabbies with fast horses took late night customers down the avenue to New Village and the gypsies. Later the "Aquarium" was converted into the Leningrad Film Studio, also the home of FEKS (Factory of Eccentric Actors) and the well-known movie directors Trauberg, Kozintsev and Gerasimov.

Foreign concessions came to town. In school we wrote with Hammer pencils, not aware that this stood for Armand Hammer rather than the hammer and sickle. Armand Hammer, an American businessman living in Moscow, was president of the A. Hammer Pencil Co.

Mologoles — a German concession with headquarters in Petrograd — managed big forests along the Mologa River. The passenger ship "Preussen" of the Stettin Steamship Company maintained regular cruises between Petrograd and Stettin; the ship's landing was on the Neva River just below Nicolai Bridge.

By 1922 the German Red Cross had left Petrograd. Father entered the employ of August Bolten, a Hamburg Shipping Company, as its Petrograd Harbor agent. Albrecht Holl represented German paper mills which imported lumber from Russia.

For a time we lived comfortably, occupying the entire apartment of six rooms. Father was head of our residential co-operative and saw to it that vacated apartments were occupied by reputable tenants. A well-known surgeon and dean of the medical school, Professor Wilhelm Adolfovich Schaak, became our neighbor on the second floor and his daughters, Tatiana and Michaela, became my sister's best friends. Some twenty years later this family would play a fateful role in the life of our family.

During these years dinner parties with dancing were held at home. For such occasions the neighbor's household help was mobilized. *Zakuski* — hors d'oeuvres — were served first with vodka; chicken broth with *pirozhki* filled with meat, rice or cabbage came next; this was followed by a fish dish, meat roast, and finally dessert. Crimean Barzak and sweet Chateau Yquem, my mother's favorite, were served. Dinner took four hours and was followed by music and dancing, lasting often until early morning when the first trams started running. Most of the guests were younger people, often members of the German Cultural Association.

On Sundays Albrecht Holl usually came for an afternoon visit; he walked from Vasiliy Island rather than take a streetcar. The men retired to father's study with pipe and cigar. Sometimes father played a famous passage from a Wagner opera or a Strauss waltz on the grand piano. In the study were volumes relating to the Great War, memoirs, and recent literary works by Thomas Mann, Hauptmann, Wassermann, and Kellermann.

Father's working hours were very irregular; he had to board ship with the customs and border police officials at every arrival or departure and to entertain the ships' captains and take them sightseeing. Afterwards they usually came to our house for dinner; once a week we had a box at the Mariinskiy for the ballet. Mother always stored cans of caviar for the captains to take home.

The Petrograd harbor where father spent a lot of his time was a restricted border zone. Depending on where the ship had docked, father used either the company car or a motorboat belonging to the German consulate. "Admiral" Jahn, also the janitor and security guard at the consulate, was in charge of the boat.

Once I accompanied father on the motorboat when the ship dropped anchor at a remote coal basin. It was a long ride passing small canals, then downriver past the wharfs until we reached the view and wind of the bay. At the distant coal basin father boarded the ship by the gangplank where a border guard was posted. Jahn took the boat to the other side of the ship where a crew member lowered a carton of spirits on a rope, duty-free.

"Don't tell your father anything," Jahn admonished me.

In 1924, after Lenin's death, the city was renamed Leningrad "by popular demand." Later in the year, in September, it was inundated by a big flood. Sustained winds from the west stopped and reversed the flow of the Neva River and the waters rose. A hundred years earlier in 1824 a similar flood had occurred and was immortalized in Pushkin's poem, "The Iron Horseman."

School closed early the day of the flood; at home in the afternoon we all waited anxiously for father's return from the harbor. He arrived in time — the water in our street was just a few inches high. The driver of the car left for home but had to abandon the car and return to our house. By that time the water in our street was about four feet high. Everyone in the house congregated in the stairwell and watched the water rise; it stopped just short of the first floor apartments.

Overnight the winds diminished and the water receded; because many city streets had wooden pavements — sextagonal or brick-shaped wooden blocks placed over lumber floorings — they were flushed away. A captain whose ship arrived days later told us how they encountered the floating lumber in the Bay of Finland.

\* \* \*

Some days I went from school directly to Blumenfelds where we had French lessons with Tante Jeanne, a dwarfish old governess who lived with them. We read "Tartarin de Tarascon" and prepared skits for Christmas. Besides our French lessons there were piano lessons for Alfred and violin lessons for his brother George. If I happened to stay for dinner, which was rare, there was always conversation with their father on some subject such as music, literature, or archeology.

My favorite place — where I went most often — was Volik's. During the NEP period Wild West movies were imported from the U.S. and became very popular. Toilet paper also became available again. For these reasons Volik and I started making movies. On a roll of toilet paper I drew cartoons, Wild West style, frame by frame; then frame by frame they were unrolled past a window in a box; in front of the window a big magnifying glass was installed and, for five kopeks, grownups could enjoy our production.

All these homes were part of my growing up and were very different. Yura's place was sad; Volik's was lively and fun; Alfred's was more sedate — his mother was often unwell. My own home was just home: everyone was at ease and on good terms with mother. She maintained family ties and I often saw her sitting at her desk writing letters to relatives and friends abroad. Father was always preoccupied with his work, the house, and his activities at the German Cultural Association.

When we grew older we perused magazines which Uncle Robert brought from the Consulate: the "Berliner Illustrierte," "Die Woche," "Film Woche," "Das Neue Universum," and "Sport und Sonne." The twenties were the heyday for silent movies and Berlin a major center of film production where Fritz Lang, Lubich, Murnau, von Stroheim, and Pabst worked. Alfred and I cut pictures out of the magazines and published our own film magazine to circulate in class. With Volik I went to all the Wild West movies starring Hart and Roland. We also read stories about the Wild West by Mayne Reed, Brett Harte, and Karl May.

Volik's father was second in command of EPRON, "The Expedition for Special Underwater Assignments" which raised the cruiser "Oleg" sunk in the Bay of Finland in World War I and the "Narodovolets," a hospital ship which inexplicably overturned while moored at the Vasiliy Island embankment.

Iosif Ivanovich and Dagmara Ernestovna loved fun and good company. They often hired an *izvozchick* to go to the "Aquarium" night club or the "Donon" restaurant, to the movies, or just to a pub for beer and crayfish. After suppers with friends at home — there was always a carafe of vodka on the table — Dagmara Ernestovna played the piano. Sometimes she was accompanied by her unmarried sister, Magda, who sang everything from gypsy songs to opera arias. Magda was also a striking woman. Tall, slim, temperamental, with a beautiful voice, she was courted by Brabets, a well-to-do businessman. We boys admired her too; perhaps that was the reason Brabets gave us his teakwood flat boat which he had used for hunting ducks at Lake Ladoga. To our regret Magda left for Riga in the mid-twenties where she became a professional opera singer. When, in 1944, I was in Riga as a soldier I saw her name printed in big letters on battered prewar posters of the Riga City Opera.

Dagmara Ernestovna always slept late until it was time for Annushka to fetch a fresh warm *baton* (baguette) from the Lohr bakery. Sometimes during vacations we were assigned this chore with an allowance for the bakery's famous *crème brulées* (toffees).

The summer of 1926 I spent with Volik and his family in a village near Krasnoye Selo, the former summer camps of the Imperial Guards and the place where Vronsky raced his horse in *Anna Karenina*. Here we also rode horses bareback with the village boys to the fields for grazing at night where we lit bonfires and dug potatoes, then baked them in the hot coals.

By the time I was fourteen Volik and I had a rowboat, a kayak, and a small flat-bottomed teak boat with a one-cylinder inboard motor. We kept this equipment on a barge which was Mr. Fesenko's headquarters and spent many spring hours there repairing and painting our boats. In the rowboat we went downriver to the bay and Lakhta beach. We tried to sail the kayak by attaching keels to it but gave this up after a school friend overturned and nearly drowned; two sailors pulled him out of the water. Looking back I often think how lucky we were. I was not a good swimmer nor were we properly clothed on such occasions; the Neva River was cold, its currents swift.

In the fall of 1927 August Svirbul, our best gymnast, drowned; he and Paul Maar had borrowed Volik's kayak. They overturned in the vicinity of the naval air station after having come too close to a landing seaplane; only Maar was rescued. Our entire class went to the funeral; later we assembled at the home of his older sister for the usual "pominki," the Russian wake. Great amounts of food and drink were consumed on this occasion; there was music — August's brother-in-law was a jazz-band pianist — and singing. I had never been at a wake before and found the noisy atmosphere of the party disturbing.

My friendship with Volik was a close and congenial one, but never restrictive or exclusive. Years later, even when our interests diverged — his was engineering while mine tended towards the arts — our friendship included Irina and Lida, our wives. Volik was the stronger character, the more determined to achieve whatever goal he had set himself; I was more pliable, with more imagination and less affected by failure to reach objectives. This, in a way, was the foundation of our friendship — we were equals and neither one ever had the upper hand. Later it also determined our respective fates. The strong one perished while the adaptable one survived.

## TRAVELS ABROAD

By 1923 the ruble had become a convertible currency and it was possible for us to visit mother's relatives in Germany. Ira needed ear surgery as a consequence of having had scarlet fever and it was to be performed at the University Clinic in Göttingen. In June we boarded the freighter "Hildegard" as guests of its captain.

I would have preferred to be with Volik who was leaving with his father on an expedition to the Caspian Sea. A caravan of ships and barges had to navigate the ancient Marinskiy Canals to the Volga River and the Caspian Sea. Iosif Ivanovich was in charge and posted his twelve-year-old son on a barge as a helper to an old sailor.

But a sea voyage has its attraction for a boy too; even more so if sailing on a freighter. I could visit any place aboard, including the engine room, boiler room, radio station, and the bridge. I could follow the ship's progress in the map room, visit the galley and sailors' quarters. We ate at the captain's table. Everybody was friendly with the exception of a stoker who once came up out of a hole in the deck, dirty and sweaty, to take a drink of warm gruel from the kettle. "Enjoying the sun, little brat?" he said to me.

We had blue skies all the way and entered the Bay of Kiel on the fourth day, disembarking at the entrance to the Kaiser Wilhelm Canal. The change of landscape between Europe's east and west was quite remarkable: the red-tiled roofs submerged in the greenery of gardens and forests along the undulating seashore; the blue bay dotted with many sails and ships waiting to enter or exit the canal at the Holtenau Locks.

We visited Gertrude Eilers and her children — my Teriyoki playmates — in Luebeck, then took the train to Göttingen for Ira's surgery and stayed with grandmother. Grandmother lived in a comfortable home with her sister and her oldest son, Uncle Otto. My Cousin Tito from Argentina and his mother were also visiting. His father, Uncle Willy, had left for Argentina as a young man before the Great War and was now raising cattle near Santa Fe.

Uncle Otto found bicycles for Tito and me and we spent our time riding around in the quiet neighborhood streets shaded by trees and paved with small stones in intricate patterns.

Germany in 1923 was in the throngs of hyperinflation and political unrest and I remember going with Uncle Otto and his companions all World War veterans on their marches to some distant destination. The men carried weighted backpacks, sang marching songs, and practiced martial skills along the way. Uncle Otto, now around forty years of age and still unmarried, worked as a handyman for his well-to-do cousin, a game warden and owner of a game and fish store. I liked Uncle Otto although he often had an aura of sadness about him in contrast to his jolly cousin, the game warden, who occasionally took off for some hunting expedition in his hunter's green and feathered hat with two rifles around his shoulders,

After Ira's surgery, we visited my aunts in Eisenach and Bremen. The sea voyage back was stormy. Mother was seasick and remained in bed. The steward took care of Ira who was as lively as ever. Once we reached Kronstadt the familiar landmarks — St. Isaak's golden cupola and the spires of the Admiralty and the Fortress — gleamed over the flat dimly gray horizon. I was home again.

During the summer of 1924, mother, Ira, and I visited my paternal grandfather and the Schmiedebergs in Tallinn, Estonia. The train trip from Leningrad to Tallinn lasted most of the day. George Kennan, who arrived in Tallinn on official duty in the 1920s, wrote: "Tallinn is a lovely old Hanseatic town — a northern replica of German Luebeck — surrounded incongruously but not unattractively by Russian suburbs. It lies on a bay of the Gulf of Finland, some sixty miles across the gulf from Helsinki. Two hundred and fifty miles away, at the head of the gulf, stands Leningrad." [7]

As they had in Petrograd before leaving for Estonia, Grandfather, Aunt Vera, Uncle Rolf, his parents and sister Erna all lived together in an apartment on the upper floor of a suburban house. In 1923 my cousin Edith was born.

The family depended on Uncle Rolf's small business, an auto repair shop which employed about a dozen workers with grandfather as business manager. Uncle Rolf also designed and manufactured narrow gauge diesel locomotives for the peat fields, the most important Estonian industry.

On summer evenings and weekends the Tallinnese streamed out to the nearby park, Kathrinenthal. Its main av-

---

[7] George F. Kennan, *Memoirs 1925-50*. Little, Brown and Co., 1967, p. 25.

enue, lined by trees and dotted by pubs, garden restaurants, and a tennis club, ended in a *corso*, a big loop of the road on an elevation overlooking the bay with its sunlit midsummer northern horizon. Here the Tallinnese promenaded — weather permitting — on foot, on bicycle, in horse-drawn carriages or in cars, stopping on their return at the outdoor eateries. A few miles out along the bay stretched the big popular beach of Brigitten which could be reached also by steamships and motorboats leaving from the harbor.

I spent many days in Tallinn's harbor, only ten minutes away from home. It was a busy port and of particular interest was the docking of two big liners, the Finnish "Ariadne" and its German sister ship "Ruegen," which regularly plied the Baltic waters between Helsinki, Tallinn, and Stettin. On one such occasion I recognized Paul Nemirovskiy, with whom I had shared the school bench that year, among the passengers on board. He was returning with his parents from a trip to Prague, Czechoslovakia.

In 1925 I traveled again to Tallinn, this time with father who only stayed two weeks while I remained for the rest of my school vacation. I traveled home by myself; I was 13 and had completed the lower school.

## LAST YEARS OF SCHOOL

By 1927 the NEP was on the wane; it was the beginning of "Reconstruction," the year Stalin expelled Trotsky from the Communist Party. Before that time there had been little intrusion of politics into our school life except for the obligatory participation in the May and November demonstrations. The demonstrations were fun with their band music, the singing of the "International" and with banners and effigies of capitalists and imperialists hung from gallows carried aloft in the procession: Churchill, Poincare, Baldwin, and Lloyd George among others.

In 1927 *Pravda* published an article which attacked our school as a "reactionary remnant of the old regime" and soon our school was reorganized, teachers fired, and a new administration installed. Students from a formerly Catholic school — commonly referred to as the "Polish school" — were transferred to our building. (The former Polish-Lithuanian provinces had a predominantly Catholic population.) Political economy, economic policy, and Marxism replaced the old subjects of history and geography.

In June 1928 Alfred and I graduated from the 41st Soviet Unified Labor School, the former Petri Schule. Our little group of friends, including Alfred, Paul Nemirovskiy, Walter Goldman and Henry Banse, did not stay long at the graduation festivities. The school was not what it had been and we were happy to be out. After getting our diplomas we bought cigarettes and went to a restaurant. Although it was late at night when we parted, it was light outside as this was the time of the "white nights." For Alfred and me it was farewell to our other friends since we were to leave soon for Germany to continue our education there. I was just sixteen and Alfred was fifteen years and nine months.

* * *

During the summers of 1927 and 1928, I had taken a job coaching three younger students from my school in the German language at their dacha in Siverskaya, an hour by train from the city. Siverskaya was described often in the writings of Vladimir Nabokov whose family had their estate there. The dachas of my employer and his mother-in-law — who had twelve children — occupied a sizeable lot with fruit, vegetable, and flower gardens. There was a tennis court and good swimming nearby in the Oredezh River. We went camping overnight and caught crayfish to be consumed with beer at weekend parties. On Saturdays members of the clan came from the city and there was always something to celebrate: name days, birthdays, holidays. On Sundays everyone except me went to church; upon their return the boys and I were put to work making ice cream, a favorite dish of the master of our house.

On the master's birthday a particularly big crowd assembled; there was much singing and drinking with dinner served on the big veranda. When at dinner's end the master demanded more ice cream but none was left, he angrily climbed onto the table and began to throw everything in his reach at the guests who fled from the veranda. Eventually his wife calmed him down and master and guests resumed singing and promenading in the gardens. It was a memorable day.

Siverskaya offered an additional attraction — perky blond Asya, my master's young sister-in-law, nineteen years old and married to a well-known soccer player. She came from Kiev for the summer and I fell in love for the first time. Asya played tennis and went swimming with us; she joined us on nighttime expeditions to catch crayfish. Saturdays she went with us to the railroad station to meet those coming from town. Weekend evenings the railroad station was the place to be seen promenading up and down the platform all dressed up. On rainy days we played endless card games spiced with flirting by Asya.

Then suddenly one day she was gone; this shocked me more than the news that my request for a travel passport had been turned down. However Alfred received his passport. I traveled to Leningrad to see him off since nothing kept me any longer at Siverskaya. Alfred embarked at Vasiliy Island at the landing of the Stettin Steamship Company and we waved him goodbye as he sailed down the river on the "S.S. Preussen." I would not see him again until thirty years later in Washington, D.C.

In 1929 uncertainty and an expectation of change were in the air. It was the first year of consecutive "Five-Year Plans of

Industrialization." In the capitalist world, Wall Street collapsed and the depression began. Soon the fate of millions would be determined by Stalin and Hitler.

I think that father had welcomed the 1917 revolution and shared the euphoria of the Russian intelligentsia which was reflected in the literature and arts of that period. NEP dampened revolutionary enthusiasm; politics was out, the good life was in. The time called for an apolitical stance: "We don't engage in politics" was then a common attitude. But now in 1929 it changed to: "Who is not with us is against us."

At home political opinions of foreign visitors were always listened to without comment. Although father had worked many years for German institutions which had made life easier for us during the bad years, he was more inclined to criticize foreigners than to listen to their negative opinions about Russia. Mother had always liked life in Russia. Even later, after she had gone through tragic times, I never heard her speak a bitter word about Russia.

It was different at Volik's. References to "the rabble" were common, as were deprecating comments about Communists and Zhidovka, the wife of Petrograd's party boss, Zinovyev. She lived one flight up and was picked up every day by her car and driver wearing her commissar's leather coat. Zinovyev was one of the three most prominent leaders of the revolution along with Trotsky and Lenin. Like his successor, Kirov, he was later killed by Stalin. Zinoyvyev was Jewish, as were Trotsky and many European communist leaders throughout Central Europe, and this encouraged latent anti-Semitism in those opposed to communism. We listened to criticism about the Soviet state of affairs by Herr Wegerer, a German national who resided in what used to be our drawing room before living space was rationed in the late twenties. His observations were from his trips to Karelia or wherever his business had taken him, and included accounts of disorganization, inefficiency,

mismanagement, or political interference into production matters. I was liable to get into an argument defending the pro-
gressive aspects of our social system. After all, the situation in
other countries was not rosy either with all the unemployment
and political unrest. Herr Wegerer's German papers — the
*Berliner Tageblatt* and *DAZ* — were full of unpleasant news
from abroad. Usually such discussions were curtailed by father
admonishing me to restrict my opinions "to subjects I know
something about."

In any case, pessimism and criticism were not compatible
with my frame of mind. Nor did I procrastinate at the dinner
table but instead rushed off to meet my friends. On the way I
would notice a car parked at our street corner. We knew it was
there to follow Herr Wegerer when he left the house in his car.
In the morning at breakfast, mother, looking out the window
at the man watching our house from the opposite side of the
street, noted that "our friend is already here." Nobody was really bothered by it.

With the demise of NEP and the departure of most foreigners, father was out of work. He took up language teaching
at the Berlitz School of Languages, Military Aviation School,
and Communist Academy, the latter an institution of higher
learning for Party executives who had no prior education.
Mother tried to increase the family income by knitting; her
popular Orenburg shawls[8] became a thriving industry. She also
learned to do manicures — practicing on me — and provided
dinners for those with whom we were forced to share our
apartment. Living space had become rationed and soon food
would be too. Oscar and Nadya Goldin moved into our dining room and Herr Wegerer occupied one of our rooms while
in town.

I was 16 in the fall of 1928, fancy free, and out of school;

---

[8] Large woolen shawls, a specialty of Orenburg, a city in the Urals.

the affairs of the world did not concern me but I knew what I wanted to do and even more what I didn't want to do — no pressing of school benches. Stage and cinema were on my mind.

Father wanted me to study Spanish at the Berlitz School but my mind was set on film-making, the new art of the 20th century. I also participated in stage performances of the German Cultural Association, commonly known as the Verein. It was founded in 1922 by members of the German-speaking community in Petrograd and had about 300 members. Professor Alexander Wulfius, our former school inspector and history teacher, was its president. A well-known personality about town, art connoisseur, excellent dancer of the mazurka to the tango, and an admirer of female youth, Wulfius also represented the German-speaking colony in Petrograd vis-a-vis foreign visitors.

The Verein was located on the fifth floor of an apartment house. Besides a library and other smaller rooms, it had a big hall which accommodated a stage and about 100 seats. Lectures, musical events, and a very active amateur/professional drama section made use of the stage. Distinguished German visitors were frequent guests: Hindemith performed with his trio; Kuhlenkampf played his violin. Famous German conductors who came to direct the Leningrad Philharmonic were frequent guests of the Association. Our family friend, Isidor Becker, gave popular recitals of German lieder. At monthly family evenings, also popular among Russian guests, the big hall became a dance floor, the associations's jazz band made music, and the buffet served sandwiches, pastries, and wine.

Some of the most popular events were performances by the drama section. Father starred in many of its productions of plays by Goethe and Schiller, Lessing and Kleist, Bahr and Sudermann, Hauptmann and Hoffmansthal, and Goetz and Kaiser. The classics were directed by old Mrs. King who had come to St. Petersburg as an actress from the famous Weimar Theatre long before World War I and married Mr. King, a Petersburg lawyer. Younger ambitious directors staged contemporary plays or wrote plays based on Arthur Conan Doyle and O. Henry stories. Among these younger directors were Werner Christiani and Eugene Rokotov.

At the same time Eugene Rokotov was organizing an International Theatre to produce plays in foreign languages at various clubs. I participated in its first production, "From Morning to Midnight," a contemporary play by Georg Kaiser. To compensate me for my activities (there was no money yet to pay salaries), Rokotov, who made his living as a photo correspondent, delegated some of his photographic assignments to me.

Equipped with the necessary permits, I photographed the arrival of the plane which inaugurated airmail service between Berlin and Leningrad. I climbed the towers of the Smolny Monastery to take pictures of the bells scheduled to be removed for industrial use, and drove to Pskov with a German motorist who had come in his Mercedes to Leningrad as his final destination in the Baden-Baden international tournament.

That winter I spent little time at home; I slept late, left home, came back for dinner at six in the evening, and left again for rehearsals. I usually got home after midnight and this did not please my parents.

I did not see much of Volik who was in his last year of school and preparing to enter the Technological Institute. He pursued this goal with his usual determination and worked during the summer as an excavator mechanic.

I had letters from Alfred who was now enrolled at the Berlin Franzoesisches Gymnasium which he still had to attend for two years until graduation. I was glad that I did not have to sit on a school bench any more but could tread stage boards instead. At this moment in time I wanted "to do things." As Stendhal said, "I must act a great deal and not give myself time for reflection."[9] It was at this time that I met Aleka, Werner Christiani's fiancée.

* * *

When the 1928-29 theatre season was over, Rokotov's International Theatre closed down. The hoped-for financial support from government agencies did not materialize. My application for admittance to the Photo-Kino-Technicum was denied; Werner's efforts to join LENFILM were unsuccessful. In September 1929, when an exhibit of "German Laboratory Equipment" opened in Leningrad, we were glad to get jobs, first as interpreters and later as company representatives with various exhibitors. Harry Pufahl, Albrecht Holl's nephew, joined us. One of the companies Werner worked for exhibited x-ray equipment for the examination of metals. When the exhibit ended the equipment was bought by Leningrad's Plant No. 7. Werner was hired to install and maintain the equipment and gave up his cinematographic ambitions.

That winter the atmosphere at home was not a happy one. Father had lost his position at the Military Aviation School. Later he also lost his job at the Communist Academy for reasons unknown to me at the time. He spent more time at the German Cultural Association, now under pressure by the authorities to merge with the "Club Eugene Levine," an organization sponsored by the Communist Party. The Association's lease was cancelled; it had to move to distant quarters on Vassily Island. Its performances were now staged at the House of Teachers, the former Yusupov Palace where 70 years ago old Eilers had started his Russian career. The Palace theatre, a miniature copy of the imperial theatres, had a well-equipped modern stage.

---

[9] *The Private Diaries of Stendhal*, W.W. Norton & Co., 1954, p. 525.

In 1930 another aspiring cinematographer, Andrey Behrens, joined our small group of friends. He was about four years my senior and came from the south near Odessa. Besides cinema, he loved poetry and literature and introduced me to the poems of Bagritskiy and the stories of Isaak Babel. Andrey had just finished a short subject film for the Office of Tourism and he had ideas up his sleeve of how to get funding for other short subject films.

In the evenings we congregated at Werner and Aleka's place for discussions, drinks, or tea. Harry Pufahl, who did photography and had acquired a Leica — probably the first one in town — often joined us. Volik was seldom there; his engineering studies took up all his time.

# 4

## *Leningrad*

### 1930

The first time I was arrested was in October 1930. I was eighteen years old. It was exactly one month after they had taken father and had arrested Herr Wegerer at the Beloostrov train station on the Finnish border. He had been a buyer of Russian lumber for German paper mills since before World War I and also had an office in the Finnish city of Vyborg where he lived for most of the winter months.

That October evening my friends Aleka and Werner came after supper and we had tea with mother, sitting around the dinner table in front of the bay window. We talked about Wegerer's release from prison a week ago when he had come back to his room in the morning, repacked his suitcase, and left again in the evening for the train to Helsinki.

We were now sure father would be home soon too. Mother complained about the Blumenfelds: when mother went to see Elsa Blumenfeld to tell her about father's arrest, Elsa barely let her come in, she was so scared. Her husband, Robert Blumenfeld, who was my godfather and whom I called Uncle Robert, was legal advisor to the German Consulate in Leningrad. Since Wegerer was a German citizen, Uncle Robert knew of his arrest. Board members of the German Cultural Association had also been arrested that September.[10]

Mother was optimistic as usual. I disliked the subject matter; those things happen, mistakes are made. Our house and Herr Wegerer had always been under surveillance; usually they followed his car. They knew all about us; there was nothing to hide. Why did they watch us? God knows, but that's their business. The conversation at the table was both in Russian and German. Mother's Russian was fluent but she had not lost her German accent during the twenty years she had been in Russia. Aleka understood but did not speak German, and I preferred talking with her about other things — the end of the rowing season and whether she would also start skiing. (Would she renew our broken relationship?)

Werner and Aleka were just preparing to leave when the doorbell rang. It was close to midnight; the house entrance had been locked since nightfall. Mother put the bottle of alcohol which Werner had brought from his laboratory on the cupboard — she would later make elderberry liqueur from it. (Lately vodka and foodstuffs had been in short supply.) Perhaps it was a neighbor; my sister Ira was spending the weekend with our neighbors, Professor Schaak's daughters. I went to open the door, but Nadya Goldin (the Goldins now lived in our former dining room) had already opened the door. And there they were again! The same commando who had ar-

---

[10] A summary of events compiled by *Osteuropa Magazine* in 1990 reads: "The waves of arrests, the first one on Easter 1930, the second one during the night of September 1, targeted the remainder of the Russo-German intelligentsia (medical doctors, men of the church, teachers, scientists, businessmen)." *Osteuropa Magazine*, Sonderdruck. Deutsche Verlagsanstalt Stuttgart, 1990, p. 56.

rested my father: the navy officer, a border guard soldier with a rifle, and our housing block administrator. They had a search warrant. Nadya retired to her room in a hurry.

Now Werner and Aleka had to stay and sit around the table with mother and the guard. I was told to accompany the navy officer to my room. We only had three rooms since living space had been rationed. Last time, when the night visitors came for my father, they rummaged a long time through everything in father's former study, now my parents' bedroom. They took out all the books, papers in the desk, and clothes. This time the task was limited to my desk, photographs, and darkroom. Eventually a protocol was filled out for the requisitioned items; it included my camera, photographs, and also the bottle of alcohol Werner had brought. The housing administrator signed as witness. Then I was shown my arrest warrant.

"Go and change into warmer clothes," the navy officer told me and went out to the hall to call for the Black Raven, a van to transport prisoners.

I was just pulling up my pants when Aleka came into my room. She kissed me and whispered: "Everything will be all right. I love you."

The guard barged in. "Citizen, you are not allowed to talk with the prisoner." We returned to the living room for me to say goodbye.

"You must button up your fly," mother observed — to make light of the moment. We heard the car arrive. Putting on my overcoat in the hall I looked back once more through the open door. It was all a *déjà vu*, but a month ago it had been more dramatic and sad — to say goodbye and stay behind.

Then, on that day a month ago, Herr Wegerer had asked me to accompany him to the train station to help with the luggage. His car and driver were urgently needed at the harbor where a ship was to depart. At Finland Station, while Herr Wegerer was buying his ticket, I carried his luggage to the Finnish sleeping car, the only car to cross the border. After Wegerer boarded the train, a uniformed guard asked me to follow him to the station office where I was asked to produce an identity paper. I showed them my factory pass, they made some notes, and I was free to go.

That same evening Isidor Becker had come over to sing his beloved Schubert and Schumann lieder. He sang for my mother; he was fond of her. Anisya, our maid who had come to us from her small village, leaned over the end of the grand piano and began to howl; music always made her cry. Herr Becker had a beautiful tenor but earned his living as a chemical engineer. If it were not for his unfortunate figure he could have sung in the opera but, failing that, he sang at recitals, often at the German Cultural Association.

Then, a month ago, I had accompanied him downstairs since the house entrance was already locked. Upstairs again, my parents and I were just about to say good night when the apartment doorbell rang. And there they were, the navy officer with his crew, who had come to arrest father.

Now, a month later, I looked back and saw the brightly lit room with mother, Aleka, and Werner standing far away in a haze of cigarette smoke. Downstairs the housing administrator had unlocked the house door, held it open for us to pass, and stayed back to lock it again.

The Black Raven was at the gate; the guard opened the rear doors. The housing administrator came through the gate, said "Good night," and was on his way home. I stepped through the rear door into the empty car and sat down on one of the wooden benches. Behind me a door with a small window was slammed and locked. A guard sat down behind it in a small rear compartment, his rifle between his knees. The rear door was slammed and locked and the car moved. It was cold inside. We rattled over the cobblestone pavement of our street; then, after a left turn, we rolled smoothly over the wooden pavement. Gears shifted; it must have been Trinity Bridge, now Bridge of the Revolution, then a right turn. It must be Million Street and we would pass the Hermitage and the Winter Palace. The destination was clear now: Gorokhovaya 2, famous GPU[11] headquarters. When the car stopped and the doors were opened, I got out and stood in a courtyard.

"Get moving," the guard said.

We entered a big lobby. It was warm, the lights dim, and it was quiet; the floors were carpeted. A wide elegant staircase dominated the lobby.

"Stop."

At a small desk with a green-shaded lamp, occupied by a guard, the navy officer transacted some business. Another guard, smartly dressed, appeared. "In order," he said to the guard with the rifle who turned around and disappeared.

The navy officer motioned to us. "Let's go," the new guard said. We followed him up the grand staircase to the top floor and down a hall flanked by doors. At the corner of the building was a small hall with a wooden bench. "Wait here," the navy officer said, and he and the guard turned the corner into the next corridor.

I was alone and sat down on the bench. It was probably about 2 a.m. now. They will interrogate — that was clear — and fine with me; maybe I'll be home in the morning. I was nervous about the alcohol. What should I say? Where did it come from? If they asked me and I said it came from the exhi-

---

[11] CHEKA, GPU or OGPU, NKUD, NKGB, MVD, and KGB were all acronyms for the Soviet secret police at different times in the history of the Soviet Union.

bition, then they would interrogate Werner. How would he know what my answers had been? I had to keep him out of this altogether. But how? Simple. It was just there in the cupboard and I didn't even know about it. Or maybe Herr Wegerer had bought it at the "Torgsin," the store for foreigners. Then there was the camera which had been brought from abroad by the German vice consul. It's true that no custom duties were paid for it; I had just "borrowed" it; I needed it professionally. I'll pay the custom duty if I can have it for my own.

It was warm and I was sweating; I took off my overcoat and stretched out on the bench. I began to think about Aleka. If I were home by the next day the first thing I would do is call her. She would say: "Darling, where are you? When shall we meet? Come right away. I'll meet you on the river quay; I have to tell you something. Remember what I told you yesterday. It will be all right." I'd run, catch the streetcar, jump off at the end of the bridge. I would see her far away coming down the embankment. There would be no one but her, her slim figure slightly bent forward, walking slowly, waiting for me to cover the distance between us, smiling, eyes and lips and teeth. I would be running and it would be wonderful to feel the air moving, the muscles flexing, the rhythm of the run. It was really like flying; easy, breathtaking, the river to the right, the familiar facades on the left flying by and only Aleka there in front, smiling.

"Citizen, you are not permitted to sleep here. Get up, get up." The guard was pushing my shoulder, shaking his head. "Get up, take your belongings and move." He motioned me down the corridor. I was drowsy. We passed a few doors.

"Stop." He knocked at the door and opened it. "The arrested is here, Comrade Chief."

"Let him in."

I entered a middle-sized room with two windows overlooking the courtyard. To the left there was a desk with a green-shaded lamp and a middle-aged man in uniform was sitting at the desk, two rhomboids on his collar, a general's rank. Near the window was another desk with the navy officer sitting behind it; on his desk sat all the requisitioned items, including the alcohol.

"Sit down. Before we go on with the business, do you have anything to say? A clean-hearted confession will be to your — and to your father's — advantage."

"I don't have anything to confess, Comrade Chief." I said, shrugging my shoulders.

"I am not your comrade," he said, his voice slightly raised. "For you I am Citizen Investigator. Remember that. When you have confessed and when you have been appropriately punished by the Soviet powers and have wholeheartedly renounced your crimes or mistakes and have returned to live among the honest citizens, then you may call me Comrade Weinschrot and thank me. *Dass ich sie vom Schlimmsten bewahrt habe* [I have kept you from a worse fate]," he added in German.

"Citizen Investigator," I said, "I don't know what I should confess to. You probably know everything about my life. I have nothing to hide. I can answer all questions you have to ask."

Weinschrot slammed his hand on the desk. "It's always the same story. Later they cry when it's too late." He stood on his feet leaning over the desk.

The interrogation went on for a couple of hours, mostly about father, Albrecht Holl, and Herr Wegerer. No questions about the requisitioned alcohol or the German Vice-Consul who had once invited me for lunch with some dancers from the ballet and from whom I had received my camera. I had also learned that the Vice-Consul was a homosexual, a criminal offense in the Soviet Union. I certainly didn't want this subject raised, and it wasn't. Later, when I had a glimpse of the other desk, I saw that the alcohol had disappeared. This was a relief.

Towards the end of the interrogation I was given a piece of paper and a pencil. "Write down all the names of people you know who have visited your home or whom you have visited." I sat down to write; it was a long list. Early in the morning Citizen Weinschrot called home and talked with his wife — family talk — maybe just to impress me how *gemuetlich* it might be to be back home. Once more a final question: did I have anything to confess? Then a guard was called.

## IN PRISON

I was taken downstairs again to sign out and was led into the yard. The Black Raven was waiting and we were off to the famous Shpalernka, Leningrad's House of Preliminary Detention. Another yard, another reception area without windows, but with many doors. There were a few soldiers behind desks. Papers changed hands. I had to clean out my pockets, then undress; I was examined to see whether I concealed anything on my body and then was ordered into a cell behind one of the many doors, standing room only. Time passed slowly, then the door opened and my clothes were thrown in, minus the belt and boot laces. "Get dressed." Then came another period of waiting again in the small cubicle.

Eventually I was led out of this area and, with a soldier behind me, I ascended a staircase enclosed on one side by a wire fence. At the third floor, a gate. Another soldier came down the corridor, his steps clicking on the stone floor, and opened the gate. We entered a broad corridor, no daylight. On one side were big grated arches; and there, behind the grate in the dusk lit by one yellow bulb, were many people. It looked like a zoo. Right where we entered I saw Professor Wulfius, my history professor from school, hanging onto the grate; I noted his ironic smile. "The chickens come home to roost," I heard him say as we passed by. We continued down the corridor. There was another cell and another one and then a gate was opened and I went in.

A few people rushed toward me. Over one hundred prisoners filled the cell. There were twenty-one cots ranged against the walls, two tables in the center of the room with benches, and in one corner a toilet enclosed waist high by corrugated steel. Most prisoners moved slowly counterclockwise around the tables; some sat at the table and played chess; small groups stood in the corners and talked. Two windows were shielded on the outside so that one could only see a strip of sky above and a strip of courtyard below.

I was led to the elder of the cell. He told me the rules and assigned me a place to sleep next to the cell gate. In the evening I would get a straw bag to put on the floor; the last to arrive here received the worst place to sleep. The gate opened to the inside of the cell and most interrogations were conducted at night. Every time someone was called or came back from an interrogation, I had to get up and move my mattress. Maybe a dozen times a night, maybe more. With time one moved up the prison ladder and, if there long enough, one might end up sleeping on one of the twenty-one cots. Prisoners were sentenced or transferred and sometimes even released. This occurred during the daylight hours.

There was always hope for a discharge; only a few knew for sure that they were guilty of something. For most, it was just guesswork. Some signed "confessions," others did not, but even those who did sign, did so to "ease their fate," to have the Citizen Investigator put in a good word for them before the "Troika" — the three high officers of the secret police who looked at the evidence and passed sentences. Maybe they would release you or at least let you go home for a few days before leaving for the place of exile. Hope springs eternal.

There were those who had been through it all, the veterans with no illusions. They were in solitary first, the quiet place with carpeted corridors, no sound of stepping heels or clicking locks, no calls, no voices. "Like a first-class old hotel," Mr. Molvo told me. And he knew about that; once a page at the Imperial Court, he had been more recently maitre d' of the Astoria Hotel for foreigners.

The worst was to be called "with belongings" at night. This was then the end of the rope. It happened later to Lyova, my neighbor on the cot. His was a bad case. He hoped for a "ten" but he got "seven kopeks." Ten years was then the maximum prison sentence; seven kopeks was the price of a bullet. Interrogators liked these proverbial sayings: "Moscow doesn't believe in tears," "seven kopeks worth," "put on debit" etc. Lyova was a telephone executive and he sold "on the left" — for his own profit — telephones which belonged to the military. He was called at night with belongings and he kissed me goodbye. A few of us watched the courtyard below from the window — whatever we could see. There was the Black Raven and we saw people getting in, handcuffed, silently.

The general prison felt more like a hospital. Clean and polished stone floors, oil-painted walls, the carbolic smell; a small desk at the end of the corridor, a green-shaded lamp, the officer on duty like a nurse in a hospital. At the end of the corridor was a window with a view. From there one could see the street, but only in a short glance when being escorted to a doctor.

When one passed by other cells, prisoners clung to the steel bars; they wanted to see if there was anyone they knew, anyone connected with their case. It was news time for prisoners. Someone called out of a cell in a subdued voice: "Sasha got five" or "Sasha got out" or whatever the news might be. One looked for new faces or for those missing.

It was a high-class crowd in this prison: intelligentsia, medium-rank officials, and a few party members. Mostly "fifty-eighters" (Article 58 of the old criminal code with its fourteen paragraphs covered all "political" crimes). No common criminals, no peasants.

In time, one joined one of the many groups or cliques which form in any such assembly. There were also solitary types who kept to themselves; they didn't trust anyone, everyone might be a stoolie, better not say anything. They also didn't like to share their *peredacha*, packages from home with clean underwear and food — whatever their loved ones could provide for them. There was a general rule that those who got packages gave something to a fund maintained for those who didn't get anything. Twice a day there was food; tea, bread, sugar in the morning, and *balanda* — a soup — in the afternoon. Three times a day we left our cell: once to store our straw sacks and to wash, once to pick up the straw sacks again in the evening, and once for a half hour walk in the courtyard, in pairs, no conversation. The rest is talking time.

## ALEKA

In a prison cell there are many stories; some are personal — even intimate — about wives, family, lovers. And there is plenty of time to think, to remember, to dream. I dream mostly of Aleka.

Why did she so abruptly break up our relationship that day before the boat races when she promised to come in the morning while I was sick in bed. Instead she called that she could not come.

"Why can't you come?" I feel immediately that something is wrong.

"I'll tell you later when I see you."

"Why not now?"

"I don't want to."

"With whom are you going?"

"With no one."

"It isn't true."

"It is."

"When will I see you?"

"I don't know, I'll call you."

Aleka hangs up; she doesn't call all day. The next day I have no fever and in the afternoon I am on my way to the club. She must be there; I couldn't get her on the phone. As I approach the clubhouse I see a car parked in front and Aleka with two men get into the car and drive off. I stay all evening in the club and wait but Aleka does not return. The next day she calls me. She will meet me in a park downtown. There she tells me that her feelings towards me have changed; she needs time to be alone.

"Is there someone else?"

"No."

"That isn't true.'

"It is."

"Then why?"

"I don't know."

"Don't lie."

"I am not lying."

And so it goes; I am not satisfied. With whom did she leave the club in the car? Somebody gave her a lift, she says, and names some people from the club.

"When will I see you again?"

"I don't know; give me time."

"Promise me."

"I told you. Give me time."

Why? It isn't because of Werner.

Only a few weeks earlier, in July, Aleka had called: "Let's go this weekend to Sestroretsk — we can use mother's room and go on Saturday. Werner will come Sunday; he can't make it Saturday."

Returning from night shift Saturday morning I take my swim trunks and towel, say goodbye to mother, and jump on a streetcar at the intersection. It is nearly empty but the rail station is busy. I wait on the steps overlooking the plaza. There is a brisk wind, a gust lifts a cloud of dust and sand into a turning column, a small cyclone; it drifts across the plaza, then another gust comes from the river and tears it apart; the dust and litter are chased down the street. Deep blue shreds of sky pierce through layers of clouds, cumulus, cirrus. It is warm in the sun but the wind is cool.

A streetcar comes and there she is; we rush to the platform and the train. The cars are full; we push through the crowd and find a place at the window; standing room only, but it's good to stand there so close together. The train moves; there are arguments whether windows should be closed. "Close it on the other side," says the passing conductor; our window remains open and the breeze feels good. A man sitting next to us at the window offers Aleka his seat. "No, thanks; we are comfortable where we are." A conversation starts. He is an engineer, tests aircraft engines. "Are you students?" he asks. "Let me guess," he smiles. "I bet you are newlyweds." "You guessed it," Aleka laughs.

Sestroretsk is right on the border with Finland. The white sandy beach is divided by a barbed wire fence; the beach continues into Finland, the barbed wire fence way into the shallow waters. Far away one can see people on the beach in Finland. It is July, sunny, but breezy and cool. Nobody tests the water and there are very few people on the beach. We dig ourselves into the sand and read. Aleka brought books; I read Dos Passos' *Manhattan Transfer.*

Our room in the sanitorium where Aleka's mother works part-time is a glass-enclosed porch. It is the time of the white nights and, for the first time, we spend a night together.

Out the window one can see the gate of the border post and a booth with a soldier. The next day at noon we meet Werner at the station. He doesn't care for the beach; it is too windy. We all take a long walk through the pine woods, eat at the rail station restaurant, and return to the city.

I remember another day Aleka and I were together at the Winter Palace, then part of the Hermitage, when we walked arm in arm from window to window looking out onto the Neva, the fortress, and the bridges.

"Why did you have to marry?" I asked.

"Silly, I didn't know I would love you," she laughed her short ironic laugh. "Remember, you tried to get into the taxi with us. I had to push you out and to tell you to get in front with the driver."

"Sure I remember. And your aristocratic friends laughing at me."

"Those laugh best who laugh last," she said. She looked around; there was no one to be seen. She stepped in front of me, kissed me, and laughed in my arms. We wandered farther along the endless flight of halls from one window niche to another. Then her mood changed and we stopped. "I remember standing here with my mother. Mother in a Red Cross uniform. And there," she pointed down the hall, "the Czar and Empress were coming with their daughters. We used to live here, across the Winter Canal in the new Hermitage."

"You never told me you lived here," I said.

"No. What does it matter now?" We looked out the window; across the Neva River the Alexandrine gold needle glistened in the afternoon sun.

"We should walk here all night when the sun never sets," I said.

"I have to go now," she said. We turned around and went toward the grand staircase.

That summer of 1930 I am eighteen, in love, and every day — rain or shine — is a beautiful day. Everything is a pleasure: walking the streets and parks arm in arm or waiting for the streetcar which will bring her and take us both to the rowing club.

Rowing on the river! The feel of the boat sliding through the water and dipping slightly with the oars' pull, the whole body working in concert with the crew, the simultaneous click of the oars, the up and down of the boat and its increased speed. It feels a bit like riding a horse in a gallop. Afterwards, showering the sweat off and sitting on the balcony overlooking the river watching others row past in sculls and doubles, in fours and eights; the girls carrying out their boat and placing it on the water. Her crew.

Whenever there is a symphony concert and I am not at work, I get tickets for Aleka and me. Bruno Walter, Klemperer, Zemlinsky, Knappertsbusch, Ansermet, Stiedry, Hindemith, Kuhlenkampf and others came in those years to conduct the Leningrad Symphony. And it is not only the musicians and the music which thrill me. To go there with Aleka is exciting because of the attention she draws by her appearance, and I am certainly vain on this point. Philharmonic Hall is the former Assembly of the Nobility and an elegant Empire structure. The parterre, where the audience sits in comfortable armchairs, is surrounded on three sides by rows of white columns. During intermissions one promenades in the wide passageways behind them. Philharmonic Hall has an elegant audience. One goes there both to listen and to be seen; we always have good seats. During one concert Lev Oborin plays a piano concerto and looks in our direction whenever possible. At intermission I tease Aleka about the looks she got from him. She laughs at me. "You don't know a thing," she said. "He only likes boys."

I had known Aleka from school, but only by sight. Although we graduated together in 1928, she had come to our school only a year earlier with the Polish Catholic School contingent. For political reasons, the Catholic School had been combined with our St. Petri School, a former German Lutheran school founded 200 years earlier under Peter the Great, thus ending our school's long history.

Aleka was known for her Louise Brooks looks, keeping to herself, and walking alone with a book during intermissions. There were rumors that she used to "go out with older men," those who had graduated some years earlier.

During the last days of school a group from our class was hired as extras for a short subject film produced for the city's police traffic department by Werner Christiani. He was about a dozen years my senior. I knew him from the German Cultural Association where he was one of the younger set of ambitious theater directors and where he had staged A. Conan Doyle and O. Henry stories. Tall, slender, very agile, with a pale complexion and beautiful hands, Werner was much admired by the young set. He dressed smartly. His gray double-breasted suit, impeccably ironed trousers (he put them overnight under his mattress), spats over shoes, and rim of his felt hat bent low over his brow gave him the appearance of a film star.

During the filming we became better acquainted and, once I was back in town in the fall, I looked him up to discuss plans for other short subject movies and schemes for procuring a professional movie camera. With a camera of our own, possibly to be procured in Germany, we hoped to get a foothold at the LENFILM studios.

One day when I visited Werner while he was ill with a tooth inflammation, he asked me to deliver a letter addressed to Aleka. I knew that he was divorcing his first wife. Aleka lived with her mother, grandmother, and younger brother on Million Street near the Hermitage. Her father, a former Navy officer, was then in exile in Siberia. Aleka recognized me and asked me to wait while she wrote an answer. Would I please deliver it to Werner?

From that day on I saw more of Werner and Aleka. I was active at the "International Theater" and our rehearsals took place not far from where Werner had his room. I learned that they were getting married as soon as Werner got his divorce.

I dropped in quite often at Million Street. Somehow it was always on my way between city and home and I liked the atmosphere there. Usually, besides Aleka, only her grandmother was at home. Aleka's mother, once a lady-in-waiting at the court, worked at an orthopedic hospital where during World War I, she, like other society ladies, had served as a nurse. Aleka's grandmother was a *grande dame* straight out of a Goya painting. It seemed that the encumbrances of daily life did not penetrate the thick walls of this old place. There were no servants but, as if they were there, their tasks were accomplished unnoticed. There was an air of formality in the house and little or no talk about everyday boring subjects and no complaints. Unpleasant subjects were ignored.

Aleka's father, a former imperial naval officer and once a naval attache in Constantinople, had been banished for three years to a Siberian town, a common fate for former officers. If they had served in the White Armies during the Civil War, they were likely to end up on the island of Solovki, the famous concentration camp.[12] He returned home early in 1929.

Werner and Aleka's wedding took place in April at St.

---

[12] The Solovetskiye Islands — Solovki for short — was a former monastery in the White Sea at 65 degrees latitude; it became the first Soviet concentration camp and the origin of the Gulag Archipelago. For a detailed description of it see Alexander I. Solzhenitsyn's *The Gulag Archipelago 1918-1956: An Experiment in Literary Investigation III-IV.* New York: Harper & Row, 1973, pp. 9-24.

Simeon Church; I was Werner's best man. St. Simeon is a small old church. At the altar it was all gold and candles; I held a crown over Werner's head and Aleka's brother held one over her head. Behind us stood Aleka's parents and the guests and, in the back, a crowd of old women always present at such ceremonies, chanting, praying, and crossing themselves.

I rode in a taxi with the newlyweds to a reception at Aleka's house. Afterwards they just walked home; Werner had obtained a room in a big apartment. There was no honeymoon.

My romantic involvement with Aleka began one rainy day in the late fall of 1929 when I dropped in as usual to see her. She was on the couch reading under the lamp; it was already getting dark. I sat down beside her and chatted about one thing or another. She looked at me with a smile, her usual smile, but only her mouth smiled while her big dark flashing eyes retained their piercing, questioning, intelligent look. Then she took my head with both hands, lifted herself to my face and kissed me and, when the kiss exhausted us, we both broke into tears. My awakening passion suddenly seemed to change everything — the cherished friendship of the three of us, clear and simple just a moment ago. When I told her, looking at her tears, that now I had to go out and find Werner to tell him "everything," she just shook her head. "You do not need to tell him anything — he'll know," she said. We never talked about it again. That same evening the three of us went out together to see Louise Brooks in Kortner's film "Lulu" based on Wedekind's "Pandora's Box." It was shown only at the Film Producers Association and had movie celebrities jumping excitedly in their seats.

Early into the New Year, Aleka came down with scarlet fever. I was with her for two evenings until the rash appeared. That evening when Werner came home we called the ambulance which took Aleka to the hospital. She stayed there for weeks in the old barracks of the isolation station. One could visit her by looking from the outside through a window. I went there daily, sometimes with Werner; when she was better and came to the window I wrote notes which she answered with "yes" or "no," since she had nothing to write with. We communicated as lovers do. Soon after Aleka came home from the hospital she became pregnant and had an abortion.

At that time I was mobilized for labor duty. It was the year when unemployment was outlawed in the Soviet Union and I was unemployed; the international theater where I had been active didn't get any state subsidy and folded. I reported to the Labor Exchange Board and was sent to the Max Hoeltz Plant[13] to be trained as a lathe operator. The plant manufactured cigarette machines and linotypes.

Work went on in three shifts and each week we were assigned a different shift. When I worked evening or night shifts I spent my free time with Aleka. We joined a rowing club, we went to symphony concerts, and danced at the German Cultural Association or at Hotel d'Europe. When I had money we took a taxi to the Strelka — land's end — or went to a cafe.

* * *

Now when I receive my first *peredacha* — package from home — I find a handkerchief in the package scented with Aleka's familiar *Quelques Fleurs d'Houbigant.*

In prison, day in and day out, it is the same routine: clean up, wash up, food distribution, and half an hour walk in the yard. And listening to other people's stories.

A geneticist, a religious man who worked at Vavilov's Institute for Plant Breeding, was dispatched by Vavilov to Moscow

---

[13] The factory was named for a German communist.

for a few days away from the coming *chistka*[14] which was to be conducted at the Institute. He had a sleeping car ticket for the Red Arrow; there was only one other passenger in the compartment, an intelligent, pleasant young man. Tea and zwieback were brought to the compartment; they settled down for a long night and talked about science and religion, debating whether they were compatible, about theory and faith, holy order and holy man, freedom and research. The geneticist was asked if his philosophy was compatible with his scientific work.

"You mean that I will not be honest in my research because I believe in God? Proof doesn't depend on faith, theory depends on proof." And so they talked long into the night.

In the morning after he and his companion had tea together, the latter showed him his identification and said: "I must ask you to come with me." There was a car waiting at the station which brought them to the Lubyanka. Later the scientist was brought back to Leningrad in a boxcar.

"They certainly don't spare any expense," someone remarked.

Now, in prison, the geneticist debated the same issues with a former Party man decorated with the Order of the Red Banner, an educated man who had held high positions, a true believer who had "deviated." Here they were: two believers — one Marxist, one Christian. They argued and shared *peredachas*. One could say they loved one another here in prison but were enemies outside.

Gorkiy had called prison the "university of life." In the 19th century, Prince Kropotkin, the anarchist, called it a

---

[14] *Chistka* means "cleansing" and was an investigation by party organs into the political, philosophical, and intellectual purity of a scientific organization. It looked for right or left deviations or outright counterrevolutionary tendencies.

"university of crime maintained by the state." There was always something to listen to in the big cell. Architect Katzenelenbogen lectured about form and function, style and modernity, Bauhaus and Hannes Mayer; others told us how to eat if there isn't enough food — chew every bite sixty times — or how to exercise in solitary confinement. A group of us exercised every morning.

I was never called again for an interrogation at Shpalerka and was sorry to leave the place when they transferred me to Kresty Prison, a modern, American-style building forming a cross — that's where the name comes from. Steel galleries ran along the inner perimeter five stories high with about 800 cells originally built to house one inmate each and every one containing one iron bedstead, a drop leaf table, a chair, and a *parasha*, a covered pail standing in one corner next to a ventilation shaft.

Our cell had a view over the Neva River and Smolnyy Monastery. There were four of us — a carpenter, an agronomist, an accountant (a former Czarist officer), and myself. The officer taught me chess and told stories about the Great War and his time as a POW in Germany. There is more tension in a small cell than in a big one and less activity. Nothing seems to happen to anyone. At Kresty the "cases" were mostly closed; prisoners were just waiting. Only downstairs near the "pressure cells" on the first floor was there any activity; the guards there were GPU soldiers. The "press" — as it was called — had cells, standing room only, for as many prisoners as could fit in — men and women — and a loudspeaker. They were suspected of hiding gold or foreign currency, usually didn't stay very long, and went home, at least for a while, after having given up their treasure.

I stayed at Kresty for two months. In April I was called twice for short interrogations by the navy officer. The first time he wanted me to sign a prepared protocol. I refused to do so without putting in some changes. The next day he brought the corrected protocol and I signed it. He told me that I would be set free but had to sign a paper stating that I would not leave Leningrad.

Our guard smiled when I told him on the way back to the cell that I would go home. He said, "The doors here are wide open to come in but the way out is tha-a-a-t narrow." And he put two fingers into a narrow slit in front of his squinting eyes. At Kresty the guards were regular prison guards, not soldiers of the secret police, and this typical Russian peasant type was always friendly to prisoners.

Waiting was hard for me. Doubts set in: was it true or just a trick? Did I overlook something? Why did he say that I would be set free? They usually don't promise such things. And then why tomorrow and not right away?

I didn't want to show either my doubts or excitement. I knew my cell-mates were thinking: "Why him, not me? He is young, no wife, no kids waiting for him. Or why is he nervous? He knows he will be free, if not today, tomorrow, next week." Or "could he be a stoolie?" For them, everything was still uncertain. What will they get — three, five, ten? When will they see their families again? I no longer shared their unknown fate and this put me at a distance. Only the former officer, my chess partner, seemed free of resentment.

Somehow the day and night passed. Next morning, on my return from the washroom, a guard was at the door waiting for me "with belongings." Quick goodbyes, down five flights of iron stairs past the interrogation cells and through the first iron gate to the warden's office. A discharge certificate and pass are issued, belt and shoelaces returned. And now one can go out of the building through the courtyard to the main gate. There the guard looks at the pass. "Home," he says and opens the small door in the big gate.

I step out. In front of me is the choppy river, to the left and right the high brick prison walls. It is April.

I turn right and start running, downriver, to Finland Station where the streetcars are. There is tram number six and, as I get on it, I am suddenly conscious of my five-month beard and bag of dirty clothes. I stay on the platform, turn my back and look out the window as we pass the familiar streets, the bridge, the buildings; nothing has changed, everybody walks around as usual as if nothing had happened.

There is my street and I jump off the moving streetcar. I run down my street, through the gate, doors, up the stairs and ring the bell. It is Ira who opens the door. "Oh my God. You look like Jesus Christ," she screams and hangs on my neck. Mother comes, everybody comes, big tumult. Then telephone calls are made; Volik, my best friend, is there in five minutes.

# 5

## Interim

On the day I returned home from prison in April 1930 Martha Holl arrived at the house to share the good news. She was certainly glad to see me, she said, but what about my father? He'll be coming home too, I answered; it was all some mistake. But Martha didn't buy that; she had just come back from a visit to Germany where everything was also out of order with unemployment and political fighting in the streets; God only knows who can restore order there. But her ruminations do not interest me. I want to hear news about my friends and about Aleka.

Volik tells me the news. Aleka and Werner are separated; Aleka now lives again on Million Street with her family. He has seen a lot of Aleka this winter while going to concerts and movies together. A second German exhibit of laboratory equipment has opened; Werner and Harry are working there. I call Aleka's home; her grandmother answers: Oh how wonderful, she is so happy. No, Aleka is not at home; she is visiting friends in Tsarskoye Selo but will be back tomorrow; I should come at noon. She will not tell Aleka anything; I should surprise her. I call the exhibition hall and talk to

Werner. We will meet there shortly but first I have to go to the barber to take off the beard. Ira and mother don't want me to, but I can't stand it any longer.

At the end of the day I meet Werner and Harry at the exhibit of German laboratory equipment and later walk with Werner along the university embankment. He tells me about his separation. They still are friends, no hard feelings. Should he look for work for me at the exhibition? Well, I have first to check in at the Max Hoeltz Plant.

I could hardly wait until noon of the next day. When I came to Aleka's place, her grandmother opened the door. When Aleka saw me she cried and came running for an embrace. Then she wanted to go for a walk with me and talk. We went to the river and she told me about an old family friend whom I knew casually. Aleka was moving for the summer to Tsarskoye Selo where this man and his mother had a place for the summer. This would give her time to think and rearrange her life. Although he wanted to marry her, he had promised not to pressure her. He was an older man, dispassionate, not in good health; but he was a gentleman and his mother a kind lady. She still loved me, Aleka said, but she had to get away from it all. From what, I thought, and why? But I did not ask.

As we walked along the river from the Hermitage to Trinity Bridge and back again, she told me all of this bit by bit. I felt hurt, but maybe not to the degree I would have expected. Give me time, she said, and so there was hope.

In the evening Herr Becker came and we sat and talked. Mother told us of her "conversations with Herr Weinschrot." He had summoned her twice.

"Sometimes he tried to frighten me but it didn't work," she smiled. "We spoke German; he has a Viennese accent. Actually he was quite polite." Herr Becker protested. How could she talk about him so calmly as if he were a decent person?

"If he had been a German K&K officer[15] in 1918-19, he might have stayed downstairs in our house on the way back home to Vienna," mother said. But probably he was not an officer, just a Jewish boy from Vienna drafted into the K&K army and taken prisoner by the Russians. Weinschrot became a "soldier of world revolution" while a Russian POW. He rose to the position of Chief, Special Department (Foreign Intelligence), of the Leningrad GPU. In later years, whenever he came to mind, I mused how Weinschrot had fared in 1934 or 1938 when, after Kirov's murder, the Leningrad GPU was purged, or in 1938 when Yagoda, the top boss, was executed.

Many years later in Germany mother told me the whole story about him and my father. When NEP ended and my father lost his job with the German Shipping Agency, he must have seemed to Weinschrot a good prospect for hire: Russian born, master of many languages, close relatives abroad — father and sister in Estonia, brother in Finland, friends and wife's relatives in Germany. Also a patriotic citizen — since he had not emigrated — and a liberal, maybe an anarchist, but with no attachment to the old regime.

Probably Weinschrot summoned father as early as 1928 only to find out that father was not a soldier of world revolution, that he had been brought up in the conviction that "gentlemen do not read other people's mail." This was the problem.

What could the two have talked about during father's year of solitary imprisonment? Certainly not just about father's acquaintances and his conversations with them. Did they discuss Soviet-German relations; the postwar status of these two countries which had both lost the Great War, their business and military relations, the political prospects in Germany?

---

[15] *Kaiser und Koeniglich*, i.e., imperial and royal officer.

Did they consider the depression, wars between left and right, perhaps the prospects of "building socialism in one country" rather than world revolution? At that time the German Communist Party, the "strongest among the Communist parties in Europe, became a castrated giant whose brag and bluster only served to cover its lost virility." [16] But why was the German-speaking community of Leningrad targeted for dissolution at that particular time? And why was our neighbor, Professor Schaak, who had also been arrested, then released upon intervention of the famous surgeon Professor Fedorov? Maybe it was the return of Schaak which fed our hope concerning my father. We were wrong. For 11 months father continued to be kept in solitary confinement at Leningrad's Nizhegorodskaya Prison before being transferred to Kresty Prison Hospital.

In any event, after one-and-a-half years in prison for alleged espionage under Article 58, paragraph 6, usually punishable by execution, Weinshrot had father sentenced to three years in exile with one-and-a-half years already served. This was in 1932, on the threshold of Stalin's Great Terror, and of Hitler's ascendancy to power in Germany.

* * *

My job at the Max Hoeltz Plant was waiting for me when I returned, but I didn't want to stay there. However, I had to go there to get my papers and first went to the front office to get the back pay due me. At the shop my appearance created a small sensation. Uncle Petya was all smiles and took me immediately to Plekahnov's booth; all the foremen congregated there were curious to hear an account of what had happened to me. When they learned that I was quitting they tried to change my mind. I was sorry to leave and appreciated how

---

[16] Arthur Koestler. *The God That Failed.* Bantam Matrix edition, 1965, p. 48.

they had accepted me into their midst, but I had made my decision and my friend Andrey and I had different plans.

Andrey Behrens was working at the optical plant which was manufacturing the first Soviet cameras. The acquisition of a camera required the advance purchase of a bond — full price — with delivery of the camera later. Andrey had suggested that the optical plant might make a promotional film. He wanted me to apply for work on the assembly line until the movie plans materialized. I was hired and worked at assembling cameras until the administration learned that I spoke German and I was summoned for a different activity.

The plant employed a number of German immigrant workers, members of the German communist party who had come to the Soviet Union through the help of the International Society for Revolutionary Assistance (MOPR). The Germans were specialists employed as foremen and controllers and constantly came up with problems of inefficiency, quality control, and lack of tools. Other problems were of a more sensitive political nature. As foreigners they had special privileges: better food rations, better housing, and vacations. This was contrary to their ideas of a classless society; it separated them from their Russian comrades and caused envy, discontent, even enmity. For me to convey their complaints to the administration was a rather thankless task and I was greatly relieved when the time came for me to take over as cameraman of our film project.

There were three of us: a friend of Andrey's who had experience as a writer and director of short subjects; Andrey, who knew camera work; and myself, whose ability to handle a movie camera was mainly theoretical. Our production center was the Photo Kino Technikum where Andrey knew the administration. While the students were off on summer vacation we took over the lab, developed our film, printed copies, selected archival material, and cut and edited our production.

In two-and-a-half months of intensive work I acquired practical experience working with the camera which proved to be of great advantage to me in the years ahead. Needless to say, we had fun.

I liked Andrey, the "Odessite" in him who loved to wheel and deal. His hero was Ostap Bender of the "Twelve Chairs," a popular novel which made fun of bureaucratic simpletons while praising — tongue-in-cheek — man's resourcefulness and adaptability. But Babel and Bagritskiy, the contemporary revolutionaries, were his heroes too.

Andrey always had new ideas for employing cinematography and photography and had already made short subject films for the trade unions, tourist office, the yacht club, and a concrete factory. Now we looked together for opportunities to use film as a research tool at the Leningrad Ballet and at technical institutions of higher learning. Eventually Andrey organized a photo-film laboratory at the Polytechnical Institute and I took up similar work at the model basin and wind-tunnel of the Technological Institute.

It was particularly important to be fully employed now because of the pending introduction in major cities of the internal passport system for which a place of work and residence were preconditions. Persons who did not receive a passport had to leave the cities for the provinces.

Since my job at the laboratory did not occupy all my time I also found work through Werner at the Institute of Standards for the Construction Industry. The head of the Institute was also Dean of Architecture at the Art Academy and, with his help, I hoped to become a student there in the fall of 1933.

At home we no longer had the substantial financial support provided by Herr Wegerer who had paid us for his board when in town in Torgsin bonds; with these bonds we could go to special stores to get scarce food. But we were still well off financially. In addition to my three jobs, mother earned money knitting her popular Orenburg shawls. Isidor Becker brought us German patent applications and other papers on technical innovations for translation. Among them I remember a report on Berlin's new water treatment plant.

The summer weeks and months went by, but father did not return home. Mother went regularly to the Nizhegorodskaya Prison with *peredachas* which were just as regularly rejected; finally in August they were accepted when father was moved from solitary confinement to a common cell.

Towards the end of the year our neighbor, Professor Schaak, informed mother that father had been ill with thrombophlebitis and had undergone surgery by a well-known colleague of Schaak's. Soon we were notified that father had been transferred to Kresty Prison hospital. In March father received his sentence: Three years of exile, including the one and a half years already served while under investigation, under Article 58, paragraph 6, "espionage."

One day when mother brought a *peredacha* for father, she was told that we could visit him at Kresty Prison hospital. When we went there a nurse took us to a separate building through a long corridor well-lit by big windows to a room with several beds, one occupied by father. He looked pale and had a swollen bandaged arm, but got out of bed as soon as he saw the three of us and came out to the corridor. It was an emotional encounter with all the usual questions and irrelevant answers. Then, after a while, father began to talk about guilt, transgressions, and God's punishment. I was stunned. To my mind father had been engaged in a struggle, a combat with Weinschrot to endure and to prevail, and father was the winner. Wasn't his sentence a vindication, a confirmation of his innocence, his victory? Why now the flight into religion? We had never really belonged to a church; we never went there except on Christmas. When Alfred Blumenfeld and I were sent to confirmation classes I dropped out after the first two Sundays and didn't even attend Alfred's confirmation. Father never objected. Now I was embarrassed by his surrender as I saw it. Certainly I lacked compassion.

I went to a window and looked out on the Kresty Prison which I had left a year ago, rather than listen to what father had to say. Then the nurse returned and said that our visit was over. This was the last time I saw my father.

I think mother and Ira visited him one more time but I did not. In April he left on a transport to Alma Ata. From there he wrote that he was employed at a Turksib office, the Turkestan Siberian Railroad still under construction. We all felt relieved; mother and Ira would visit him in Alma Ata in summer. Andrey and I had already planned a trip to the Caucasus during our upcoming leave in August.

In the summer of 1932 I also joined Harry Pufahl on some occasions to do photography at various sports events. All these part-time jobs filled most of the hours of the day way beyond the regular eight hour work day, but I had a feeling of independence and accomplishment and the monetary rewards made it all worthwhile. Harry's father, an accountant, was also a tinkerer. He built small organs, assembled motorcycles from old parts, and his most recent hobby was putting together radio receivers. Harry had one of these receivers and we often listened to pop music: the latest hits transmitted by Motala, Hilversum, or Berlin stations.

Harry's Aunt Mary worked as an interpreter and translator at the Soviet Institute for the Metallurgical Industry and was secretary to one of the American engineers. Mr. Weindl, who was Austrian-born, spoke German and was a frequent guest at Harry's home. He brought one of the first Leica cameras from Germany and gave it to Harry who, like all of us, was interested in photography.

A Leica at that time was a revolutionary tool. While the

old sports photographers came with their big cameras and a dozen glass negatives, we shot several rolls of film, selected the best pictures for the sports magazine, and sold prints to the participants in the event — soccer players, bicycle racers, swimmers, boxers, hockey players. After such events, Harry and I worked through the night in his little darkroom enlarging hundreds of prints to sell. The only problem was film supply. One needed connections to cameramen in film studios who could "spare" some film for the black market. We became acquainted with Stilianudis, a cameraman and Greek national working on documentaries with Dziga Vertov, a well-known Soviet producer. They had been shooting a documentary in Germany and Stilianudis had returned from Germany with his own supply of film. He also brought a British motorcycle and pornographic postcards from Constantinople. Through him our supply of film was assured.

Mr. Weindl also brought us American pop records, a most valuable addition to our social gatherings: "Ro-ro-lling Along," "Betty Coed," "Somewhere in Old Wyoming," Gershwin tunes, and many others. Volik's mother, having listened to these records, often played them later on her piano. Whatever free time our little group of friends had — Werner, Volik, Andrey, Harry and myself — was usually spent together.

Werner had married again. In the spring he had visited his home town of Pskov and came back with his third wife, Nina, a sturdy provincial trained nurse. They lived now in a room of the former Holl apartment; the Holls had moved into the house of the Swedish Consulate.

❋ ❋ ❋

At the end of the school year mother and Ira prepared for a trip to Alma-Ata to visit father, but their preparations were abruptly interrupted.

One morning, while mother and I were still at breakfast,

the doorbell rang. When I got to the door, Nadya Goldin was already there and the postman had handed her a telegram.

"It's for your mother," Nadya said. A telegram could be only bad news, I thought. I opened it. The telegram read: "Gherman Yakovlevlich Saal died. What should be done with his belongings?" I showed it to Nadya and went back to our room.

"What happened?" asked mother when she saw me.

"A telegram," I answered and handed it to her. She was shaken but never lost control; I don't think I ever saw her cry.

"How shall we tell Ira?" she said after a while. "She'll take it very hard." My sister was out of town visiting friends.

Shortly afterwards Andrey told me in confidence what he had learned from Werner who, at the time the telegram arrived, was on a business trip in Moscow. When Werner returned he was summoned for his regular interview with the secret police. The agent wanted to know about our reaction to father's death and revealed to him that he already had a detailed account of what happened at our home that day. It was clear to me that only Nadya Goldin could have been his source. I didn't tell mother about my discovery because I didn't want to implicate Werner.

Soon thereafter, in August 1932 Andrey and I went on vacation to the Black Sea. Andrey still had documents from the tourism office from filming the Volga cruise. We decided that these papers could still serve us well in getting free accommodations at tourist facilities in Sochi and Sukhumi. It was a ruse that worked. At Sochi we were provided with free room and board. After two weeks we boarded a boat at Sukhumi for Odessa; from Odessa we took a train back to Leningrad. We had sleeping car accommodations and did not learn anything about the famine which was sweeping the Ukraine. At some stations we noticed women and children with bundles huddled around station houses waiting for an opportunity to board a train. But one was accustomed to such sights even at city stations. The total control of information completely obscured the disastrous state of affairs in the country. Stalin called it "dizziness from success."

## LAST DAYS IN LENINGRAD

For the winter of 1932 to 1933 our group of friends rented a house in Toksovo which was in the direction of the Finnish border and a good place for cross-country skiing. We went there on weekends, Werner with his wife, the rest of us with occasional girlfriends. We all met at Finland Station with our skis, toboggans, rucksacks with food and drinks, camera, and a record player. On two occasions our group attracted the attention of the railroad police and we were called in for identification.

During this period I met Olga, one of the girls among our athlete friends and a student at the Institute of Economics, and we became good friends. She was a member of the women's ice hockey team at the Dynamo Sports Club. Olga joined our occasional parties at home; together we attended a big New Year's party at the house of champion bicycle racers.

One early February afternoon while waiting for a streetcar at one of the main intersections, I recognized Olga standing at the tram stop. She didn't see me; I approached her from behind and put my hands over her eyes. She turned around, whispered "go away," and moved towards the front end of an approaching streetcar. I saw her enter the front platform reserved for police and streetcar personnel followed by a man wearing a civilian overcoat over military boots. I hung on to the rear platform of the streetcar and watched Olga and the man exit a few stops down the avenue at the "Big House," the new high-rise GPU headquarters adjacent to the Shpalernaya Prison.

I called on Olga the next evening. She lived with her parents on Vasiliy Island; she was at home and asked me to accompany her to the Dynamo Sports Club for her ice hockey training. The Dynamo Sports Clubs were actually sponsored by the GPU; they were the best equipped and financed clubs and therefore attracted the best athletes from all walks of life.

We walked across the river and part of the way to the club before boarding a streetcar. She told me what had happened the day before: at the Institute she was called to the Special Section where a man was waiting to accompany her to the "Big House." There she was given a warning; if she wanted to remain a student she had to terminate her association with our group. She didn't really know what to do; we had become quite fond of one another.

I waited in the club's cafeteria until her training session ended and brought her home. It was after midnight when I approached my house. There was light in all our windows. I knew what that meant. For a moment I thought of turning around and going somewhere else but did not; after all, I had nothing to hide.

At home there was the familiar scene: a guard with rifle, the housing administrator shaking his head as he saw me (I didn't know whether with a sense of consolation or accusation), and a GPU officer conducting a search. This time the officer seemed to be of lesser stature; he had a threatening attitude born of inferiority. But this was of no consequence. He had a search and arrest warrant for me. After a change of clothes and goodbyes, I was again in the Black Raven and driven once more to Shpalernaya Prison.

## PRISON AGAIN

During the next two months at Shpalernaya Prison I was called for three interrogations — always at night — by the man who arrested me. There were the usual threats with pistol on table, prolonged periods of standing face to the wall, and the appearance of a second interrogator with the two of them trying to confuse me by firing questions in fast succession. But their script was no good; it lacked any sense.

I was to admit that I was the organizer of a Hitler youth movement. Hitler had taken over the German government on January 30, 1933, a week before my arrest. There was the issue of listening to foreign radio: weren't we receiving instructions by radio? I didn't understand how one could get instructions over a radio station. Mannerheim was pulled out of their bag of tricks too — we were supposed to have spied for him while skiing in Toksovo. I didn't know much about him. Wasn't he president of Finland?

It was all too silly. Meanwhile one learned about the standard interrogation methods: threats, promises and enticements. As long as there was no beating or other physical harm, one was not scared enough to comply with the interrogator's demands which usually included signing prepared "confessions." Even the walk to the basement and standing there face against the wall after having listened to some theatrical threat was unbelievable, if frightening. One knew that "the case" didn't amount to much, as did the low-ranking interrogator.

At the end of March came the last interrogation. No silly accusations this time, just "How well do you know Andrey Behrens and Citizen von Grass?" Yes, I knew Andrey well; I met him often and we worked together. Citizen Grass I barely knew at all and hadn't known he was a "von." A protocol was written to this effect and I signed it. Then I was told that Andrey and Grass had signed confessions; the investigator read me some excerpts. They admitted belonging to a counterrevolutionary organization and having spread counterrevolutionary propaganda; Grass stated that he was a monarchist.

This seemed to close the case. I had the feeling that sentencing would come soon and that I would not be going

home. From the interrogations I gathered that Volik and Harry also had been arrested, but heard nothing about Werner or
Olga. I had the feeling that everything was falling apart and
didn't care that much whether or not I would go home. Even
home was not the place it used to be, and I knew that mother
would be able to take care of herself and Ira, without me.

I thought back to Aleka. I had never learned why she had
left me. But, when I saw Olga step on to the front platform of
the tram followed by the man in civilian overcoat with boots
beneath it, I remembered Aleka getting into a car accompanied by two men in front of the rowing club. The two images
overlapped. Olga told me that she was ordered to cut our ties.
What about Aleka? Did she keep it a secret?

Eight years later in Moscow Aleka sent me a note: She re-
gretted that I hadn't looked her up when I was in Leningrad.
How had she known that I had been there? The carrier of the
note told me: "Aleka is working two jobs. You know what I
mean." Was this a note in line of duty or perhaps a note for
old love's sake. Like history, life is full of assumptions feeding
fantasy or prejudice. When love is intruded upon by govern-
ments, it becomes operatic stuff where everything can be explained according to the conventions of storytelling. But in
life everything remains conjecture: Why? Who? How?

✳ ✳ ✳

On late winter days or early spring mornings when the air
is filled with a new transparency, a delicate veil reverberating
with new sounds and penetrating the thickness of any wall,
even the inhabitants of a prison cell become aware of nature's
changes and are even more haunted by memories of the world
outside.

The places near the windows from where at least a narrow
strip of sky was visible above the window blinds were never
empty. They were a refuge of loneliness in the thicket of the

prison crowd, respected by the crowd like an altar where every one was entitled to a few moments of solitude and fervent flight. Meanwhile the others pursued their daily chores and needs: lining up for a place at a table, awaiting their turn at the toilet, or joining the ranks of those who had already started the ceaseless movement around the tables as soon as the floor was swept and the routine prison day took shape.

One April morning there was the familiar clattering of keys, the snapping sound of the lock, and the appearance of the officer on duty. As usual all movement in the cell stopped. In the sudden silence, the officer called out my name. A morning call was unusual unless it was "with belongings."

Old timers who gathered at the gate were unanimous: "You will get your sentence." When the convoy came we did not follow the usual route for interrogation but went downstairs through several gates close to the exit. One did not know where the exit was but sensed the different circles of the prison by the way the guards behaved and by the air, the smell, the noise, maybe just the draft: The noiseless, softly lit carpeted gangways of the solitary block, the wider forbidding halls of the interrogation block with their tense traffic regulations, and the even bigger halls of the common prison with the arches of human cages and faces behind the bars, where everything was polished and clean except the air. Towards the exit everything got dirtier but the air got cleaner. When we passed a shutterless window, I felt already half free.

We entered the commandant's office, a room with one big window and view of a yard, a big desk in the center of the room, doors on both sides to other offices, and two benches left and right from the entrance. Volik was sitting on the bench to the right, his face pale, a sparse beard, his expression more dour than usual. When he saw me he nodded his head and managed something of a smile. I had to sit down on the

left bench. There was a coming and going of uniformed females who didn't pay any attention to us; then a tired looking
officer came in. He sat down behind the desk, looked through
some papers, called Volik's name, and read the sentence: "By
decision of the Troika of the OGPU... convicted in accordance with Article 58, paragraphs 10 and 11, to five years at a
corrective labor camp." Volik had to sign a paper; the guard
said "come along" and they left the office.

As they were leaving, another officer entered, a tall young
lieutenant in a floor-length great coat, a heavy Mauser pistol
and two leather field cases on his belt supported by shoulder
straps. He had the look of a battlefield soldier, not the polished neatness of uniformed prison personnel but a sense of
the steppe, of restlessness and an unsheltered existence not at
all fitting into the prison surroundings. He greeted the commandant; they both disappeared into an adjacent office, then
came back carrying folders. The officer signed something, put
some papers into his field case, looked at his wristwatch, and
went out leaving behind him an (imaginary) smell of sweat
and hay, of places far away. I could not know, of course, that
during the month to come we would be crossing a continent
together.

Now my name was called and I was read what I had heard
already when Volik had been called. It was also five years.
Let's get on with it, I thought, while walking back to my cell.

It was time to say farewell. For the second time I was leaving this place where sorrow, hopes, regrets, enlightenment,
contemplation, weakness and fortitude, and the whole scale
of human emotions was laid bare, begging for compassion or
crying for contempt. It had provided me with mentors and
educational examples not available out there "in freedom"
where teaching was restricted to sterile abstractions, slanted or
perverted from their true meaning.

Here in the vaulted halls of the new monastery I had become aware of the classless brotherhood of men in need, men with true compassion and honest contempt but without hate, where an honest word without fear or an honest silence out of fear gave the day a true meaning.

In the afternoon I was called "with belongings" and transferred one floor down to a nearly empty cell. Volik was already there. We huddled in a corner and he gave me news of what happened after my arrest. He was arrested a month later when they came to his house for the third time. On the first visit they took his brother Oleg, on the second his father, and only the third time around was it his turn, leaving his mother alone at home. Nothing during his interrogation concerned his family. It all related to Harry, Andrey, and me and was about the same silly stuff they had asked me. Harry was the first one arrested after me; Andrey got panicky and told everybody that "if they put me into solitary I'll sign anything they want." Of course he was the only one to be put in solitary.

So it was Andrey, the "weak link," he who had introduced me to his favorite writers Bagritskiy and Babel.

> Upon whose path are we now strewn?
> Whose feet will trample down our rust...?
> Roll on through the fields,
> Chant in the steppes!
> Follow the gleam of bayonets glancing...[17]

Andrey, the civil war romantic, who fancied his "Galife" britches and knee-high laced American airman's boots. Of course, it was irrelevant who the "weak link" was, just as im-

---

[17] From Eduard Bagritskiy. "By Our Black Bread, Our Faithful Wife," *Modern European Poetry*. New York: Bantam Books, 1978, p. 419. Eduard Bagritskiy (1885-1934), the poet, and Isaak Babel (1984-1939?), the fiction writer, joined the Red Army in 1918 and romanticized their exploits.

material as what our "house watchers" or "tails" had reported; police statistics to support a conviction. What did it matter who had supplied it? Not so for Volik; he cursed Andrey and hated his weakness. Volik was desolate; it was his last year at the engineering institute. His only hope was that we would be sent to one of the well-known nearby Gulag projects, either the Svir Canal or the Belomor Canal.

More prisoners kept arriving at the cell, all with about the same sentences. Everyone now expected the *svidanye* (the last meeting allowed the prisoner with his family before departure) and the *peredacha* for the road. This came the next day. About a dozen of us at a time were escorted down to a meeting room. There was a wire fence across the room on our side, a wooden barrier some distance away on the visitors' side, and a guard controlling the area in between.

Volik and I went down together. To our great amazement we saw not only our mothers but also Iosif Ivanovich and Oleg, Volik's father and brother who had been released just a day earlier — Oleg was to choose a place of exile within a week; he chose Berdyansk on the Sea of Azov. We were told that Harry and Andrey had also received their sentences: five years of exile to Totma. They came home for a week before departure. It was difficult to communicate because of the noise around us, but mother told me Proskuryakov, my boss at the model basin, had requested the OGPU for my transfer to the OSTEKH Bureau. The *Osoboye Tekhnicheskoye Bureau* ran prisons in major cities where prisoners with special qualifications were kept to perform assignments in their fields of expertise. It was a nice but unsuccessful try — I had no qualifications for such a special assignment. There was not much else to say except to wish one another well. We were actually glad when it was over. Later in the day the packages came and we spent a second night in the transit cell.

It was "get ready with belongings" for all of us the next

morning. Two Black Ravens were waiting in the courtyard for the two dozen prisoners in our cell. After a short drive to another prison, we were unloaded at the entrance to one of the wings. There were already several hundred prisoners inside filling the ground floor. Convoy soldiers — all Mongolian faces — stood around; at the center of the prison were tables where the transfer of prisoners' papers was in process. It took hours of waiting. When our turn finally came, there was again the officer who had come to the prison commandant's office the day before. He was commander of the transport and of the Mongolian guards.

In late afternoon our turn finally came; we were escorted into the yard where open trucks waited with motors running. We boarded a truck and were ordered to squat; two soldiers with rifles in hand boarded with us and squatted at the rear corners. Truck after truck left the yard proceeding along the river, over the bridge along Liteinyy Prospekt to Nevskiy Prospekt and the railroad yards at Moscow Station. It was dusk, the evening rush hour, the trams were filled. As we passed the streetcars the passengers' astounded faces stared at us for a brief moment. People waiting at tram stops or walking on the streets turned their heads to watch our moving caravan.

## HEADING EAST

At the Moscow Station switching yard a crowd had assembled in the dark near the warehouses. Word had spread through town and, from a distance, relatives and friends watched their loved ones depart. Under the lights, a train of about twenty boxcars with one passenger car in the middle stood ready to leave. Soldiers were posted around the area where trucks unloaded sixty men to a boxcar; then the doors were shut and bolted.

Inside the car it was dark; in one corner near the ceiling a grilled opening let in a little light. Mostly by touch I found out that at both ends of the car were wooden platforms about five feet high and five feet deep; in the middle of the car was a square foot hole in the floor — a toilet.

When we climbed inside the boxcar, a dozen sailors already occupied the platform next to the opening; the opposite platform was also occupied, mostly by criminals, as we found out. We crawled under the sailors' platform and slowly settled down in the semi-darkness, placing our belongings against the wall under our heads. With fifteen lined up next to one another, there was only about one foot in width for each of us.

The next truck brought a load of peasants. It was still dark when the noise of arriving and departing trucks ceased. At daybreak the train started moving, swaying and rattling. The navy sergeant sitting by the open window called out the names of stations we passed. Guessing our destination became a general preoccupation. Where were we going? Was it the Belomor Canal, a well-known Gulag project? Or maybe Svirstroy? Volik hoped for the latter; he had worked there as a student last summer and prisoners were also employed there.

Next to Volik on his other side was a highway engineer, a friendly man in his forties who had recently returned from the Far East where he had worked along the Manchurian border on road construction for the military. He tried to entertain us with his experiences and stories. But once we had passed Volkhov and continued traveling east, Volik became uncommunicative. The day we passed Vologda and it became clear we were heading for the Ural Mountains, his pessimism changed to depression. He fell silent and refused to eat, even from our own provisions of bacon, salt pork, dried bread, and sugar.

Once a day the train stopped; the car door was opened enough to pass through a container with soup and sixty rations of black bread, three hundred grams each. When we were lucky enough to stop at a station, we would also get a container of boiling water which was particularly welcome since the soup was made of salted fish with millet. The navy sergeant made it his business to distribute the rations which was, in a way, ironic, since he and his sailors had gotten five years for complaining about poor food at their Scheusselburg Naval Station.

One morning a few days after our departure a fight erupted at the other end of the car; the criminals had stolen provisions from the peasants. When our navy sergeant tried to intervene and was in turn attacked by the criminals, the sailors came rushing to his aid and soon order and authority were reestablished. This led to the setting up of a food fund for those who had no *peredachas* — mostly the criminals — and by using carrot and stick this way, law and equity were established for the remainder of our journey.

On the day it was my turn to sit on the upper deck near the window, I enjoyed seeing the beauty of the Ural Mountains, their red stone and green firs. Sometimes on curved stretches one could see our entire transport with the guards in the elevated brake houses watching over the roofs of the train. We were leaving Europe; before us — from the Urals to the Bering Sea — Siberia stretched over six thousand kilometers. I tried to convince Volik that since we had come this far we might as well "see the world." He smiled his ironic smile, but his energy and resolve slowly came back and he began to eat and talk once more.

Our only entertainment, besides singing by the sailors and criminals, was swapping stories. One interesting story was told by Alex, a student of the Leningrad Civil Aviation Institute. Alex had graduated from a teacher's college and had been sent for three years to work in Uelen on the Chukchi Peninsula to teach children of the Chukchi tribe, nomads who live by fishing, hunting, and keeping reindeer. The small colony of Russian officials at Uelen essentially ran a trading post, collecting furs and skins from the natives in exchange for ammunition and other supplies. Dog sleds and kayaks were the only means of transportation. When the Uelen Party Secretary fell from a dog sled during a trip in the tundra and his hand froze and developed gangrene, Alex, the only one who had some knowledge of biology, was ordered to perform an amputation. The only medical doctor had left Uelen on the last boat and a new one had not yet arrived.

"With my 'wife,' a Chukchi girl, I cleaned and disinfected my school room, a former chapel of pre-revolutionary settlers, prepared the tools, and placed our victim on a big table. Alcohol was an important ingredient of the operation which was successful. The secretary returned to the "big land" with the next ship." The *bolshaya zemlya* (big land) referred to the rest of the country which could be reached only once a year by the supply ship.

Alex had other interesting stories about life in this remote region, including one of particular interest because it dealt with America. One year, when the supply ship failed to arrive at Uelen, they ran short of essential supplies for the colony as well as for the natives. An expedition to Nome, Alaska, was organized to exchange furs and skins for food and ammunition; Alex was part of the crew in charge of the engines.

"It was a seldom-used cutter and we spent time preparing it for the voyage. We had a stormy passage and, on the approach to Nome, were met by a U.S. Coast Guard cutter. It signaled us to follow it and later arrested us. On arrival in Nome we learned that our cutter had once belonged to some Americans who went on a hunting and fishing trip to the Russian coast, a common practice at one time. However, this time the Americans were detained by Soviet authorities on their arrival and, although they were allowed to return home, the boat was requisitioned. Now, during our trip, the storm had chipped off some paint and the boat's original name and home port were visible. However, when Nome authorities learned that we had come to do business in furs and skins, we were welcomed and feted and deals were made. We could keep the boat, get our supplies, and return home safely."

When, after his three-year stint, Alex returned to Vladivostok, he was arrested and accused of illegal travel abroad and of having performed unauthorized surgery. Eventually both charges were dropped; he returned to Leningrad and enrolled in the Aviation Institute. His "wife" remained at Uelen; she didn't want to leave for the "big land."

Among our other passengers of interest were two young Latvian Communists who had fled prosecution by Latvian authorities and come to the Soviet Union. Eventually they became students at Leningrad University where they could not refrain from voicing their opinions on all subjects. But they went too far and were accused of some deviation — whether left or right they did not know themselves — and got five years for antisoviet propaganda.

We also had a radio officer and two young sailors from the merchant marine. Their story was more salacious, a fact they obviously enjoyed. Their ship was in a French port for repairs and they were granted shore leave for a few days in Paris. In a cafe they met a man who spoke some pidgin Russian. Since the sailors were short of money he offered them a deal: Girls and money if they could perform for the benefit of a camera and voyeur customers. They were only too happy to oblige. How their escapade had become known to Soviet authorities they never knew. Although Wiegand, the radio officer, had declined the offer, he was held responsible for his mates. On arrival in Leningrad they were arrested and got five years, though not for antisoviet propaganda.

The only ones with "tenners" — ten years was then the

maximum prison term — were the peasants convicted in accordance with the "Law of August 7" (1932) for stealing government property, i.e., gathering grain remnants on harvested collective farm fields for private consumption.

On the tenth or twelfth day we reached Novosibirsk. The train left the main line and stopped at a switching yard. We thought it was our destination but it was only a stop to visit a bathhouse. Boxcar by boxcar we were processed through the bath while our clothes were thrown into a chamber of dry heat to eliminate vermin and lice. It took about fifteen minutes for this procedure and then we were back in our boxcar; after sixteen hours we were again on our way east.

We crossed the Yenisey River at Krasnoyarsk during a spectacular sunset and passed the imposing forests near Tulun and Zima and beautiful Lake Baikal. By the end of the month we had passed Karymskaya. "That's where the Manchurian railroad veers off," said our highway engineer. It was now familiar territory to him and he got quite excited. "If they don't ship us all the way to Vladivostok and then north to Kolyma, everything will be all right. If we are assigned to a road building project, you boys come with me. I know all the local bosses in this region and we will be all right." He told us about his past exploits and praised the local women as being "healthy and handy."

# 6

# *Baikal-Amur Labor Camp (Bamlag)*

## ARRIVAL

On a cool sunny morning the train stopped at a small station. Behind the station the ground swelled into a chain of low rounded hills. There were no trees, only the golden yellow of a steppe under a deep blue sky. A sailor waited at the door expecting the distribution of food or water, but soon it became obvious that this was no usual stop. The train moved short stretches back and forth, then the doors were slightly opened and there was much commotion outside. Near the track in the field stood a row of roughly hewn tables. A group of people dressed in quilted garb were walking alongside the train with the convoy officer and his soldiers. We had arrived somewhere. A man came by and asked how many "live souls" we had. This must be a camp joke, I thought. No one had died in our car. Soon the car doors were opened on both sides and we were permitted to get out and relieve ourselves. On the adjacent track stood several green railroad cars labeled "Sanitary Train."

The unloading of our train had begun at the rear end with women prisoners escorted first to the sanitary train. Before our turn came, a man in a quilted jacket over his officer's uniform told us to line up.

"Welcome to Bamlag!" he said.

The Baikal-Amur Correctional Labor Camp, situated between Lake Baikal and the Amur River, was organized in 1932 for the construction of a new railroad line to substitute for the Manchurian Railroad, now in the hands of the Japanese. According to a 1992 issue of the Russian journal *Otechvennyye Zapiski*, the Bamlag population rose from 62,000 in 1933 to 190,000 by 1935. The article listed the size of transports from different cities: Moscow, 1483; Karaganda, 1162; Vyatka, 701. Our transport numbered about 1200 prisoners.

"You are now under my command. You'll proceed five at a time to those tables. Keep order. You'll be registered. Later you'll get the sanitary treatment. Afterwards, you get food. You are here to redeem your guilt before the Soviet Motherland. You'll be given plenty of opportunity to do so; your future is in your hands. You are here to be rehabilitated, not punished, as far as we are concerned. As you can see, there are no guards around any more. You are leaving your past behind you. Now you have the opportunity to reforge yourselves into useful citizens..." and so he went on, giving us the first of many pep talks most of us would hear for the next three, five, or ten years.

In single file we moved up to register. There were the usual questions: name, age, education, qualifications, and work experience? The scribes were prisoners and handled us with authority. While not unfriendly, they didn't treat us as equals either. Eventually we were led to the sanitary train. We undressed before entering the train, leaving our belongings on the ground. We went through a car with showers, soap, and hot water; then came the barber who shaved every bit of hair off our bodies.

We left the train naked and lined up in a row to wait for our disinfected belongings. It was a sunny afternoon and the temperature was agreeable. After the long tense confinement in box cars, it was good to have this moment in the sun. We laughed at the hairless bare figures standing in the pristine landscape under a blue sky, slightly shivering but happy. We had known them before only in crumpled clothes with beards and long hair. "Look at that Apollo of Belvedere!" shouted someone pointing to one of our oldest companions. When we got our clothing it was hot but not much cleaner.

In the evening we got soup, a pound of bread, a piece of sugar, hot water, and pressed Chinese tea, and went back into our car. The first day was over. As darkness fell and it got colder, the car doors were shut; soon most inhabitants were asleep; only a few stayed up for a while to exchange bits of information gathered through the day. What did they want to know? What kind of work could one expect? Will we stay together? Where do we go from here? There was no camp here except for a few tents next to the Urulga station. It must be just a distribution point. We had passed Lake Baikal days ago and it was still thousands of kilometers to Vladivostok.

I didn't care much where we went as long as I went together with Volik. Tomorrow we would see.

The next morning we were called out one by one with our belongings and reassigned to different boxcars. Volik and I were separated. I found myself in a car with only a few passengers, mainly middle-aged educated men among whom was Wiegand, the ship radio operator, and the Latvians. Eventually a new train was formed and we proceeded eastward. The doors remained ajar and we traveled in comfort.

We saw no settlements, no people, only railroad stations

with a few houses around them. We passed a few camps: Log barracks or rows of tents surrounded by a barbed wire fence with an arch over the gate featuring a slogan painted on red canvas and a soldier at the gate. Smoke rose from log cabins outside the fenced area. These were sights to be repeated hundreds of times in months to come.

One by one, boxcars were uncoupled and left standing at stations we passed until ours was the only one left and we were attached to a freight train going east. On the third day we arrived at Mikhailo-Chesnokovskaya; our car was pushed to a side track and a small camp, a few tents enclosed by a barbed wire fence. We disembarked and remained in this camp for the next two weeks in relative comfort with straw mattresses, blankets, and plenty of space and water.

Occasionally these days of waiting at the isolation camp were interrupted by work, the unloading of trees which arrived by rail on the adjacent track. For most of us it was a welcome activity; only the Latvians refused to work and their daily bread ration was reduced to three hundred grams. When big heavy tree trunks arrived, none of us knew how to handle them properly and some of us barely escaped injury.

Towards the end of our stay here two commanders and their retinue arrived and we were ordered to line up for inspection; again the Latvians refused to cooperate. Their refusal, however, did not create any stir. After looking us over, the visitors went to the tent where the Latvians were resting and engaged them in conversation. They listened patiently to what the Latvians had to say about "prisoners' rights under International Red Cross regulations."

Prisoners from the personnel department came to fill out cards relating to our work experience. Once, while we were at work unloading lumber, I was approached by two men who asked me about my experience as a cameraman. I had registered as a film cameraman and photo correspondent.

After two weeks in isolation camp we were escorted to a big camp a mile away at the foot of a range of bare hills. About two dozen barracks were separated by barbed wire fences into several areas. At the gate guarded by armed soldiers we were met by a few prisoners who led us to the bathhouse. There we were examined by female medics, our own clothes were taken away for disinfection, and we were issued underwear and gray quilted prisoners' clothing. Afterwards, our small group was broken up and assigned to different barracks.

Inside my barrack were three rows of two-story platforms. There wasn't much light since the windows were obstructed but there were several light bulbs along the passages. I was told where to fill my sack with straw and to keep my belongings under the sack. It seemed that the barrack was not fully occupied. An old man was sweeping the floor. He showed me where the canteen was. I had received tickets for my daily bread ration and my pail of soup.

Behind the barrack along the barbed wire fence was a long ditch with an equally long guard rail at the height of a chair. This was our toilet in any weather. Not far away stood a washstand, a long water container with rods hanging from the bottom; by pushing the stick up, water poured out to wash hands and face. At the canteen I got six hundred grams of bread, a piece of sugar, and an aluminum bowl filled with soup. A fish eye looked at me from the center of the bowl; the soup was the same salty water with millet which we had received on the train. It didn't look too good.

Towards night, the camp — desolate during the day — filled up with prisoners returning from work. There were large groups escorted by guards. Other prisoners came in small groups or alone and usually went to two barracks of a different design closer to the gate. These were the ITR, the engineering and technical personnel. As I learned later, their barracks were more comfortable; they had smaller rooms for six to twelve persons with individual cots.

I didn't see any of my traveling companions this evening. The prisoners returning from work to my barrack didn't show any interest in a newcomer. They were busy following their camp routines: getting food, washing up, inspecting or repairing their belongings, relieving themselves, and finally disappearing into the darkness of their sleeping space. So did I, and next morning was awakened by the call for lineup.

In the camp everything seemed to be run by prisoners; no military uniforms were visible. Except for food, the situation did not seem too bad; it was not much different from what I could have expected had I been drafted into the army. I hated uniforms and following orders but, after all, I had no choice. At lineup I was wondering what kind of work was in store for me when my name was called and I was ordered to go to the gate. There a small group of prisoners had assembled. A guard took us through the gate and escorted us to headquarters. We learned that the guard was also a prisoner.

Headquarters was a long two-story brick building on the outskirts of the town of Svobodnyy, which in Russian means "free.".

Originally the building housed administrative offices of the Trans-Baikal Railroad, a secondary one-track line skirting the Manchurian border for about 2,000 kilometers. The Trans-Siberian main track crossed Manchuria via Harbin on the way to Vladivostok. This shortcut was called the Chinese Eastern Railroad and had been owned by Russia. Its headquarters were in St. Petersburg and my father had worked there before the revolution. Now Manchuria and the railroad were occupied by Japan. A new 3,000 kilometer-long Baikal Amur mainline or BAM was to be built from Lake Baikal to the Sea of Okhotsk.

## FILMING AGAIN

At headquarters I was directed to URO, the personnel department where the man who had visited me in isolation camp was looking through some files with a personnel clerk. While I waited, they looked me over as if I were a sheep for sale. Then the man approached me.

"I am Savenko, here on assignment from Moscow, and I need a camera assistant. You think you are qualified? I need a hard worker. It won't be easy work but it's better than digging earth or cutting trees. Tell me once more what you did and which camera you are familiar with." I was excited about doing camera work again and told him whatever he wanted to know. Savenko seemed satisfied with my answers, took a folder from the clerk, and went out.

A woman came in. The prisoner clerk addressed her as "Maria Vasilyevna;" she obviously had come to have a look at me too. She appeared to be about thirty years old and was a Russian beauty with a head full of blonde hair, high cheekbones, blue eyes slightly slanted, and a strong full figure dressed smartly in a businesslike suit with an impeccable white blouse. She was friendly, asked me a few questions about Leningrad and my family, and told me that she was Savenko's wife and a cinematographer herself.

Savenko returned and ordered me to follow him. In the long corridor we sat down on a window sill. He had asked the higher ups about me. The problem was that I was a 58er "to be rehabilitated through hard work." Savenko had promised that I would be made to work hard.

"Now," he said, "we'll go to Comrade Dikiy, Chief of the Third Department, who will have to make the decision." We went to the end of a wing of the building and Savenko went into a room while I waited outside. After a while he called me and took me past an office occupied by well-dressed female secretaries into a room where a general was sitting behind a desk. For a while the general looked me over.

"How old are you?" he asked me.

"Twenty-one, Comrade Chief."

"Well, we are not comrades," he said, "but anyway at twenty-one you would do military service. Right? Instead you are here and you'll serve your country here; we will make you an upright Soviet citizen yet. Savenko is a good Bolshevik and knows how to go about it. It's all right — " he turned to Savenko, "take him."

He wrote something down on a piece of paper on his desk. We both said "thank you" and left the feared office.

We went back to personnel. There was paperwork to be done and I was told to collect travel rations back at camp.

"See to it that you get good travel rations," Savenko admonished. "Do not count on me to feed you. I will meet you at the gate tomorrow morning. There will be a lot of work to do. We leave by train in the afternoon."

The next day was a busy one: supplies had to be packed, equipment and luggage brought to the station by horse-drawn cart, and tickets procured for the journey. Besides being Savenko's camera assistant, I was also his manservant. Still, I was happy not to be behind barbed wire any more.

The Trans-Siberian Railroad had two passenger trains which ran daily through eight time zones and about seven thousand miles from Moscow to the Sea of Japan and the city of Vladivostok. Express train No. 1 was usually occupied by VIPs. The other train was primarily for people with travel orders. Passengers without travel orders usually camped for days or weeks at a station until they could board a train. At stations, the ticket windows were usually closed and one had to approach the station master by the back door. Trains arrived with all doors locked; to board, one had to look for a door where passengers or a conductor were alighting. Savenko, of course, had the required papers and necessary clout. Everything was arranged long before the train's arrival and the three of us boarded the train with the station master's help.

We left for Takhtamygda, a small station where a supply rail line was being built due northeast to Tynda which was located on the only highway in the region, an unpaved road which went to the Lena gold fields and to Yakutsk, a thousand kilometers due north.

We arrived at Takhtamygda, Bamlag's Third Division headquarters, the next day. Surrounded by forests, headquarters consisted of a few block cabins and a camp of barracks enclosed by barbed wire. On a side track a steam excavator was being assembled. We reported at the division chief's office. Savenko and his wife were given a room in one of the block cabins. There was momentary confusion as to what to do with me. "Put him with Tyemkin," the captain ordered, but there was no time for me to go anywhere. Savenko wanted to start work immediately.

The camps of the Third Division were spread north in the taiga along the Oldoy River. Equipped with saws and axes, spades and wheelbarrows and some horses, prisoners were cutting a trail through the taiga and building camps for themselves and a roadbed for the rail line. Here the permafrost reaches its southern boundary; to dig a hole in the ground is harder than to quarry stone and everything has to be blasted with ammonal. At the turn of the century the Panama Canal was built by steam engines; at Bamlag, things were done, as the saying went, by "farting steam." The vast forests and mountain ranges of this area were then uninhabited except for families of Orochones, native nomads, who lived in bark tents hunting and fishing, not unlike American Indians in times past.

By the time we arrived, the trail already extended for thirty kilometers with camps along the trail about ten kilometers apart. In clearings close to water — a spring or the Oldoy River — barracks were erected of newly cut logs to house four to five hundred prisoners behind a barbed wire fence. Outside the fence stood log cabins for the camp chief, his assistants, the guards, and a kitchen. Prisoners worked, spurred on by their foremen and the promise of 1200 grams of bread for exceeding work assignments. There was no escape from these camps and the guards, prisoners themselves, were here only to secure law and order in the camp and to protect supplies.

The day after our arrival we set out for the taiga with me carrying tripod and camera and the Savenko couple hurrying in front and arguing about where to go, where to stop, and what to shoot. It soon became clear that the terrain, the mosquitoes, and Savenko's decision-making did not agree with Maria Vasilyevna. She remained at home and devoted herself to problems of supply and public relations.

Savenko and I set out on our trek north by horse and wagon with an old prisoner to take care of the horse. The trek through the wilderness would have had its exciting aspects; however, I suffered from a bad case of diarrhea and Savenko was constantly finding more work for me to do, which added to my discomfort.

Wherever we stopped Savenko was a guest of the camp chief, the only military officer in the wilderness. I was usually quartered with his technical assistant, an engineer and 58er, or with the "political assistant" in charge of propaganda, a former party member and non-political offender. Our arrival was an extraordinary event for them and everyone in authority wanted to appear on the record in the best light possible.

I made the preparations for the shots, reconnoitered the best locations, interesting activities and people, and brought the equipment to the sites selected. Savenko directed the action and manned the camera. One day, on a reconnoitering mission, I was surprised by the sound of an airplane. In this forlorn vastness, where the only line of communication squeezed in between Manchuria and the Arctic was the width of the rail track, a plane was an unknown sight. But there it was, flying over my head like a big white bird and disappearing behind the treetops, its noise slowly receding.

Days later I read in the paper that Jimmie Mattern, an American pilot, had flown over the region on a round-the-world flight. He crash-landed near Uelen on the Bering Sea, was rescued, and brought to Nome in Alaska.

This summer the big event was the arrival of Naftaly Aronovich Frenkel, to replace Mrachkovskiy who was a former associate of Trotsky. Frenkel came from Belomorstroy with a big retinue; once a prisoner himself, and now a general accorded the Order of Lenin, he was a favorite of the Kremlin's "khozyain." *Khozyain doma* is the usual expression for master of the house. In those years the word *khozyain* was often applied to the big bosses instead of their given name. The biggest *khozyain* was, of course, Stalin, but the expression was used also for Frenkel[18] or for anyone else who wielded power over other people such as Matvey Berman.

Soon after Frenkel arrived, Berman came from Moscow on an inspection tour. Berman was head of the Gulag, the Main Administrative Office of All Corrective Labor Camps. Savenko and I met his special train at Takhtamygda; we followed him and his retinue wherever they went to inspect, advise, condemn, or praise; present red banners to shock brigades; look into kitchens and talk to prisoners, primarily the 35ers (common criminals convicted under Article 35 of the Criminal Code). Unlike the feared Frenkel, Matvey Berman, with his silver-knobbed walking stick in hand, played the role of benevolent "master reforger of human souls."

We traveled on his train to Bolshoy Never and from there

---

[18] For the extraordinary life story of Naftaly Aronovich Frenkel, see Solzhenitsyn, *op. cit.*, pp. 138-141.

on the Aldan Road, Berman in his open Lincoln car. We followed by truck over mountain ranges and wide valleys blooming in magnificent colors, stopping here and there to let a family of bears cross the road. Tynda was the end of Bamlag country. Berman continued north to the Lena gold fields. Savenko and I turned back; he was eager to develop the exposed film and for this we had to travel all the way to Vladivostok, 2000 kilometers to the east.

In Vladivostok we reported to the local GPU office. Savenko stayed at an hotel in town and sent me to a camp at Vtoraya Rechka, a few train stops away and a transit camp for prisoners awaiting shipment to Arctic regions. (Five years later Mandelstam — the great Russian poet — arrived and died at this camp.)

I was issued passes and railroad tickets to travel between Vladivostok and Vtoraya Rechka. The next day a storm broke loose in Vladivostok: On the developed film, the images of early takes had nearly disappeared. Savenko immediately smelled sabotage and I was under suspicion until the lab told him that it was a common problem with Ferrania film — an Italian product which Savenko had brought from Moscow — if it was not developed promptly.

Before we left Vladivostok we visited Chinatown; I accompanied Savenko and a local GPU officer who went there for lunch. It was an authentic Chinese quarter in those years, a maze of narrow alleys crowded with unidentifiable businesses. One rarely saw an occidental face. Women in traditional clothes with bandaged feet were carrying children tied to their backs. We ate very well; waiters shouted their orders to the kitchen at the top of their voices; Savenko was jovial; the local GPU man played host. Afterwards, we had tea and hot towels.

After the incident with the Ferrania film, Savenko decided we would develop the film ourselves. He procured an outsized railroad boxcar for a laboratory. It was my task to have the car equipped, insulated, and partitioned into three parts: One for Savenko, one for the lab — to develop, fix, wash and dry the film — and a small one for me to sleep in.

By the time our moveable lab was ready, winter had set in and the main problem was to keep the car warm. I had the usual camp stove installed — an old ammonal barrel — and a storage space built for firewood and coal; but we had no opportunity to use the lab before the first real frost. Savenko left for Svobodnyy and the boxcar was now my responsibility. I had to see to it that it got attached to freight trains and it took many days to get to Svobodnyy. Except for the cold, I didn't mind it. In the evening I loaded my stove with wood and covered myself for the night with everything available; in the morning I jumped out of my bunk, sprinkled kerosene on the wood, threw in a match, and sat next to the stove until it got hot. At night the temperature outside reached thirty below zero Celsius.

When the first one hundred kilometers of rail line had been laid up from Takhtamygda to a mountain pass up north, Savenko and I returned to the Third Division. Division headquarters had moved to Camp Red Dawn at the end of the new line. The first time I rode to Red Dawn was on a truck and I nearly froze to death.

It was a long ride, maybe five hours, on a cold starry night. I was in the back of the truck, the cabin being occupied by more important passengers. We stopped at a heated cabin, the only remaining structure of a former camp. I stomped in my felt boots through knee-deep snow; inside the house the snow on my boots melted. But back in the truck for the last stretch of the journey, my felt boots froze stiff; slowly the cold engulfed me. First I suffered from the cold, then all sensation in my limbs disappeared and I fell asleep. I woke up in a bakery lying in front of the open hearth; the wood had just burned down and the loaves of bread were loaded onto the red coals. My felt boots were off and, luckily, there was no frostbite on my feet. On cold days it was common practice to notice a white spot on someone's face and to alert this person; the remedy was to rub the spot with snow until circulation returned. Maybe the people who carried me down from the truck and took my boots off had rubbed my feet with snow.

The next time I rode to Red Dawn together with Savenko and we went on one of the first trains. It was a slow ride in an old passenger car with a stove aglow in the middle of the car. At the end of the ride the Red Dawn Camp below the mountain ridge, aglow with hundreds of electric bulbs in the vast darkness of the land, was a stirring sight even for a prisoner.

We had come to record the biggest explosion yet to be detonated in BAM land: The blasting of a cut through the highest ridge on the way to Tynda. The day of the blast was a very cold and sunny one. Savenko was nervously looking at the thermometer; it was forty below. The day before, together with the engineers, we had selected our location. Because of the cold Savenko wanted to stay inside as long as possible, but wanted me to go out with the equipment early to be ready for shooting on time. I was reluctant since I expected the film in the camera to freeze and become brittle. We argued about it.

"You keep the camera warm," Savenko told me.

To my regret I was right; by the time Savenko arrived the film was frozen and it was my fault of course. The blast was postponed. I ran back to camp to reload the camera; eventually everything worked out. But for Savenko it seemed important to put the blame for the delay on me and he requested my transfer to "general labor." However, I was lucky again; the division chief knew me well and had witnessed the morning's events. Contrary to Savenko's request, he ordered papers issued for "return to Svobodnyy for reassignment by KVO (Cultural Education Department)." With my papers I ran down the road to get my rations — bread, some salted fish, pieces of sugar and tea; a truck driver was also there getting his travel ration.

"Where are you heading?" I asked.

"To Takhtamygda."

"I'll come with you."

"All right with me."

I traveled light now, nothing to carry this time. We took off right away and it was a warm ride in the cabin. At Takhtamygda I went to Tyemkin whose place had been my pied-a-terre since I had first come to Takhtamygda.

Tyemkin was the "publisher," editor, and writer of the division's news sheet; every division had one for propaganda purposes. He occupied a small shed outside the camp with his typesetter/printer. It was an office, shop, and sleeping quarter in one. Tyemkin and I had become good friends. He had been a student at Moscow University, a Komsomol member of course, but had shown an undesirable interest in Trotsky and now also had a fiver — Article 58, paragraph 11. He hailed from a small town past Minsk, a Jewish settlement and now a restricted border zone. He was well read; his main interest was Russia's social and political history. Tyemkin loved to engage in philosophical talk and was happy to have me as an attentive listener, although I knew little about these subjects. Once he took me for a walk into the nearby forest to show me where hundreds of frozen prisoners' bodies were stacked like wood, layer upon layer, probably awaiting spring to be buried or whatever other method of disposal was feasible. I had wondered how bodies were disposed of since under the best of circumstances many deaths occurred in our camp population, yet no cemeteries were to be found anywhere.

The next morning I jumped on a freight train which slowly passed the station going east; at Skovorodino I caught a passenger train to Svobodnyy.

## AT THE PHOTO BUREAU

While working for Savenko I had learned a lot about camp life, its ways and means, and the relationships of people in positions of responsibility, whether officers, free employees or prisoners. Walking the next day from the rail station to headquarters I thought about my situation and decided not to report to KVO, the department for which Savenko was nominally working and which had little use for 58ers, but to go straight to personnel. I knew the clerk there and asked for assignment to the photo bureau where I knew two photographers with whom I shared the barrack on my occasional stopovers at camp.

It was a small office consisting of four photographers; in charge was an old-timer at the end of his "tenner" who wanted to stay on in his position as a free employee. For those who had spent long years in camp and had lost their family ties, the Gulag was the best employer. Here they felt secure and in familiar surroundings.

The bureau responded primarily to headquarters administrative needs: mug shots for personnel or Third Department files, identification photos, enlargements of our leaders to be hung on walls, and last but not least, taking private shots for the higher-ups and their families. I had more ambitious ideas.

With Frenkel's arrival, Bamlag had been assigned a new task: rather than building a new main line in the north, a task accomplished only fifty years later, Bamlag was to build in the shortest time possible a second track for the existing rail line: 2,500 kilometers from Karymskaya to Nikolo-Ussuriysk. I had learned that there was a great need for photographic documentation.

A few days after I started work at the lab, a man dropped in at our office. He wore a military type of tunic of the kind worn by Stalin and was friendly, clean shaven, and clearly not a provincial. He brought with him some magazine pictures of a futuristic monorail train propelled like an airplane and asked us to make reproductions for the engineering department. We had not seen him before and wondered who he was.

A few days later he caught up with me in the corridor, told me that he was a prisoner, but not a 58er, and hoped to become chief of the photo bureau as soon as the old-timer "got the boot." His name was Vengerovskiy. He was a Muscovite and had "invented" the photomaton, that is, had copied an American design. It was not the copying which was his crime, but making lots of money under false pretenses. He took me into his confidence in order to assist him in his ambitions and, on occasion, shared with me his philosophy: "When in charge, first ask everybody their opinion — that is democratic — then do it your way.... If somebody speaks of the common good, he has his own interests in mind.... If he says he has your interests in mind, be careful, he is a damn liar.... Ask others their opinions so that you know where they stand.... Opinions grow in a vacuum, therefore exercise your authority properly. I do not like to be asked for my opinions by my boss. I would rather take orders. "'Yes sir, comrade boss.'" He saluted and smiled.

Vengerovskiy soon took over the photo bureau; I shared with him my own plans and we agreed that he would send me out to do field work.

In early spring, 1934, as I was preparing to leave for field work and was talking with an employee at the engineering department, I learned by chance where Volik was. He was chief mechanic at a gravel and sand pit in Ksenyevka, the only place where heavy equipment was used. Volik had always been fascinated by excavators and steam shovels and I remembered the collection of American prospectuses he had had, Marion steam shovels in particular.

Of course, I decided to go to Ksenyevka, headquarters of the second division and about one thousand kilometers west. It was a typical station with a siding, warehouse, water tower, and a few houses for railroad employees. Not far from the station, a new barrack housed division headquarters. I reported there and asked where I could find Volik.

"Fesenko? The mechanic? In the hospital," the clerk told me. "Right down the road past the station, the big tent."

"Why in the hospital?"

"Typhoid fever I guess."

I ran down to the tent in time to see two female nurses helping Volik out of a tub and, wrapped in a bed sheet, to his cot. He looked pale and drawn; he was surprised to see me but too weak to get really excited and managed only a feeble smile.

"He is all right now, on the road to recovery," the nurse told me. Later at the office I learned some good news. As soon as he recovered he was to be transferred to Svobodnyy.

The next morning I began work by walking eastward along the tracks to photograph the construction of bridges and extensive earthmoving operations. All work was done by manpower: rock blasted by ammonal, earth and stone moved on wheelbarrows; cement was mixed with shovels. Photography then was also different. My only luggage was a camera with twelve cassettes, a tripod, and ten packages of glass-plate negatives. For a darkroom I had a square bag of light-proof cloth with two sleeves attached so that I could put my hands inside in order to empty and reload the cassettes. I usually did this at the end of the day.

Most of the camps — they were now called phalanxes — were near the objects I had to photograph. Taking a dozen pictures was usually my day's work. It took time to photograph bridge construction, and I often mused at the irony that, as a prisoner, I could photograph structures which were normally off limits and always guarded by special troops.

Nights I spent at a camp and was fed there. I never starved, and though I went hungry on occasion, I always had enough *makhorka* (Russian tobacco) to suppress any hunger pangs. I suffered from scurvy and swollen feet but was never incapacitated.

At the camps where I stopped I was always well-received by the small bosses. They wanted to make a good impression on someone from headquarters. I learned a lot about ordinary camp life. Some camps were run by decent people; work was well-organized and life tolerable. At other camps, the criminal element had taken charge in collusion with the bosses. By heading the work brigades, the kitchens, and supply stores, they terrorized the laborers, mostly peasants who were victims of collectivization. Those who rebelled could die from hunger or exhaustion, by accident or by a knife.

On the long stretches to and from Svobodnyy, I had to get on the daily long distance passenger train. There were no local trains. As a Bamlag traveler, I would usually hang on the footboard of a departing train and bang on the locked door. Eventually the car porter — always a woman — would let me in. They were familiar with the terrain, knew that we were "campers," and let us ride as long as we were in Bamlag territory.

Riding on the trains I met other passengers, some of whom were traveling to or from Leningrad. Talking with them, I felt the pain of all exiles: I wanted to go home. But later, when mother and Ira were expelled from Leningrad and there was nothing left to go back to, I was freed from such longings. Only once, when I met a nice girl returning to Leningrad and we talked through the night about life in the big city, did I have the urge to hide in the train to go back there.

Volik arrived in Svobodnyy soon after my return from

Ksenyevka. Bamlag was getting more heavy equipment and Volik became Chief Mechanic of the Office of Mechanization with all the privileges of an ITR (engineering and technical *zek* personnel): quarters in the special ITR barrack and access to the ITR mess hall outside the camp. I didn't have such privileges but between us we made an arrangement that whenever he was traveling and I was at headquarters I would occupy his cot and keep the pass for his mess hall.

His sleeping quarter was a room for six; the occupants there were all older men some of whom, victims of the early sabotage trials of the twenties, had already served many years. They were members of the old intelligentsia who liked Volik, and accepted me because we were different from their younger colleagues, former Party or Komsomol members. On occasion there were discussions between an old hand and a young enthusiast. I remember one such exchange.

"I hear our young komsomolets is trying to convince us that he came here by mistake," one of the old men said. "I agree. But he has no need to convince me, he should have better convinced his investigator. And let me tell you another thing young man; it is all baloney, your revolutionary philosophy. All that revolutionists want is to get what they haven't got and what others have. Redistribution of wealth, all right, but what's so saintly about that? Now they have it and others don't. You always tell us about social justice, the corruption of the old system, about your high ideals and all this stuff. Do you know that there were high ideals before, long before you were born. And there is corruption now.

"And what do you know really about the old system? You say you are an economist. Redistribution of wealth. Fine. And it is easy as long as there is any wealth to redistribute. I know it all — 'from everyone…to everyone' — ability, needs, all this stuff. And who shall decide? Power is power, and nobody parts with it unless he has to. You see, young man, they say your abilities are needed here. But I doubt it; probably your investigator needs your apartment or maybe he wants to sleep with your wife.

"Let me tell you a story, a true one, about redistribution. Although I am an engineer I was also a *pomeshchik* (landowner) as you call it; I had an estate. I inherited it. It was a nice place; my grandfather had owned serfs you know. He took some of them to Italy and Germany to learn crafts. Native talents, you know. We had our furniture made by them, musical instruments too. They created wealth and we took care of it. It was worth thousands. In 1918 they plundered the estate. They were cold so they chopped it all for firewood. That's a reevaluation of values for you according to one's needs. To redistribute wealth is no accomplishment; to create it is what matters. And speaking of economics, from you they couldn't get anything except your freedom. From me at least they got my antique furniture. They know nothing about its value but they have something to put under their asses. No, I am not interested in your rebuttal. In thirty years, if you survive, you will be wiser too. Don't give me your learned wisdom; you haven't learned anything yet, you specialist. As Prutkov said: A specialist is like a swollen cheek, his plenitude is one-sided."

The speaker turned around on his cot with his face to the wall. The young economist looked at him with his mouth open for rebuttal, but then only shook his head and looked around the room. Finding no encouragement, he got up, said good night, and left the room.

"You want to sleep on Vladimir's cot?" one of Volik's friends asked me. "I guess you will not object boss?." He turned to the oldest man, the one in charge of the room.

"Boss, boss," the old man grumbled, "turn in now all of you and put the light out. And if somebody is going out at night to the outhouse, check on Korney, that he fills the stoves properly. It is a cold night."

Throughout the summer and fall of 1934 while traveling the length and width of Bamlag, I had only short stays at headquarters. Once I accompanied Frenkel on his special train to Khabarovsk; on the way he inspected new projects. In Khabarovsk he conferred with Gamarnik, Chief Political Commissar of the Red Army. Three years later Gamarnik committed suicide when most of the Red Army high command was executed.

In addition to technical photography I also took pictures for KVO to illustrate the progress in reforging us criminals. Such pictures were used by the Bamlag press and some went with official reports to Moscow. I accompanied KVO Chief Belskiy to meetings of "shock workers," pep rallies where rewards were distributed, mainly to 35ers. Belskiy was by far the best speaker I had ever heard; he could excite even an audience of prisoners.

On other occasions such propaganda efforts failed. Once I was asked to accompany a committee visiting a women's phalanx which had a poor work record. The chief engineer of the division was in charge of the committee. He was a diminutive man, quiet and kind, a turn-of-the-century type with his pince-nez looking a bit like Chekhov; they called him Antosha Chekhonte, a sometime nom-de-plume of Chekhov.

When we got to the phalanx the women were spreading gravel on a stretch of finished roadbed. Some had left their brigade and were lying stretched out in the sun on a steep roadbed slope. Antosha spotted them and took off along the bottom of the slope in their direction; I followed him. He stopped at the feet of a sleeping woman, a sturdy wench of about thirty years. She opened her eyes and he began to give her his little prepared speech about the joy of work, the pride of getting the "big loaf" after a day's work, the highest ration of bread weighing 1200 grams and half of the usual loaf baked in camp bakeries. She listened, smiling, and when he finished, winked at him.

"Daddy-O, please move; your shadow is in my way." Then she lifted her skirt above her bare stomach.

"Look oldie, here is my big loaf."

Antosha nearly lost his pince-nez. He turned around, shrugged his shoulders, and stomped away.

A year later Antosha was killed at Skovorodino when a quarry tunnel loaded with explosives was blasted off prematurely and he was hit by flying stones.

## SKOVORODINO

In the winter of 1934-35 I was assigned to "shock project Skovorodino," a big switching yard. Here trucks were used to bring the rock from a quarry to the construction site. Two roads were graded and watered for a smooth ice surface so that trucks could speed around the clock. They were loaded and unloaded by special brigades working three eight-hour shifts. Captain Levit was in charge of the showpiece project.

I left for Skovorodino with William Vronskiy, also a prisoner and former pickpocket, now a reporter with the camp newspaper. Tyempkin, the printer from Takhtamygda, was already in Skovorodino in a boxcar loaded with printing equipment; Vronskiy moved in with him. I got quarters in a tent where an invalid stoked a barrel stove. Skovorodino is the northernmost point of the rail line; in winter, temperatures average 30° below Celsius. The next day I was joined in the tent by five artists assigned to do propaganda art work, paint slogans, and service labor scoreboards for the daily output of best brigades. The artists included a safecracker, a pickpocket, and an artist from Moscow named Kolya Kryuger, a handsome young man with a hoarse voice and an aggressive stance acquired in camp life. I soon became friends with the latter.

Our group, as well as Vronskiy and Tyemkin, became pets of Captain Levit who was also a Muscovite, well-educated, and interested in our work for self-serving purposes. After a big clubhouse had been built, we got quarters there and the artists decorated it with big panels depicting heroic labor. Kryuger painted in the style of Deyneka; Misha, the safe-cracker, in a cubist manner. The demands of "socialist real-ism" had not yet penetrated the far reaches of the Gulag.

Except for suffering from scurvy, we could not complain. Courtesy of Captain Levit, we were provided with an ample supply of bandages and a daily ration of garlic. We spent evenings on our bunks helping one another bandage the boils erupting all over our bodies. It was also story-telling time. Mischa and Kolya usually supplied the company with enter-tainment: Mischa with witty stories of his "professional life" as a safecracker; Kolya, who had the looks of a Nordic sea wolf, with tales of his life as a merchant sailor voyaging to far-away lands and peoples. Some years later in Moscow I learned from Kolya's parents that he had never left Moscow before be-ing shipped to Bamlag.

I did all the needed photography and covered projects in the vicinity, including one run by Galina Tsvetkova, known for her good looks and high productivity. She was a protégé of the high bosses and well supplied. I spent a day there and at day's end had a sumptuous supper served in Galina's private quarters. A guest room was prepared for me for the night un-til a telephone call came that KVO Chief Belskiy was on his way. Instead, Belskiy stayed in the guest room overnight.

Belskiy left the next day in his train and I left for Skovoro-dino in a horse-drawn sleigh, compliments of Galina. Noth-ing is more enjoyable than a sleigh ride on a sunny day over a snowy country road.

A few days later I barely escaped being killed when a premature explosion in the quarry sent a rain of stones and claimed several victims. I survived unscathed. An electrician was blamed for the premature explosion and executed.

**✻ ✻ ✻**

In December 1934 Kirov was assassinated. He was Leningrad's popular Party Secretary and a potential rival to Stalin. As a reprisal, thousands of Leningrad residents were ordered to leave the city for faraway places in early 1935; among them were my mother and sister. I do not remember when I learned about this, but since we had mail privileges I eventually found out that they had ended up in Aryk Balyk, a Kazakhstan village about 100 kilometers from the nearest railroad station, which was Kokchetav. Ira was then fifteen years old. That winter she went to a one-room school in Aryk Balyk but, after Stalin declared that "children are not responsible for the crimes of their parents," she was free to return to Leningrad. Our neighbor, Professor Schaak, took her in and two years later made it possible for her to get into medical school.

Mother wrote from Aryk Balyk that she managed pretty well, mainly by continuing to knit the big popular Orenburg shawls; Isidor Becker sent her wool from Leningrad and whatever else she needed. Food rations were abandoned by 1935 and the State Commercial Stores were well stocked, although for new commercial prices. The old price for rationed butter was 2.50 rubles a kilo; the commercial price was 25 rubles. Stalin had declared that "Life is getting better. Life is more fun." Even modern western dances were now tolerated in public.

* * *

When I returned to Svobodnyy, things had changed at the photo bureau. Vengerovskiy had been transferred but no one knew where to. In his place was Belyavskiy, now a free employee after having served a term at Belomorstroy. Belyavskiy had been an assistant to General Dorfman, BAM's Chief of Finance, and photography was his great hobby.

The bureau had moved to more spacious quarters inside the camp where a barrack had been rebuilt to accommodate new equipment. Orekhov, the photographer who did most headquarters jobs, showed me the new darkrooms. On the enlarger he projected a photo of two dead bodies he had taken for the Third Department. I recognized them; they were the Latvians with whom I had arrived at camp.

"Poor fools," Orekhov said. "They tried to escape across the Manchurian border. How could they make it across the Amur River? They should have consulted me." Poor fools indeed. Why hadn't they stayed in Latvia?

I knew Orekhov's home was in a village close to the Soviet-Estonian border and that he had been in the border-crossing business on behalf of Soviet intelligence. He had also engaged in a sideline of profitable smuggling for himself which eventually brought him to the camp.

By the summer of 1935 the second track of the Trans-Baikal Railroad had been completed from Karymskaya to Svobodnyy and most camps were now moved east of the Zeya River. Berman was coming for his second visit and extensive preparations were made at headquarters. A new settlement had been built for headquarters employees: Two-storied apartment buildings, a hospital, theatre and movie house, and a new stadium. New streets, graded but unpaved, now had wooden sidewalks, slightly elevated so that in spring or after rains employees could walk to work without stalking through the mud. All structures were built of lumber after Finnish models. I knew the architect, a young zek of German parentage from Leningrad.

The camp's theatre group was preparing a new production. To my happy surprise Kolya Kryuger arrived in Svobodnyy to join them. Levit, now head of the automotive division, brought him to Svobodnyy. Kolya moved into the theatre barrack, the only one where male and female prisoners lived together. I knew most of its inhabitants, among them a well-known actor from the Tairov Theatre, a ballet soloist from the

Bolshoi, and a director of the Leningrad Operetta. Many of them had three-year terms because they were homosexuals. The group usually performed for the Bamlag headquarters employees and occasionally I had taken pictures of their performances. Now, for the Berman visit, a popular new play, "Platon Krechet," was staged at the new theatre.

## IRINA

At the opening of the theater I was sent to take pictures of the play. The heroine of "Platon Krechet" is a young komsomol girl and the part was performed with success by a seventeen-year-old student from Moscow who was in Svobodnyy visiting her parents. I had met her before when I took pictures after a headquarters concert. Her name was Irina. She had also studied the ballet and danced to a Chopin étude at the concert. Irina was friendly, petite, and a bundle of energy and determination. Her easy blushing didn't deter her from asking for and getting what she wanted.

At the performance I took many shots of her and of scenes with other actors. To complete my task, I took shots of the empty set, which had been designed by Kryuger, then noticed that while most people had already left, Irina was still around. When I started packing my equipment she came smiling and said: "I want to ask you to come to the party at headquarters."

"You know I am a zek and not invited there."

"I know, but I am sure it can be arranged. Some actors are there too. If you come with me I will talk to Sulin."

I knew Sulin, the young aide-de-camp of Berman's. So we went together to the party at headquarters and Irina got what she wanted. My boss was also there and took pictures so I was superfluous and didn't feel comfortable among all the brass. Irina introduced me to her parents and I sat down at their table. I had met her father before; he was an engineer with the automotive department, a free employee but a Belomor veteran. Her mother, I learned, worked in town as an accountant with the gold mining administration.

I left early and went to the camp to have my pictures developed. The next day Irina came to the photo bureau. She knew Belyavskiy and asked whether she could see the pictures and take them to show around at the actors' barrack.

Over the weekend the Berman festivities continued at the new sports arena and I was sent there to photograph the events. Kryuger, Vronskiy, and Irina were there too and Vronskiy told me that he was in love with Irina. Later that day we had a good time picking hazelnuts which grew in profusion behind the new stadium.

It was the end of August and Irina told us that she was leaving soon to begin teaching school in Moscow. She had just graduated from teacher's college and was to teach German at primary school. During her last days there we met on several occasions and she asked me to come to her parents place for supper the day before she was leaving.

In the Russian language, as in most European languages, there are two personal pronouns for the English "you." One is a formal address while the other is used in intimate relationships. This last evening after supper, she walked with me on my way back to the camp. Somewhere we stopped, embraced, and kissed goodbye. This was when we switched to the intimate "ty." She said she would write me via her mother.

This last fall and winter at Bamlag I stayed mostly at headquarters; once in a while I stopped at Irina's parents' place, one of the improved barracks on the way between headquarters and camp. Her parents were always very friendly; during those visits I learned more about the family: Her parents — it was actually her stepfather — had been arrested in Moscow when she was twelve years old and she now lived with a distant relative. Her stepfather was a former naval officer and aide-de-camp to Admiral Kolchak; when taken prisoner by the Reds in Siberia his life was spared due to the intercession of his sailors. Irina's mother came from a former Krasnoyarsk merchant family.

I expected my term to expire during the first quarter of 1936. Kryuger and Vronskiy had three-year terms and Volik's term was cut in half; they were all due for discharge before the end of the year.

Former prisoners could not live in the six major cities, the areas surrounding them, or in border zones, i.e., within 100 kilometers of the Soviet border. Vronskiy chose Kalinin for his residence, a city between Moscow and Leningrad, and told me that he planned to visit Irina on his way to Kalinin. I didn't tell him about my involvement with Irina. Kolya Kryuger chose Tashkent as his residence, since he was not allowed to live in Moscow. He wrote me that life was pleasant there and suggested that I join him. Volik left to join his parents who had moved from Leningrad to the Moscow-Volga Canal, also a Gulag enterprise, where his father was now employed. They lived outside the Moscow restricted zone. When my time came, I chose Kalinin. But first I had to visit my mother in Aryk Balyk.

In March, before my release day came, there were a lot of goodbyes to be said. Irina's parents gave me an old pre-revolutionary overcoat as a farewell present; it was made for a person twice my weight but was of good cloth with a large karakul collar for warmth. Irina had written me that she had seen Sulin at Gulag headquarters and was promised a two-week Moscow visitor's permit for me.

*Eilers' "New World" gardening staff. Hermann Eilers, back row far left; Jacob Saal, back row, second from right.*

*Petersburg around 1900. Rear left to right: Robert Blumenfeld, Robert and Hermann Saal, Fritz Schotte.*

*Jacob and Johanna Saal with one of their children at their dacha in Terijoki, 1890s.*

*Tennis court in Terijoki before 1914. Includes Vera and Robert Saal; Constantin (in hat), August, and Erica Eilers (center front).*

127

*Saal family, 1908, St. Petersburg. Standing left to right: Robert Saal, uncle Leo Saal, Else Seeger, Hermann Saal. Seated left to right: Jacob Saal, Johanna Saal, Vera Saal.*

*Christmas 1917. Hermann and Else Saal with the author.*

*Left to right: Rhoda Schotte,
Hermann Saal, Else Saal, unknown,
Fritz Schotte, soldier in front of
monument to Peter the Great, 1911.*

*Photograph above left, Old Eiler's house, Litseyskaya Street, Leningrad.
Photograph above right, Petri School, Leningrad.*

*Constantin Eilers' dacha in Terijoki, 1917. Top row: Else Saal and Gertrude Eilers. Middle row: the author, Bruno Eilers, Karen and Irma Eilers below them. Bottom left: Zevig children.*

*#14 Litseyskaya Street (later Roentgen Street), St. Petersburg, about 1912.*

*Photograph above, Litseyskaya Street, 1921. Back row: Else and Hermann Saal. Seated, left to right: the author, Jacob, Johanna, and Ira Saal; Vera and Rolf Schmiedeberg. Photograph at left, Jacob and Johanna Saal with Ira, #14 Litseyskaya Street garden, about 1921.*

*Else Saal and Elizabeth Pufahl in Litseyskaya Street drawing room, about 1926.*

*Left to right: Volik, Aleka, Ira, and the author in Leningrad, 1930.*

*The author and Ira, 1926.*

*Else Saal, the author's mother, 1929.*

*The author with Aleka and sister Ira, 1930.*

*A performance of the German Cultural Society at Yusupov Palace, Leningrad, 1928. Actor at far right, Hermann Saal.*

*The author in a German Cultural Society production, Leningrad, 1929.*

*The author listening to American records, Leningrad, 1931.*

*Volik, 1932.*

*The author, 1928.*

*Left to right: Nina (Werner's third wife), Werner, the author, Volik,*
*1932, Leningrad.*

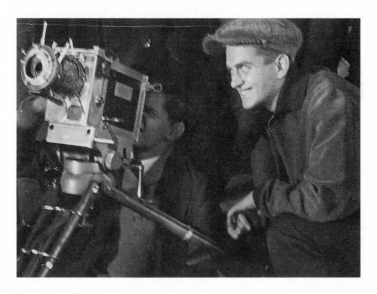

*The author filming with Andrey in Leningrad, 1931.*

*Photograph above and below: prisoners at work, Bamlag, 1930s.*

*Photograph at left: Frenkel on inspection with officers and prisoner engineers, Bamlag, 1936.*

*Irina with Andryusha, Moscow, 1939.*

*Warsaw, October 1942.*

*Photograph above left: the author in Koenigsberg, 1944. Photograph above right: the author and Zorin, Kranz Beach, 1943.*

*Walter Goebel, Misha Vogt, and the author in Grossraum barracks at Christmas, 1943.*

*Hermann Baun, Chief, Strategic Reconnaissance, Eastern Front, 1949 photo.*

*The author in Riga with "Commando Zeppelin," 1944.*

*The author with Misha Vogt in Lindau, 1946.*

*Ira, 1979.*

*The author's second wife, Rosemarie, 1951.*

*Aunt Nina, Kratovo/Moscow, 1960s.*

# 7

## Free Again

When I got my camp release certificate, travel rations, and a requisition slip for a train ticket I was a free man, though not permitted to reside in the six major cities or any restricted zone.

Walking to the railroad station I was joined by only one other ex-prisoner. As usual the ticket office was closed. My companion was inexperienced in the way one could board a train. I instructed him in how it could be done and he followed my advice; we hung on the footboard as the train left the station. When the woman conductor who let us in learned that we were going all the way, she told us that we could travel without tickets only as long as it was Bamlag territory. After Karymskaya, strict controls would not permit us to continue without proper tickets. She suggested that one of us should try to exchange the requisition chits for tickets at Shimanovskaya, our next stop.

I remained in the train with our luggage while my companion ran to the ticket office. He failed to return before the train departed. I was now without my requisition chit and decided to go no further than Ksenyevka where people knew me and would issue me a new one. In Ksenyevka I learned from the head conductor that an express train would overtake us there and with luck my companion could catch up with me. The express came at night; I saw the chief conductor getting off and told him about my missing companion.

"There was a prisoner who tried to hitch a ride but I threw him off way back," he told me.

I stayed overnight at the nearby camp office. In the morning I got a new requisition chit and a ticket. I left my companion's luggage at the station master's office; it had its destination marked.

What I remember of the long Siberian train ride were the crossings of the big Siberian rivers, the foul air at night while sleeping on the *galerka* (the top third shelf designed for luggage) and running at train stops with a borrowed kettle to fetch *kipyatok* — hot boiled water provided for the passengers at one end of a station's platform. My travel ration included a hard bar of pressed tea which was highly appreciated by kettle owners.

I was not aware then of how lucky I was to have been arrested in 1933 and discharged in 1936. Had I been arrested in 1935, a certainty after Kirov's murder, I would have served my full term until 1940 and most certainly have received, without further trial, an additional term. Set free now, I was able to escape the worst terror, while living "on the run" illegally in the capital.

## ARYK BALYK

I arrived in Kokchetav on a cold morning; the landscape was covered with several feet of snow. I asked the station master how to get to Aryk Balyk and he directed me to the nearby trucking station. It consisted of a large shed for a repair shop and platforms with stacked steel barrels serving as a filling station. There were about a half dozen trucks standing around and I asked for one going to Aryk Balyk. A driver who was loading barrels said he was going there and we agreed on a price.

This region of Kazakhstan is flat prairie with no paved roads, only tracks where trucks have driven time and again over the dry even surface. It took nearly a day to cover the hundred kilometers to Aryk Balyk. On the way we passed abandoned villages where nomadic Kazakh families were camping with their sheep and camels. Aryk Balyk was a village on the rim of a small lake with a low range of hills to the east; to the west the vast flat plain extended to the horizon. On top of the range stood a windmill. As we drove through the village to the kolkhoz office I noticed that half of the houses were uninhabited. At the office I inquired about my mother.

"Oh, the *nemka* — the German woman," they said and told a boy who happened to be in the office to escort me to her place, the last house on the road to the prairie. A cold steady wind was blowing. The buildings were covered with several feet of snow; trenches were dug through the snow to the doorways and windows of inhabited houses.

We entered the house through a cowshed where a cow was munching on hay. When the door to the kitchen was opened we entered in a cloud of steam. The peasant family was sitting at their evening meal. A table, two benches, and a big Russian oven were the only furnishings.

My appearance caused no surprise; I was expected. Mother, hearing the commotion, came in from her room. We embraced, the peasant family at their meal looking on, smiling and munching. The boy who brought me to the house got a reward and was sent off.

Mother's room, the only one besides the kitchen, was spacious and had three windows facing the prairie; a fire was burning in a cast-iron stove. A bed, chest, washstand, cupboard, our old trunk, a table and two chairs completed the furnishings. I recognized some pieces of china and silver which mother and Ira had carried from Leningrad on their 2,000 mile journey, the few items which reminded me of home.

We sat down for a meal and talked about what had happened to us during the last three years. Mother did not complain; she only worried somewhat about Ira even though she knew that Ira was well cared for by the Schaak family. Ira would soon graduate from school and hoped to study medicine with the help of Professor Schaak who was dean of surgery at the medical school. Considering the circumstances, Mother lived quite comfortably. She earned her living mainly by knitting Orenburg shawls, a great local attraction; she could barter them for anything she needed in her simple village existence. Isidor Becker sent her packages with everything she needed, including the wool for knitting. The villagers treated her with unusual respect; her German accent and the official version that those exiled after Kirov's murder were members of the old aristocracy gave her a somewhat exalted status.

Mother's hosts both worked at the kolkhoz and she often took care of their children, two girls about five and seven and a boy not yet two. There was enough milk from the cow in the shed and Mother cooked for herself in their oven. She was on good terms with the woman who ran the kolkhoz grocery store and also with families of other Leningrad exiles, all working-class people.

Late at night I went to sleep on a big sack of straw. During the next few days we talked about my plans. Mother asked about Irina, who had written her a few letters from Moscow. I told her that I planned to stay in Kalinin and hoped to earn a living in photography since that was what I had been doing for years. Of course I needed a camera. There was still money in Leningrad from the sale of our furniture, carpets, and china. Isidor Becker had some of this money which paid for Ira's expenses. But there was also money from the sale of the grand piano which the Holls had sold to the Swedish Consul. I could use this money to purchase a camera.

Cold temperatures and blowing snow kept us in the house all the time and our landlord, who was in charge of kolkhoz cattle, had problems; there was no hay for the livestock. Most of it had been left in the fields when winter set in. Now emergency expeditions had to be organized to dig the hay from under the snow; the longer the winter lasted, the farther away one had to go for hay.

When, on a windless, cold sunny day I left Aryk Balyk by truck for Kokchetav, a long line of horse-drawn sleighs was going for hay into the endless white plains under a brilliant blue sky. Changing trains at Petropavlovsk, I sent Irina a telegram about my arrival.


## MOSCOW

After a three-day journey my train reached Moscow's Kazan Station in the evening. Snow fell in heavy wet flakes. As the train entered the station and before it came to a stop I stepped out on the footboard. I saw Irina standing at a distance on a nearly empty platform, a petite figure, her face hidden up to her nose in a fur collar and on her head a fancy red, white, and blue knitted beret.

I jumped off the train and ran towards her and we embraced. She looked sweet and elegant in her coat with the fur collar and the snow now settling on the fur and melting on the skin.

"Don't you have a coat?," she asked.

I went back into the car and got my overcoat and plywood suitcase, feeling uncomfortable in my outfit, but passing

Muscovites didn't seem to pay any attention to me as we left the station and entered the big plaza. Outside was glistening snow under stark lights and a dark night sky. After all that time in the wilderness, the commotion, the lights and sounds of a big city were exhilarating.

At the beginning of my exile, I had often dreamt with a racing heartbeat about a return to my hometown. In time the dream had faded. Now in Moscow with Irina on my arm I felt excited about the future rather than nostalgic for the past.

We boarded the crosstown trolley. It was not crowded at this evening hour and some of the passengers glanced occasionally at us. What an odd couple we made — she elegant by Moscow standards, myself with the plywood suitcase and an oversized overcoat of prerevolutionary vintage — the term applying to a piece out of fashion as well as of superior quality.

Irina filled me in on the important news.

"First thing tomorrow you must go to Sulin. He knows you are coming and will arrange everything." This meant that I was to go to Gulag headquarters and get the promised permit for a short stay in the city.

"Vronskiy was here from Kalinin. He can accommodate you there for a few days. He is in love with me, the poor guy, but I haven't told him anything about us. You do it when you get there."

Volik had also visited Irina on a few occasions for a dinner out or for the movies. He worked on the Moscow-Volga Canal not far from the city. One could reach his village by bus but he had no telephone.

At the street corner where we alighted, the stores were still open. "Wait a moment," she said. "I'll get some fresh bread from the bakery." It was a busy corner with streetcars passing by and pedestrians hurrying to the shops. When Irina came back we turned a corner into a quiet street, entered a gate to a yard with a dozen snow-covered trees and proceeded to the entrance of an old five-story apartment house. Irina pointed to three lit windows on the raised first floor.

"That is my and Aunt Zina's room; hers is the window on the right."

Up one flight of stairs was the apartment door with big etched glass windows. Next to it an electric doorbell with directions for ringing seven different parties. One long and two short rings for Irina. We entered the apartment and proceeded along a dark corridor to the third door on the right which was open and where Aunt Zina greeted me with great friendliness. The room had a high ceiling, fancy stucco cornices, and wall embellishments; it was divided by a curtain and two wardrobes. In Irina's part of the room stood a grand piano, a couch in front of bookshelves which covered the door to an adjoining room and a table set for two with two chairs. A big floor-length mirror between two windows reflected our presence. A field cot had been made up for me on one side of the piano. After greeting us, Aunt Zina disappeared behind the partition and Irina and I had a supper of *pelmeni* (a Siberian version of ravioli) and wine.

Originally the apartment had belonged to Irina's family and she had lived there most of her life. Later that evening I was introduced to the other occupants of the apartment. A middle-aged blonde lady next door greeted me exuberantly — she was a secretary with a clouded past which concealed a persecuted ex-husband. The Rezniks, a young couple who were both engineers, also greeted me. The wife's parents had strained relations with their son-in-law; the old church-going couple had opposed their daughter's marriage to a Jew.

From the smallest room emerged a deaf-mute woman, a former maid of Irina's parents who still did household chores for whoever asked her. We knocked at the door of Irina's dressmaker, a lady with a teen-age daughter who had a substantial clientele for her not entirely legal home business. Lat-

er, when Irina and I went into the kitchen, a secret police major and his wife came there too. They occupied two rooms of
the apartment with a pre-school son. Irina had apprised the
major that I had a temporary visitor's permit.

It was late when we retired, Irina on her couch, I on the
cot. Aunt Zina said goodnight from behind the curtain and
we switched out the lights.

The next morning I woke up when Aunt Zina tried to get
unnoticed out of the room to either the bathroom or the
kitchen. Irina was already doing her ballet exercises.

"Take your time," she said. "The bathroom and toilet will
now be occupied for a while." There were fifteen people in-
tent on using the facilities, although some had washstands in
their rooms.

Zina and Irina were in a rush to leave for work — Zina to
teach math in high school, Irina to teach German in the primary grades.

"Breakfast is in the cupboard; my kettle is in the kitchen.
When I get back home we'll go to Aunt Nina's. The Rubinsteins will also be there."

Irina gave me directions to Lubyanka Street. It took a few
telephone calls, after reporting to the front office there, for
me to get my residence permit for two weeks in Moscow.
Place of residence and place of work were registered in each
person's internal passport, along with other information. Each
time one changed either one, the relevant dates had to be
stamped in the passport. Rural village dwellers did not have
passports and, in order to leave the village district, they had to
procure a travel permit from the authorities.

I wanted to get in touch with Volik as soon as possible. He
was working on the Moscow-Volga Canal Project and in
charge of excavation on the outskirts of the city. Although a
former 58er, with the help of the Gulag he had obtained a
residence permit for the Moscow region. I could not reach

Volik at work and left a note with his landlady.

Volik came the next weekend and the three of us took the train to visit his parents. They lived in a Gulag settlement for free employees, somewhat like the one in Svobodniy, in newly-built two-story apartment houses with all the conveniences not found elsewhere in these provincial areas. We had a wonderful reunion, stayed overnight, and went together to pick mushrooms the next day. Everyone was charmed by Irina.

We also made the rounds of Irina's relatives: Aunt Nina and Aunt Nera, her mother's sisters, and Irina's cousin, Aunt Nina's daughter. Aunt Nina was the authoritative head of the clan; a Siberian beauty, she had spent years in Paris before the World War and studied at the Sorbonne. Whether she was widowed or divorced I never learned. She earned her living by translating French literature and was always *au courant* with what was happening in Moscow's upper literary circles. Her daughter Ina, a biologist, was married to Dmitri Rubinstein, a biochemistry professor. Aunt Nera was married to Uncle Alyosha, a professor of literature; they were childless. Zina was Uncle Alyosha's sister and had moved in with Irina when her parents were arrested. All of them had received me with great friendliness: Nina for a regal tea served on old china with fancy sweets; the Rubinsteins, who had a cook, for a sumptuous dinner; and Nera for a health food buffet.

## KALININ

The two weeks in Moscow passed all too quickly and, with my permit expired, I had to leave for Kalinin. This city, formerly and today again known as Tver, is the only substantial city on the rail line between Moscow and Leningrad. While its residents had to carry an internal passport, there were no residence restrictions and it was a mecca for former prisoners who had been natives of Moscow and Leningrad.

In Kalinin I went to Vronskiy's place at the edge of town. He was at work. I left my suitcase with the landlady and went for a stroll through the city.

Vronskiy was glad to see me when I returned and invited me to stay with him until I got my papers; I slept on the floor on an improvised mattress.

The first order of business for me was to go to the police and have my camp release certificate exchanged for a temporary identity card and to register with the military reserve roll. With these papers in hand I could look for a room of my own.

While I stayed with Vronskiy he told me about his work as a reporter at the local newspaper. As a former petty criminal he had no difficulty landing this job and promised to make inquiries to see if there was an opportunity for me to work as a press photographer. He also confided in me about his visit to Moscow, his feelings for Irina, and his intention to marry her. I didn't tell him about my stopover in Moscow and, since Irina and I had agreed on a trip to Leningrad as soon as I had my papers, I decided to postpone telling him about our engagement until after this trip. There were no delays in procuring my papers and I found a room in the house of a woman who worked at the nearby textile factory.

On the agreed weekend I joined Irina on the night train to Leningrad where we were met at the station by my sister Ira. We went directly to Professor Schaak's apartment. It was an eerie feeling to enter the house where I had grown up, with all of its memories. We visited Oscar Goldin who, with his new wife, occupied father's former study. Anisya, our former maid, now lived with a military officer who had moved with his three children into the room vacated by mother and Ira. These were the only people I knew out of the fourteen who now inhabited the apartment that once was my home.

Irina had arranged for us to stay with friends of her family, the Vereyskiys. By coincidence, Mr. Vereyskiy was the artist whom Alfred and I had watched ten years ago making an ink drawing of the view from Blumenfelds' window for the Ogonyok Magazine. He was a well-known graphic artist and curator of prints at the Hermitage. His son Orest, also an artist, was a friend of Irina's. Orest's parents, although separated, maintained a common household which included their son and Mrs. Vereyskiy's new companion, a historian. Orest's mother was a well-known writer of childrens' books.

Irina and I were accommodated in a guest room and we all met at the dinner table where there was much lively conversation. One topic I remember was Sholokhov's novel "And Quiet Flows the Don." The book was published with Stalin's blessing; its hero, surprisingly, was a former "White Cossack." A "White" — as opposed to a "Red" — was one who had fought with the White Armies during the civil war and is not to be confused with a "White Russian," i.e., a Belorussian.

The main reason for our trip to Leningrad was to collect the money for our grand piano which Martha Holl sold to the Swedish Consul. Since, in the meantime, the Holls had left for Berlin, Martha had deposited the money with Helen Vysotskiy, Old Eilers' oldest daughter and the only one living in Russia. Whether she was widowed or her officer husband had left Russia with the White Armies I do not know, but it was to him that Old Eilers had referred in a 1912 letter when he wrote: "I summoned Helen to pay me back from her bank account the 300 rubles she had borrowed. Instead, she tearfully confessed that there was no money in the account. She had squandered it all, no doubt to support her husband's drinking habit."

Now Helen lived in reduced circumstances with her daughter and two grandsons. She didn't want me to come to her place and it was arranged that we meet on the Blue Bridge where she handed me an envelope. With the money I bought a Soviet-built Leica.

Another visit was to the Shapiros, mother's old friends

who had kept some of my clothing and a few pieces of furniture — an armchair, a floor lamp, and a sideboard which Ira didn't want. I took my clothing; the furniture would be sent later to Moscow. Then Irina and I boarded the Moscow train. I got off in Kalinin; Irina continued on to Moscow.

On my return Vronskiy informed me that, as a former 58er, I had no chance of being employed by the newspaper. Other efforts of mine to find work as a photographer for the local industry were futile, but one day while strolling through the city I was surprised to see my family name in fat letters on a poster. It announced the performances of a visiting ballet theatre and the name of the prima ballerina was Marina Saal. Our name was not common in Russia but I knew we had relatives, descendants of grandfather's brother. For reasons unknown to me there had been very little contact between the two branches of the family. Looking at the poster I remembered how way back in Leningrad Andrey and I made plans to introduce photography and cinematography at the Kirov Ballet as a training tool. Perhaps this was an opportunity for me now and I wanted to meet my distant cousin.

I went to the Palace of Culture at rehearsal time. My new-found cousin was a few years my senior, knew that we were related, and was very happy to make my acquaintance. She asked me to come for tea at their guest quarters; her husband was the company's director and would be there too. With high hopes, I went there, met her husband, and we had tea. But when I mentioned my recent past, her husband's attitude became unmistakably unfriendly; his wife was obviously uncomfortable and saddened. There was nothing else for me to do but say goodbye.

During these days in Kalinin I got several letters from Kolya Kryuger from Tashkent; they exuded his usual energy and *joie de vivre*. He asked me to come. Everything was fine; he had a room, had bought rugs, and was working as an artist at the Chirchikstroy River Dam. Life was enjoyable, he wrote, the national attire colorful, particularly on females. He had made friends, knew people of influence. In summer there was fruit in abundance: grapes, melons, peaches, apricots.

I decided to go to Moscow to see Irina and tell her that it would be best for me to go to Tashkent while I still had some funds. She agreed. She would come to Tashkent in June as soon as school was over; then we would see how things might work out.

Back in Kalinin I decided that it was time to tell Vronskiy that I had traveled to Leningrad together with Irina and that we planned to get married. He was surprised and unhappy but made no recriminations. When I told him that I was leaving for Tashkent, he begged me to lend him my camera; he needed one in his work in order to make more money and would return it to Irina. I left him the camera. When I told Irina about it on my stopover in Moscow she said that it was a stupid mistake.

## TASHKENT

It was a three-day journey to Tashkent; snow had fallen there during the night but was melting now as the train passed muddy suburban streets. Kolya was at the station to meet me, his usual happy self. He helped me with my luggage to the streetcar. He said I could stay with him for a while and asked whether I had money; he was momentarily out of funds.

When we arrived at his quarters I found out that Kolya had no room of his own. He rented only part of a room which he shared with a textile factory worker and her school-age daughter. One entered the room from the inner court or garden. A bed for mother and daughter, big dining table with chairs, chest of drawers, and a "guitar" — a frame with a hammock-type net under a thin mattress — were the furnishings. I thought of Kolya's seafaring experience; sailors on old ships used to sleep in hammocks. But there was no way two of us could sleep on that contraption. As in years before, I settled for the floor which was fine except for the possibility of scorpions. There was a communal kitchen which we did not use and washing facilities next to an outhouse in the yard. The advantage of this residence was its location a few blocks away from Central Square.

Tashkent was not as interesting a city as Samarkand or Bokhara. It was divided into two parts. The "old town," inhabited by Uzbeks, had dusty meandering streets bordered by long grey adobe garden walls and one-story houses with only a door facing the street. A covered patio opening on the garden was the center of life; *aryks* — creeks or irrigation canals — flowed through the gardens and were a major water supply. Europeans seldom ventured into the old town nor did the Uzbeks usually invite them into their homes.

The new town was built by Russians. Several avenues extended fan-like from a central circular park to the industrial suburbs. One side the park was abutted by the business district and Red Square. The avenues were wide with usually two rows of poplars on each side between which the *aryks* flowed. The avenues were lined by one-story stucco apartment blocks with enclosed yards or gardens at the center. Some parts of the city had a suburban look; large dachas surrounded by gardens provided a comfortable life for old-timers or people of influence. The working class quarters where Kolya lived had no plumbing; at every street corner was a pump to draw one's water supply.

I did not stay long at Kolya's place. Around the corner another contemporary and temporary resident had a room to himself and looked for someone to share expenses. I moved in with my suitcase and mattress but spent most days with Kolya.

Kolya worked part-time at Chirchikstroy, a construction site out of town. His job was not much different from Bamlag's Skovorodino: lettering slogans and graphic displays of "achievements by shock workers." When he was in town we worked together at arranging window displays in stores; when there was nothing else to do, Kolya drew street scenes and sketched passersby. I enjoyed watching him.

I told him about Irina, and Kolya had news for me too. Returning from Bamlag to Moscow he had met a girl on the train who came from Harbin where she grew up, the daughter of White emigrants. Harbin was now in Japanese hands and some former White émigrés were now welcomed into the Soviet fold. On the long Siberian train journey Kolya and Maria had fallen in love. Kolya brought her to his parents' home in Moscow and she had stayed with them when he had to leave for Tashkent. He expected that she would soon come to Tashkent to join him.

Tashkent was one of the few capitals without residence restrictions and a haven for exiles. It was free from the tensions, anxieties, and fears prevailing in the main cities of European Russia. The big market on the border of the old and new towns was an authentic oriental bazaar. In the shade of big trees lining the streets of the business district outdoor cafés provided the relaxed atmosphere typical of southern regions. Kolya and I often went there in the morning for a *kefir* — a kind of yogurt — and sweet buns and coffee. The girls who served there knew us and, if we happened to be out of funds, fed us on credit. If we did not go there, unleavened bread with butter and sausage or cheese was our standard fare.

It didn't take long for me to find work which paid a living wage, at least for my undemanding life. I met Vikhman, a former Czarist naval lieutenant and a long-time Tashkent resident, who knew his way around town. He headed a quasi-cooperative business which hired Uzbeks to make adobe bricks. The outskirts of Tashkent provided abundant clay to make

bricks which were dried in the sun and used for small buildings and additions to private residences. At the time we met,
Vikhman was building ice cream and soda fountain pavilions.
He wanted them "to look nice, to have architecture," and I
was to draw the plans. Vikhman suggested that I move into
his two-room adobe house located in an inner court a block
away from the central square. He had built the house for himself and his much older wife and I was to use one of the
rooms for working and living. When I told him that I expected Irina he said: "Fine, she can move in too. My wife will be
happy to have someone to talk to." He seldom spent nights at
home.

The days in Tashkent were hot and darkness fell quickly.
Temperatures dropped, the dark sky was full of bright stars,
and everybody enjoyed the evenings outside. The city had
many open-air establishments: eateries, cafes, movies, stages
for musical performances, and dance floors.

Irina arrived in June with the news that she had applied to
take the entrance examinations for the Institute of Foreign
Languages. This meant that she had to be back in Moscow by
mid-August. The Vikhmans were pleased to meet her. In the
days to come Irina was to hear in detail the wife's tale of woe.
Before the revolution she had been married to an admiral and
had an affair with Vikhman, then a young lieutenant. The admiral perished during the revolution while she and her lieutenant fled. But fate caught up with them and they were exiled to Tashkent. Now, twenty years later, her husband was
having his own affairs.

In July I exchanged my three-month identity certificate
from Kalinin for a five-year internal passport and a day later,
after a customary visit to the public bathhouse, Irina and I
went to the police station to register our marriage.

One day, returning from a walk in town, Irina told me
that she had taken a job. In the park at the open air dance

floor she met a man from Moscow who had come to Tashkent for the summer to make money by teaching Western dances. Now that Stalin had decreed life to be more fun, Western dances were no longer forbidden fruit and the rhumba was the latest hit. The man from Moscow was looking for a partner and Irina had agreed to work with him. I was not very enthusiastic but it paid well and money was always good to have. After evening dance classes, we all went for a late supper to a nearby open-air restaurant; it featured a jazz band and a dance floor. For a change I could be Irina's partner. One evening everybody's attention was drawn to the American singer Marian Anderson, who was enjoying the cool evening after her performance at the Tashkent Opera; we took turns inviting her for a dance.

Irina went back to Moscow in mid-August. I wondered how she had managed to be admitted to the exams since, according to regulations, she had to complete three years of work before becoming eligible for study at an institution of higher learning. "Don't worry" was Irina's usual answer to such concerns.

Before Irina left for Moscow Kolya and Maria, who had also married by then, surprised us by leaving the city without telling us. I discovered at the tailor's where Kolya and I had ordered new suits that he had taken not only his suit but also the fabric for mine.

Early in September I received a telegram from Irina: "Admitted, love, kisses."

\* \* \*

Just before Irina's departure an acquaintance of mine, who was head of the Construction Department of the Council of Ministers, asked me if I could do technical drawings; a Lenin monument to be erected on Tashkent's Red Square had been commissioned to a Moscow sculptor who had arrived in Tash-kent. Of course I was interested. A meeting was arranged to discuss the matter at the hotel where the sculptor was staying. When I arrived, I found a table set with vodka, wine, and a whole piglet in aspic. The sculptor, a man of fame and good appetite, unrolled the plans for his project, a large cubistic base of granite blocks combined with a tribune and topped with a large bronze statue of Lenin. My job was to extract from his drawings the component parts, give them measure-ments, number them, and deliver the drawings to the quarry. By dinner's end we were in agreement about my work and pay.

Now I was busy working on the specifications and draw-ings and visiting the quarry in the mountains near Angren where I traveled by truck. On the way we used to stop at *chay-khanas*, tea houses, shaded verandas laid out with layers of rugs on which men sipped green tea and talked business all day long. In the fields women and children were picking cot-ton.

The quarry was in a desolate area at the foot of a mountain range. We slept in hammocks to protect ourselves from scor-pions. The stone masons had come from Central Russia, from villages where men specialized in quarrying stone. They were well-organized, old masters supervising young, less experi-enced masons. I enjoyed talking with them and observing their skills.

Upon completion of my work, I had a chunk of money and came to the conclusion that to live in Tashkent with a wife in Moscow made no sense. I packed my suitcase, de-reg-istered my residence as required by law, bought a train ticket, and left for Moscow by the end of September.

# 8

## Holding on

This time there was no one to meet me at the Moscow railroad station. Irina was at her Institute and, as a rule, she came home just long enough to have a night's sleep; after attending lectures until late afternoon she gave private lessons, usually staying for supper at her students' homes. Evenings she spent at the Lenin Library just ten minutes by streetcar away from home.

My problem now was to find work and a residence permit in Moscow. I had to see Volik and arrange a visit to his parents; maybe Iosif Ivanovich could help. But even before I could make it there — it was early morning and we were still in bed — there was a knock at our door. "Who might be there so early?" Aunt Zina inquired behind the curtain. She was already up and came from behind the curtain to open the door.

Our visitors were the janitor and a policeman. They entered the room; the janitor closed the door and stood back while the policeman came close and asked for my documents. I pulled my Tashkent passport out of my jacket hanging over the back of a chair next to our couch. The policeman looked through it.

"You don't have a Moscow residence registration?" No, I didn't. "You must leave the city within 24 hours." He got a form out of his briefcase which I signed while still in bed. Then the two left. I had twenty-four hours to leave town. Where should I go? Irina had to be at her institute on time; she skipped her ballet exercises.

"What do you want to do? Get in touch with Volik." Between combing her hair, putting on lipstick, gathering books and papers, and drinking her *kefir*, she considered the next move to stay ahead of the game. "If you could only get accepted as a student somewhere. Maybe you should call Aunt Nina."

"I guess I will have to go back to Kalinin."

"What will you do there? I have to run now. I'll see you in the evening."

Out the window I saw her running across the yard. Aunt Zina was gathering her breakfast dishes behind the curtain and came out to bring them to the kitchen.

"What will you do?" she asked, standing in the door. "They will not let you live here. My sister lives in Mozhaysk; maybe you can find something there. You know, my sister-in-law also came back from a camp and my brother arranged for her to live in a village an hour by train from here. It's hard on my brother; he works late hours with his theatre groups and has to catch the last train home." She sighed and looked at her watch. "Oh my, I have to run. I have a lesson at nine."

I put away the bedding and lit some matches to the bedbugs hiding in crevices of the plaster wall decorations, a pattern of fruits and leaves dividing the wall into panels proportioned by the golden rule. Outside it was a nice September day. I wished I could get in touch with Volik, but Mnevniki was a distance and he would be on a job within the restricted labor camp area and out of reach. I could leave a note at his place and ask him to come; there would be a bus to Mnevniki about noon. I definitely did not want to go back to Kalinin which would mean seeing Irina only once a month. Maybe Volik's father could help.

I ate and telephoned Aunt Nina. When I left, the janitor's wife was sweeping the sidewalk and returned my "good morning" in a friendly way. She often did laundry for Irina who paid her well and chatted with her whenever they met. I knew that the janitor's wife was harmless but her husband was another matter; he could report to the police when he saw me. The housing administrator, whose windows overlooked the yard, could also watch my comings and goings. In an emergency I could exit the apartment through the kitchen window which was on ground level and faced the yard of the neighboring house.

Aunt Nina was asleep when I phoned but told me to come right away and have tea with her. I decided to walk and save the fare; the weather was fine. Nina was in her morning gown reclining on an Empire sofa reading some French text. The table was set with her old china.

"Plug in the electric boiler there in the corner," she said with the smile of a conspirator; she only paid for three light bulbs as her share of the communal electric bill.

"I don't like to go into the kitchen in the morning. I am trying to get my own electric meter and was promised one but that's all not so simple. It's the same as having the room painted. Look there on the desk; what do you think about the color, the emerald oil paint set off with a golden stripe? The painter promised to do the room as soon as he has enough paint but what he charges is highway robbery. Now take the silver teapot on the commode — the tea is already in it — pour carefully, don't let water dribble on the floor; it's just been polished. Come sit down and tell me your story. There is some Beluga and the French bread is fresh. Later do me a favor and make a run to the pawnbroker. I need money and have a ring to be brought there. Now what happened?"

I told her.

"That's bad; of course you don't want to live away from your young wife. It's not good for Irina either. What can be done?"

Later I went to the pawnbroker which was not far away, returned with the money, and took off by bus to Krasnaya Presna. There I had luck with the next bus to Mnevniki, found Volik's landlady at home, and left a note for him. After a long wait for the bus back, I reached home after dark and was hungry. Irina was not back yet. I went to the corner store for *moskovskiye* (hamburgers). At the next store I bought coleslaw out of a barrel. Coming out I saw Irina leave the streetcar and forgot my worries. We went home together and I held her tightly by the arm. We still had twelve hours before I had to leave town. Aunt Zina came shortly after us and disappeared behind her curtain. Irina made tea and we ate.

"What have you decided to do?" asked Aunt Zina from behind the partition.

"Well, hopefully Volik will come later; perhaps I can stay with him for a while or with his parents. Maybe his father can help."

It was late when our doorbell rang; it was Volik. We decided that he should stay overnight; the three of us went out, took the streetcar to an all night store and bought vodka, cold cuts, herring, and canned eggplants for a night's feast. When we returned, the window at Zina's was dark and as usual she had cotton in her ears, but still we had to keep our voices low. We decided that I should see Volik's father, Iosif Ivanovich. We bedded Volik on the floor next to our couch. In the morning, after four hours of sleep, we left the house together.

The direct train to Kimry was leaving around noon; I could also catch an earlier train for Dmitrov and wait there for the train to Kimry but decided against doing the latter.

There were frequent document checks in Dmitrov since it was headquarters for the Moscow-Volga Canal Camp. I took my time walking through the city, part of which was dominated by warehouses and railroad yards, small brick or wooden tenement houses, and the famous Butyrka prison. The day was gray and it started to drizzle before I reached the station. My spirits were low and my prospects seemed dim. I envied Volik who had a job he liked, a good income, and could be in the city any evening to see Irina.

Arriving shortly before supper at Ivankovo I found Dagmara Ernestovna at home and was received as usual like a son. When Iosif Ivanovich came we had a couple of drinks before supper — vodka with lemon peel from the crystal decanter which I remembered having seen in their dining room in Petersburg. We talked things over during supper. Iosif Ivanovich had an idea. There was a civil engineer and architect — from a good family, probably of Polish extraction — in charge of construction at Lock No. 4. Iosif Ivanovich would talk to him about me. I should stay to see what the next day would bring; Dagmara Ernestovna fixed a bed for me on the living room couch.

Iosif Ivanovich was successful. I was to go to Yakhroma and see the Chief of Construction at Lock No. 4.

## YAKHROMA

Yakhroma is less than an hour by train from Moscow and the house of my prospective boss was not far from the rail station. It was supper time when I knocked at the door; he and his wife were just sitting down for a meal. With Polish politeness and Russian hospitality I was invited to eat with them and made to feel completely comfortable. Yes, he needed technical personnel for the project and I could stay with them while looking for a place of my own.

"It isn't easy to find a place with our project going on here; the village is overcrowded," he said. I stayed with them for several days.

The next morning we went to the construction site. In the dugout the finished concrete walls of the lock stood high; work was proceeding on the dam and pumping station. Trucks with concrete came in a steady stream from a nearby plant. Bright lights illuminated the scene. It looked like a big ant heap with prisoners, horse carts, and trucks moving mountains of earth back into the big dugout. I was to assist a shift supervisor on the dam site where concrete was poured 24 hours a day in three shifts. Later I would take over supervision of the stone carvers, free employees who would arrive from Ukraine. On the lock's upper piers stood concrete skeletons, buildings to house controls of the gates. They were to be clad in granite with two giant steel models of old sailing ships — caravels — placed on top. Now bricklayers were in the process of raising the walls.

Winter was coming and the construction site was being winterized before the stone carvers arrived. I proposed building a monorail suspended over the roof around the perimeter of the buildings to lift the heavy stone blocks into place. My boss liked the idea and I started work immediately on the dam site. My passport and military documents were sent to the personnel office. I ate in the cafeteria for free employees, currently well supplied with wild ducklings shot by Gulag officers. It was hunting season between Moscow and the Volga. On my first free day I traveled to Moscow equipped with a temporary certificate stating my place of work and residence. I liked the job and my colleagues; everything seemed to be just fine. The stone carvers arrived; I was familiar with their ways because of my work at the Angren quarry.

Three months later my boss asked me to come by his house in the evening. There he told me the bad news: the police had refused to grant a residence registration and even the personnel department in Dmitrov could not prevail. The next day I collected my pay and papers; all my plans and hopes were dashed and I stood before the empty trough one more time. It was almost Christmas.

What was I to do? To go back to Kalinin was a solution; I had to register a residence and with the military reserves somewhere. Of course I didn't want to stay there all the time and to take a job there. I had to count on Vronskiy's help. While I was in Tashkent he had gambled away my camera; he met some old buddies, played cards with them, and lost. "I didn't have the money, so they took the camera away," he told Irina. He owed me a favor. I would register at his place and he would call me if my presence was needed in Kalinin. And I could stay with Irina in Moscow as a "visitor." Of course I had to be extremely cautious, but Irina wasn't worried; she relied on the good will of the janitor's wife.

Irina and I left the house together early in the morning. With books in hand Irina began her studies in the crowded streetcar. After we parted I wandered around for a while in the city, went to a library or sometimes to the Sandunovskiy Turkish bathhouse with its small swimming pool; both were safe places. Often I dropped in at Aunt Nina's. I didn't go back home before dark. Evenings Irina usually studied at the Lenin Library and I waited for her there so we could go home together. She didn't like my waiting at the library while she was working or socializing with fellow students and readers. I felt out of place and often jealous.

Whatever money I had brought with me from Tashkent and Yakhroma was soon spent and there came days where I wandered around town hungry. Money which Irina received occasionally from her parents was stashed away in a book on the bookshelf; it was our savings account.

## 1937

The years 1937-38 became known as the time of the Great Terror. NKVD Chief Yagoda was removed in 1936 and was replaced by Yezhov. Among other things he was accused of running forced labor camps like rest homes. In 1939, Yagoda was executed and Yezhov was replaced by Beria.

These were also the years of the Spanish Civil War, the International Brigade, and the "Popular Front" with its coterie of admiring western intellectuals visiting "the homeland of the world's toilers." Some old émigrés, Prokofiev and Marina Tsvetayeva among them, returned to Russia; I met the latter on several occasions at Aunt Nina's. Marina committed suicide in 1941.

Aunt Nina was then translating works by Henri Barbusse, a French contemporary writer. In her work she met a lot of people in the literary profession where current political issues were registered with seismographic sensitivity. She concerned herself with my financial situation and arranged a meeting with a poet friend, Konstantin Abramovich Lipskerov, who had recently returned from three years exile in Siberia for homosexuality. A scion of an old Moscow family, a friend of Pasternak's and also a converted Jew, he was now translating verse of an ancient Armenian saga. At Stalin's behest the Georgian poem, "The Knight in Tiger's Skin," had just been translated.

Lipskerov was also an art collector and liked Somov's work; original watercolors by Somov hung on his walls and he had collected prints and reproductions of Somov's art and wanted them assembled in an album. I was to work on this album in his apartment for pay and food, usually fresh bread and barbecued chicken from a delicatessen; before slicing bread Lipskerov always made a sign of the cross on the bread's crust with his knife.

For a while I was taken care of, but my situation was still

precarious; this became obvious when the police came looking for me again. Fortunately I could see through our glass
door the uniformed man and the janitor standing outside our
apartment. Instead of opening the door I went down to the
kitchen and climbed out the window into the neighboring
yard.

## ROZANOV

"Do you know a family by the name of Tamm?" Aunt
Nina asked me one day. No, it didn't ring a bell. "Strange,"
she said, "your name is not that common. My neighbor asked
me about you." The room next door was occupied by a
bedridden old man and his daughter who took care of him.
Their name was Tamm. I had met the lady occasionally in the
communal kitchen while heating tea water. One didn't introduce oneself on such occasions, one just said hello, but Nina
had mentioned Irina's married name and it was familiar to her
neighbor. One day another of Mr. Tamm's daughters was visiting and invited me in; she was curious to know who I was.
The old gentleman was lying in his bed.

"Was not your grandfather named Jacob? Wasn't he a
florist?"

"Yes, he was."

"I knew him well. We used to play whist together," the old
man said.

"And I met your father when I visited Leningrad in 1926,"
his daughter continued. "Your father showed me the city." We
chatted about Leningrad. She was an architect; her husband,
Rozanov, was an economist in a department of the Moscow
Soviet.

A short time later Irina and I were invited by the Tamms
to a family dinner. Besides the two daughters whom I had already met, there was a third sister, a stenographer with the

Council of Ministers, Rozanov, and Tamm, Jr., a State Attorney with NKVD oversight. Although without any real oversight authority, prisoners and relatives of prisoners could file appeals and complaints with the State Attorney's office, but usually to no avail. It was a Russian dinner lasting many hours, the dinner table being the only place where everybody could sit together. Old Mr. Tamm was served in his bed. There were *zakuski* and many drinks. I was flanked by the Rozanovs; Irina sat next to Tamm Jr.

Ivan Sergeyevich Rozanov, tall, heavyset, with a round face and thick rimless glasses, was a repository of Russian poetry. His favorite was Yesenin, the husband of Isadora Duncan, who hanged himself at the Hotel d'Angleterre in Petrograd. Rozanov had both feet firmly planted in reality and Aunt Nina had told him about my situation. Between shots of vodka, while Irina flirted with the prosecutor, Rozanov listened to my tale.

"'What is to be done?' — as Vladimir Ilyich said.[19] Come to us next Sunday; I will see what can be done."

"You see, everything will work out," Irina said on the way home when I told her about my dinner conversation.

"Can you draw?" Rozanov asked me when I met him again. "I was told you can. If need be, my wife can help; she is an accomplished artist. And here is what we'll do. I have funds for six posters to promote safety at construction sites. Come to my office and we will sign a contract. You are the artist, I am the technical editor, and my boss is the responsible (political) editor. You get 200 rubles per poster, I get 100, and my boss Golodov 100."

I went to the Office for Embankment Construction and

---

[19] *Chto Delat'* — "What Is To Be Done?" — was the title of two famous treatises, one by Chernyshevsky and one by Lenin.

signed a contract the next day. It was a good six months salary. My work proceeded reasonably well; by mid-July I delivered the drawings and collected my money.

During the spring and early summer Volik came to see us often with his girlfriend Lida, a pretty Jewish girl from Zaporozhye who worked as an accountant. We went out together to the movies or sometimes to a restaurant and, on one such occasion, they told us that they had registered their marriage. During the months which followed all four of us became close friends and so it hit us hard when they told us that — together with Volik's parents — they would soon leave for the Far East where Volik and his father would work on a new Gulag project to regulate the Amur River. Shortly before Irina's summer vacation we saw them off on a special train for Gulag executives and their families.

During Irina's summer vacation we traveled to Aryk Balyk for her to meet my mother; Ira would also be there on a visit from Leningrad. The weeks at Aryk Balyk were relaxing; there was not much one could do. In the woods we picked small sweet wild cherries growing in abundance on small bushes and brought home full baskets. Irina also liked to look for mushrooms.

It was the wild cherries which caused my mother to take the landlord's small boy into her custody. The older sisters, when left in charge of the boy, ate the cherries and fed the pits to the little one. Since his parents didn't seem to care what happened to him mother took the little one into her own room to look after him.

We explored the school library which had a good collection of expensive editions unavailable in bookstores; here they stood unused. We walked and talked and the lazy weeks passed quickly. In mid-August the three of us left on a truck filled with grain; Ira headed back to Leningrad where, with the help of Professor Schaak, she was admitted for study at the Leningrad Medical Institute.

## Yauza Project

On our return from Aryk Balyk I went again to see Ivan Rozanov for help in finding work.

"You have to enroll as a student," he said. "Of course you can't file admission papers but there is a way. The Moscow City Council has an Institute of Civil Engineering which has preparatory courses for competitive entrance exams. You have to pay for the courses but anyone can apply, no questions asked. You pay your dues and get an identity card like other students. With that you rent a room somewhere in the sub-urbs, get a student's temporary residence registration, and bring it to me. We need people on a new project. You apply for a temporary job as a student; there is no big questionnaire to fill out for a temporary job. Tell them you can work evening or night shift; I know the people there and will put in a word for you."

I did as he told me, paid my dues for the preparatory course, got my card, and went to Ramenskoye, the last stop on the suburban line and about a one hour ride. I looked for a room at a worker's settlement beyond the railroad depot; the houses had well-kept fenced lots planted with vegetables. Af-ter asking around I was directed to the last house which bor-dered on the rail tracks. It belonged to a middle-aged couple; the husband worked at the railroad depot.

The room I rented was smaller than a single prison cell but it had a window, bedstead, and chair. I told the landlord that I was a student, had a temporary job in Moscow, and a wife who lived in Moscow with a relative, and I would often stay in the city with my wife. Should there be need — like a sum-mons from the military authorities — I gave them the telephone number of Irina's apartment. It was all right with them. The landlady took my documents and went to town the next morning to get me registered at the police station. I was glad not to have to go there myself and it was easier for the landlady — who knew the girl at the registration desk — to take care of it, no questions asked.

When everything was settled I returned to the city. Rozanov made a call to the personnel office of the Yauza project. I went there and got a temporary job as a student technician.

The project, a dam and lock on the Yauza River in the center of the city, had just been started; the small river was diverted and the site excavated for the foundations of a dam and lock. The engineer in charge of the project was Skvortsov, a gentleman of the old school. In due time I learned that he had served time at the Belomor Canal, was freed in 1933 with special privileges, and returned to his native Moscow. I don't know what Rozanov may have told him about me, but it would not have taken long for Skvortsov to realize "what kind of bird" I was. He assigned me the job of technician in charge of blueprints.

Later he asked me to act as liaison with the architect-designer of the project, Alexander Pasternak, a member of the Academy of Architecture and brother of the poet Boris Pasternak. Engineers do not usually take much interest in the aesthetic concerns of architects and Skvortsov was no exception. He was happy to have me coordinate the demands of the architects with those of our technical staff.

My work at the construction site was interesting. It didn't include responsibility for making out job orders or computing work sheets of prices, outputs, and workers' pay. It was also noncontroversial; I had only to see that work in progress corresponded with the blueprints. When a block was ready for pouring concrete, a commission of three engineers — my boss Skvortsov and two design engineers from headquarters

— convened to check it out. I accompanied the commission on their inspection tour with the blueprints. Later, the commission convened in our office where a protocol was prepared and signed.

There was a bond of trust between these three men. The oldest among them, a Ukrainian, used carefully selected words to express his disdain for contemporary Soviet working methods and way of life. The other engineer entertained us with his observations of America garnered from a recent visit to the construction site of the Hoover Dam in the United States. He admired American punctuality and lack of bureaucratic habits in business dealings.

"A handshake is as good as a signed paper," he said. "If you are meeting someone you don't know, look at your watch. The man who arrives exactly at the appointed time and place is your man." I knew that these three men trusted me, since they let me stay in the office during their deliberations.

## CRITICAL TIMES

In November 1937 Irina told me that she was pregnant. She was unhappy; it was not the right time to have a child and would interfere with her studies; also she had set her sights on the New York World's Fair. Students in the English department were being selected for work at the Soviet pavilion as guides and interpreters. I didn't want her to apply and was sure she would not pass the political screening process.

Her pregnancy also interfered with the lighter side of life, a contributor to which was a new acquaintance, a friend of one of Irina's fellow students. He, Sasha, was a descendent of Cossacks and of light build with a long narrow face, black hair, slanted eyes, and high cheekbones — a Lermontov type, good-looking like a racehorse with Caucasian mountaineer blood in his veins. He worked as an engineer in the radio and electronics field and held a job with a cooperative which provided him with ample money and free time.

One fall Sunday, after a visit to the Museum of Contemporary Western Art — the former Shchukin and Morozov collections now considered "examples of decadence and bourgeois decline" — Sasha suggested going to a restaurant and the horse races. I had to go to work in the evening and declined his offer. Besides, I didn't have the resources for such an outing. Irina accepted. I left for home while the girls went with Sasha who, from then on, switched his attentions to Irina.

He asked Irina to give him private lessons in English and German at his place in the center of the city near the Bolshoi Theatre and once a week Irina went there for these lessons. Needless to say I was not in great favor of this arrangement but Sasha paid well and Irina would not forego such an opportunity. She was also pleased with his attention and occasional invitations to theatre, particularly the ballet.

Sasha persuaded us also to go horseback riding at Izmailovo Park. I had had riding instruction back in Leningrad and Irina took lessons at the Izmailovo Riding School. Izmailovo Park — a large wooded area at the outskirts of Moscow — was beautiful in the fall and riding through the woods was exhilarating.

When, towards the end of the year, Irina stopped riding because of her pregnancy, I didn't see Sasha for a while. Then one snowy afternoon when I was about to leave for work he came and wanted to talk with me. I only had time for a walk to the streetcar.

What was it he wanted to talk about? "Irina is pregnant," he said. Well, this was no secret.

He said it was his child. I was dumbfounded. Should I believe him? My streetcar came, I had to be at work on time, and there was no opportunity to discuss the matter further.

At midnight I hurried back home. There was still light at the window. Irina was reading.

"What is the matter?" she asked when she saw me.

"I want to talk with you. Come to the kitchen."

"No need," she said. "Zina went out of town to visit her sister. What is the matter?"

"Sasha was here."

"What did he want?"

"To talk to me."

"What about?"

"About you expecting."

"What nonsense."

"He says it is his child."

Irina looked at me and laughed. "He would like it to be his. Come on, did you believe that?"

It was not that easy for me to convince myself to the contrary. I asked her to cancel her lessons with Sasha; she reluctantly agreed.

I did not see Sasha again, but fifty-seven years later I learned that Sasha had been an agent of the secret police since his arrest in 1929, an agent provocateur, and later a double agent in World War II. In 1937, at the time we knew him, his target had probably been the Institute of Foreign Languages.[20]

Although I now felt more secure having a job and an official residence duly registered in my passport and was no longer worried to be seen at Irina's place, the general atmosphere of instability and anxiety had reached a new pitch. Everywhere one heard of "nightly visits." Irina's friend and fellow student, Nina Pletneva, confided to us that her grandfather, a famous heart specialist, had been arrested for having "facilitated the death of Maxim Gorkiy in collusion with Yagoda, the former NKVD boss." One day when I was to meet Irina at one of her private lessons at some Party mem-

---

[20] For more on Sasha Demyanov, see Pavel Sudoplatov. *Special Tasks: The Memoirs of an Unwanted Witness — A Soviet Spymaster*. New York: Little, Brown & Co., 1994, pp. 152-160.

bers, people of influence, the scared face of the student's mother looked at me through the slightly ajar door.

"Come in," she said in a subdued voice. She closed the door behind me, came close, and whispered: "Did you hear? Tupolev was arrested." Tupolev was the foremost Soviet aircraft designer. "Just yesterday he still had carte blanche at the State bank."

The great wave of terror rolling across the country soon reached us too, but I was not the one caught in its net. A cable from Svobodniy from Irina's mother read: "Papa Misha sick. Leave for Moscow on...." It was clear that Papa Misha, Irina's stepfather, had been arrested again.

I was not at the rail station when Irina's mother arrived. Irina and Inna, Aunt Nina's daughter, went to meet her and took her home to Inna's place. There was no difficulty in getting her registered because Maria Gerasimovna had a passport from the Far East Region, also a restricted zone, and the police had no way of knowing that her husband had been arrested. At Bamlag, the wave of arrests had affected everyone: uniformed officers, free employees, and prisoners at the end of their terms. No one was spared regardless of rank or position, including Comrades Frenkel and Berman as we learned later.

A few weeks later we received a telephone call. It was Lida, Volik's pregnant wife. She was in Moscow on the way to Zaporozhye with Dagmara Ernestovna who was returning to Leningrad. Iosif Ivanovich and Volik had been arrested too and were in a Khabarovsk prison.

Some days later, when Irina came home after working in the library, I noticed that something was preoccupying her. She was obviously worried and I asked her what was the matter.

"Promise to take it easy," she said.

"Never mind. Tell me."

"Kolya is dead," she said.

"This can't be."

"I know how you feel."

I cried. In spite of whatever had happened between us, Irina knew that I admired Kolya, his talent, fantasy, and joie de vivre. Kolya dead — that seemed impossible. Why him of all people?

"It must be a mistake. How do you know?" I asked. Irina told me how a few days ago she had stopped by to see Kolya's family. The old nanny opened the door, saw Irina, and started crying. She pointed to the door to the family's rooms which were sealed.

"They came and took them all, all three," she whispered, "and then came this telegram." She took it out of her pocket and showed it to Irina. It was from a Tashkent hospital. Nikolay Kryuger had died of intestinal typhoid fever.


## ANDRYUSHA

Spring came and we had to think about our growing family. Irina carried her burden well and attended her lectures until summer break. In the spring we rented a dacha in Bolshevo and, while Irina was still attending classes, her mother moved in to help her prepare for the newcomer. Bolshevo, north of the city about half an hour by train, was known for its "Commune" for homeless war orphans of the early Soviet years. It was Dzerzhinskiy's "showcase for communist upbringing" beginning at an early age. Irina chose Bolshevo for its good hospital.

Before the baby's arrival a phone call came from my landlady in Ramenskoye about a summons for military reserve training. We were trained as truck drivers at Ramenskoye and I stayed at my rented quarters there. Besides driving lessons, we took apart and put together a Ford truck from engine to differential. The training course took three weeks.

On July 23, 1938, Andryusha was born. It was the normal birth of a healthy boy. I could not see them until mother and son were discharged from the hospital and we were walking home pushing Andryusha in a baby carriage. One day before they returned I came home from work to find a big bunch of flowers standing on the porch of our dacha.

"Where does this come from?" I asked my mother-in-law.

"A nice young man left it here. His name was Sasha; he said he was a friend of yours," she replied.

This summer we lived comfortably at the dacha. I certainly didn't miss our city dwelling and enjoyed the daily train rides back and forth. But in September we had to go back to Yakimanka Street to our two-thirds of a room and it was back to college for Irina. Who would take care of Andryusha? Help came from Inna, Irina's cousin. The institute where she worked had a research facility for child development. About a dozen mostly abandoned newborn babies were cared for and observed at a facility located in an old palatial building not far from the Kremlin, the former Imperial Foundlings' Hospital.[21] For a year Andryusha could stay at this facility with Irina visiting three times a day to nurse him. The babies were attended around the clock by a staff of nurses, doctors, and psychologists. We could not have had a better arrangement.

This winter was for me a time of inner isolation. I had lost my best friends and saw very little of Irina who was away from home from early morning until nearly midnight when she returned from her last nursing of Andryusha. Her time, energy, and thoughts were occupied by work and the sustenance of a new life.

My time between work and sleep had to be filled with something, and it was the memory of Kolya which made me start drawing again. The view out our window of the yard at

---

[21] See Appendix Five.

dusk — the iron fence, bare trees with snow-covered lace of branches, and old buildings in the background — was the subject of my first brush and ink drawings.

"Where did you buy these drawings?" asked Irina's Uncle Alesha, the professor of literature, on a rare visit to his sister Zina. Irina liked to discuss with him the issue of Shakespeare versus the Earl of Oxford or Nietzsche's meaning of "Superman." "I didn't buy them," laughed Irina, "they are Leva's drawings."

"No, really. Jokes aside, tell me," insisted Uncle Alesha.

Word spread around in the family that I had talent. Inna and her husband were members of the House of Scientists and enrolled me as a relative to attend art classes there. The House of Scientists, a big old mansion on Volkhonka Street, was one of the exclusive government clubs for the privileged: scientists, actors, architects, and writers. There I attended live model drawing classes some evenings and Sundays.

Soon Aunt Zina's brother Nikolay, who was director of a provincial theatre in Kimry on the Volga as well as of several amateur theatre groups in Moscow, asked me to do stage designs for his productions. It was interesting work.

I also read a lot during these times: Dreiser's "The Genius," the story of Eugene Witla, the artist; Vinogradov's "Three Colors of Time," a book about Stendhal and his role in Napoleon's invasion of Russia; and Stendhal himself, "The Red and the Black" and "The Charterhouse of Parma."

# 9

## Uneasy Peace

Political events in the Soviet Union followed now in fast succession. After two years of terror, some people arrested during Yezhov's reign began to come home. But not all; Volik did not.

Volik's father, however, returned to Moscow. He was even given a room in town and Dagmara Ernestovna came to join him from Leningrad. We visited them once for the last time; it was a strained meeting, not at all as it used to be.

Long ago mother had once said to me: "It is hard to lose friends. They don't want to see you because they are afraid, but they are still friends. Or are they? Maybe." We were not afraid to see Dagmara Ernestovna and Lida but somehow we felt guilty having things go well for us. Do they really want to see us, Irina wondered? Weren't we salt in their wounds? Envy, like fear, is equally destructive of trust and friendship.

Soon a telegram came from Svobodniy: "Arriving Moscow...(train and date)...Papa Misha." We met him at the railroad station; he stepped out of the car on crutches but unbroken in spirit. Not only was he free, he had a voucher for medical treatment at a Crimean sanitorium. We breathed a bit easier.

Lida, Volik's wife, came to see her in-laws and hoped to learn something about her husband. I went with her to the Lubyanka "information bureau" which was full of people.

She filled out a form and handed it to a uniformed man behind a small window who told her when to come back for an answer. We came again on the designated day. Lida stood in line only to receive a small piece of paper: "...sentenced to ten years in remote camps without correspondence privileges." She did not even cry; so many others were coming out with the same answer.

For a long time we hoped against hope that one day Volik would be back, but no one ever learned when and where he perished. Some thirty years later I dreamt that I descended into a shaft. First there were steps, then only ladders; finally I began to slide down until I caught hold of something and looked down to the bottom. Volik was lying there dead. He had shot himself. I woke up in a sweat.

The fate of Volik and Kolya weighed heavily on me. Why them? Why was I still walking the streets? They were the stronger ones, more talented, more determined. For the first time I asked myself whether life was worth living. However, the demands of daily life helped pull me out of my depression. Andryusha had to come home; the research program at the nursery continued only for 12 months. We had to make a decision on Rosanov's offer to move with him and his family to Tixi Bay, the Arctic port under construction in the Lena River delta. He was leaving Moscow for the relative security of the Arctic region. He wanted us to come too but we decided against it. I was sorry to lose good friends but I was also lucky to acquire a new one. Orest Vereyskiy, whom I had met on our 1936 visit to Leningrad, had moved to Moscow after his engagement to Xeniya, a Moscow engineering student. He now worked as a free-lance graphic artist for various publishing agencies.

At the end of August, Isidor Viktorovich Becker stopped over at the Hotel Moskva on his way back from visiting mother in Aryk Balyk. We met for supper at the hotel's roof restaurant where he had arranged for a table on the balcony overlooking the Kremlin. It was a pleasant August night with a dark starry sky, the red stars on the Kremlin towers shining prominently. Becker wanted to talk with us about my mother, whose term of exile expired in 1940. She would not be permitted to live in Leningrad or Moscow; a place should be found halfway between the two cities so that mother could visit all of us.

Later in the evening there was a commotion. The maitre'd came out on the balcony and ordered all diners inside where tables had been set for everybody. No explanation was offered but one was not accustomed to ask questions or to expect answers. Shortly after everyone settled down in the dining hall the big doors flew open and a group of men was ushered through the hall to the balcony. By their clothing one recognized they were foreigners, but we were shocked to see swastika buttons on their lapels. Just recently the director of a Moscow textile plant had been arrested when someone found out that a swastika pattern could be recognized in the woven fabric of Pioneer scarves. We didn't know how to react. Was it a film production? But there were no cameras or lights. It looked as though they were authentic "Fascists" and not under guard. We soon left the restaurant and the next morning saw pictures of Ribbentrop on the front page of the newspapers and read about the German-Soviet Non-Aggression Pact.

However portentous such events are, they do not usually impact on the daily chores and needs of an average life. Not immediately, at any rate. In August we took our son home. A crib was procured for him and placed at the end of our sleeping couch. The grand piano was sold. A search for a nanny was conducted and Irina came up with a prospect; the janitor's wife knew of an eighteen-year-old girl who had just come from a village to stay with her aunt down the street. Irina hired her to stay with Andryusha while we were at work, feed him, and take him out into the yard for fresh air. Andryusha was now a full-fledged Moscow resident registered with his mother's passport.

When we brought Andryusha home, he was welcomed by all the inhabitants of our apartment who were also introduced to Nyura, our nurse, the one they would meet in our communal kitchen and bathroom, newly modernized and supplied with hot water from a central heating plant.

At home a new routine set in. We were now five in our room when everyone came home after work. Andryusha no longer had the palatial accommodations of his first year of life where a big hall with beautiful parquet floors had served as a playpen for him and his playmates. Now it was just the crib and the lap and the buggy going out with nanny. He was just like any other child on the block, joining his contemporaries and their babushkas to play in the yard or street. Irina spent more time at home. I went Sundays to art classes and worked evenings on stage design and costumes for Nikolay Sokolov's theatre at Kimry and his amateur groups in Moscow. Sometimes I spent an entire night painting stage sets.

## THE POLISH AND FINNISH WARS

Newspapers and radio brought news of events in Poland beginning with the German invasion on September 1, 1939. We didn't have a newspaper but listened sometimes to the wired radio program on a loudspeaker plugged in the wall outlet. Few people in the Soviet Union had radio receivers. The state-owned houses were wired so that inhabitants could listen to the local station, usually by way of a small loudspeaker.

At first these events seemed far removed from our world.

Whatever the political turnabout in our relations with Germany, the military events taking place were "out there" in the capitalist world, and beyond our borders which were under "lock and key." However, this didn't last long. A telephone call came for me from Ramenskoye during the second week of September. I was to report for military service; mobilization for the Polish campaign had begun. I took leave from my job, packed a few things, and left for Ramenskoye.

A motley crowd had assembled in front of the Ramenskoye police station. A sergeant ran in and out of the office collecting documents from the arrivals and checking them out against lists. There was much guessing about what was to come. "What do you do? Where do you work?" we asked each other.

Eventually the paperwork was completed and we boarded a train. About an hour later the train stopped at a road crossing in the midst of fields. We disembarked and marched to a barn and tent where our clothes went into disinfection, our hair was cut short, and we were issued uniforms. Late in the evening we marched in small groups to several villages and were assigned quarters in peasants' houses. My small group consisted of engineers and technical personnel. For a couple of days we waited while noncommissioned officers ran from village to village compiling more lists and organizing food supply. Ours was a transportation battalion; soon trucks would arrive and we would be on our way, we were told. Then one morning we were marched to a former manor house some miles away, which was battalion headquarters. A major spoke to us in a big room which may have once been a ballroom. Referring to the noncommissioned officers he said, "Those asses only run around and nothing gets done. You are intelligent people; it will be up to you to get the job done." Then he left it to his lieutenant to explain what was to be done.

On the way we had passed civilian trucks parked in a harvested field. Our task was to inspect their technical condition, availability of tools, reserve tires, and so on. Trucks arrived every day from all over the central region, mainly from collective farms, some from as far as two hundred kilometers away. Within a few days we had them inspected and checked out. Then we waited.

Newspapers reported the Red Army's successful advance into Poland and the great welcome it received from the local populace. Eventually there were pictures in the paper of Red Army officers greeting German officers on the Bug River. The Polish campaign was over; reservists were discharged; but I had to stay on to accompany the lieutenant to Ryazan where the trucks were to be stored at battalion headquarters. After a week in Ryazan and completion of all the paperwork, I received my civilian clothing, discharge paper, rations, and train ticket. I got back home by mid-October and went back to my job.

Peace did not last. By the end of November 1939 we were at war with Finland which had attacked the Soviet Union, we were told. There was no general mobilization, only reserves of the northern regions were called up; but there were food shortages in the provinces and a ring of controls was established around Moscow. Only holders of Moscow passports or those with official travel papers could travel to Moscow. When I traveled occasionally to the theater in Kimry on the Volga, I had to pass through such controls. Provincials who traveled to Moscow to make purchases had to circumvent the controls by getting off the train at a stop short of the checkpoint, walking past one or two train stops on foot, and boarding trains at a station beyond the checkpoint.

The city was full of rumors; the war was going badly and the propaganda machine ran at full speed ascribing beastly qualities to the Finns. Aunt Zina, still a believer in the goodness of the revolution, now expressed some doubts from behind the dividing curtain.

"Can you believe it? Before the revolution I spent many summers in Finland. Finns are such honest, decent people."

She believed our leaders were misled by underlings whose mistakes or sabotage had caused our problems. But what was she to make of appeals by her colleagues to Comrade Stalin demanding a "heightening of revolutionary vigilance to help the glorious Chekists purge educational institutions of Trotskyite-Bukharinite and other counterrevolutionary trash?"

Honest, decent Zina was prey to the official policy that a priori there were no poor students, only poor teachers. She had to pass poor students or face accusations of inadequacy or even sabotage. It was hard on her, as she was still beholden to old-fashioned truth rather than contemporary dialectics. For us, the younger generation, it was simpler. Didn't everybody lie every day? Wasn't it part of survival? Lying was an existential necessity, a "form of existence" Solzhenitsyn called it years later.

Soviet forces were held at bay for three months by the Finns in the Karelian snows. According to Soviet official sources, 58,000 Soviet soldiers died during this short war. Stalin freed Frenkel from prison to build a railroad behind the front. At year's end, Papa Misha was transferred from Ukhta — where he had been working at the Gulag railroad project — to Karelia. Irina's mother came to Moscow; she had a nervous breakdown and stayed for a while at Aunt Nina's. The latter eventually arranged for her to work at a sanitorium near Zagorsk as a bookkeeper. Returning by bus from a visit there, I overheard a discussion among a group of Party organizers coming back from a Party meeting. The talk was about Hitler, what a great leader he was, and what support he had among his people. No more mention of Fascists.

At work I felt I was under more pressure. Now everyone had to carry a labor booklet with a complete employment history; it was not possible any more to change jobs. Penalties were introduced for tardiness and absenteeism and strict rules were established concerning medical "bulletins" for sick leave.

I left home at seven in the morning and was back by six or seven in the evening, having had my main meal at a cafeteria. Evenings were spent working on stage sets. Sundays I went to art classes or visited Orest at his studio in town. We went together to the graphics shop of the House of Artists where his lithographs were printed or to the movies or met at a *zabegalovka* — a slang expression for a stand-up eatery — for *sto gram* (a one-hundred gram glass of vodka) and *zakuski.*

## Days of Sorrow

On a rainy April day, Andryusha came down with a fever. Before leaving for work we called the doctor. A young woman doctor serving our neighborhood came in the evening. It was just a cold she said. When we came home from work, Andryusha's condition had worsened; his fever was high. He stood in his crib, talked in his fever, had nightmares, and cried. We sent Nyura away. Aunt Zina worried behind the curtain and talked to us constantly. Eventually she put cotton in her ears and switched off her light. We stayed up half the night until Andryusha fell asleep, then slept a couple of hours. In the morning Andryusha had broken out in a rash. What should we do? Call the doctor and wait until afternoon when she makes rounds? Leave Andryusha with Nyura? He looked weak. He looked at us sadly. We had to go to work. I called a taxi, hoping it would come soon. Irina wrapped Andryusha tightly in his covers and left for the institute. The taxi came and I took him to the hospital.

At the hospital you had to wait. I asked for a note from the hospital to bring to my place of work. "Well, when the doctor has seen the patient...." was the only reply. A doctor came and looked at Andryusha. It was scarlet fever; he had to be placed immediately in isolation. We went to an area with glass-enclosed cubicles with a crib in each one. It is a place made entirely of windows and full of light. A nurse took Andryusha and I watched her putting him into the crib. Then I went out with the doctor and he wrote me a note. I left the hospital, jumped on a streetcar, and went to work. In the evening Irina and I went to the hospital. No, we couldn't see Andryusha now; come the next day. I went there the next morning on my way to work. It was early. No one was there. I waited. Then finally a doctor and a nurse came down the hall. Andryusha was dead. Complications…brain…sorry…no, I could not see him. I did not go to work. I went to Irina's in-stitute.

On a rainy April day Irina and I followed alone a horse-drawn cart with the little casket to the cemetery.

Spring passed us by unnoticed. The crib was gone with whatever else had belonged to the newcomer and filled his liv-ing space. Nyura was also gone. Aunt Zina didn't stop any more on the way to her part of the room or ask questions from behind the curtain partaking of the new life. The room seemed empty now, too big for the three of us going our sepa-rate ways.

There were unattended problems to be taken care of. Iri-na's mother had been spared the news, had been lied to over the telephone. "No, Andryusha was still ill. No, no, don't rush to visit here." Eventually she had to be told and Aunt Nina did it. My mother came back from Aryk Balyk. She stayed a few days with us on the way to Leningrad to see Ira, then set-tled for the time being in Vyshniy Volochok, halfway between her two children. Irina's mother left Moscow too. She went north to Karelia — actually to Finland — to join her hus-band in Rovaniemi; he was working on the new railroad to connect the White and Baltic Seas.

My work was more challenging now. Pasternak's design called for fresco paintings and caryatids derived from the

Greek Erechtheum. The frescos were of particular interest to me; three artists were assigned by the Artists' Union to do the work. I gave them the best plasterer to work with, since frescoes must be painted on wet plaster. The caryatids were made at a Moscow "art factory," a former brick plant. The main production line there consisted of Stalin and Lenin figures placed all over the Soviet Union at clubs, offices, factories, and kolkhozes. The genial leaders' plaster heads, bellies and legs, were lined up in long rows to be shipped and assembled in place. It was an amusing, if rather pathetic sight. Our order, not to be mass produced, was made of cement rather than plaster.

Abroad it was an eventful summer. France surrendered and German troops moved into Denmark and Norway; the Baltic states were incorporated into the Soviet Union. In the Moscow subway one saw visiting groups of students from Estonia, Latvia, or Lithuania who were immediately recognizable by their dress and comportment, talking in their native languages, exchanging views among themselves, uninhibited. A stark contrast to the dour silent Muscovite passengers, turned inward, not looking at anything except station names and only furtively at the newcomers as if they were a forbidden sight.

Irina left for a Caucasus vacation in July; I had three weeks of leave in August. Orest suggested that we go together to the Valday area and rent a house in the village where his parents always rented their *izba*. Orest's wife, Xeniya, and Tatiana, a friend of his and an accomplished watercolorist, would join us. I could learn watercolor technique from Tatiana.

The Valday Hills region is one of the loveliest parts of Russia; its hills, woods, and lakes are the source of the Volga River. It is both far enough from and close enough to the two big cities to be favored by the *cognoscenti* of the Russian landscape. There I did my first painting. At the Morozov collection Orest had introduced me to Cézanne and Van Gogh, and Van Gogh's painting of fields with road, horse cart, and a train on the horizon had made a great impression on me as did the simplicity of Marquet. Orest's parents were also at the village; his father with a collection of prints by Rembrandt and Jongkind from which he never parted. One day we were invited to their *izba*; a big table was cleared and cleaned and a big folio of prints was opened. In very slow procession, each print was moved in silence from side to side. No talk, no commentary. Just the five of us standing at one side of the table as in silent prayer.

At the end of our vacation, Orest and I went to Leningrad. It was to be my last visit to my home town. I went to the Hermitage again and spent the day walking through the Winter Palace. Out on the quay it was one of the brilliant northern autumn days, breezy, with green skies and white clouds, the sun gold on the choppy waters of the river, the air clean and transparent. I walked up and down the river as I used to do years ago with Aleka.

Irina arrived in Leningrad from the Caucasus and on September 7 we celebrated both her and Ira's birthdays with students from the medical school where Ira studied. At midnight Irina and I took the Red Arrow train back to Moscow. The rail station was empty but railroad police were everywhere. I remembered how in the twenties we used to visit the busy station restaurant famous for its bliny

My mother came to Moscow for a visit and to talk with us about the possibility of emigrating to Germany; she had heard that this was now possible. I doubted that it was, nor was I interested. What could I expect to do in Germany? Was it true that unemployment was no longer a problem there? Hopefully — given our new friendship with Germany — our political climate would revert to the way it was in the twenties.

During Molotov's visit to Berlin in November 1940, Orest

and I went to the movies. A newsreel showed his reception at the rail station, the drive through the streets and arrival at the Reich's chancellery. The uniforms, sabers, and goose-stepping guards were impressive. No hungry, poor, and unemployed we were accustomed to seeing in films about the West. The world had changed; we left the movie house dumbfounded.

In the fall the artists who had worked on the frescoes asked me whether I wanted to moonlight on their new assignment painting ceilings of the Kursk Railroad Station. The traditional Russian floral design had to be painted lying down on one's back high up on the scaffolds. It was a well-paying job and I agreed to join them after I completed my construction job.

By year's end the work on the dam and lock was finished and I was transferred as shift supervisor up river to work on concrete embankments. It was an unpleasant job since, as supervisor, I now had to deal with job orders. For falsifying job orders one could be sentenced to five to ten years imprisonment. However, inflating job orders was a general practice. Piece work was common for all laborers and, to assure reasonable pay, work orders had to be inflated by a variety of means. If supervisors failed to do this workers complained to the union or the party and supervisors were accused of failing to organize "shock work," or worse, of sabotage.

During 1939-1940 many new labor laws were passed. Beginning in January 1939, all workers and employees had to possess labor books. These contained the dates of changing employment, reasons for leaving or dismissal, and pay.

On June 26, 1940, the work hours were extended from 200 to 208 hours per month; piece rates were to be adjusted so that the worker would not earn more from the hours added. On June 28, 1940, a law established provisions against job quitters. Absence from work called for a penalty of six months correctional labor with a 25 percent cut in wages. Managers who failed to report delinquent workers were subject to prosecution. A decree of July 10, 1940, established that, for poor quality or nonstandard goods, factory managers and chief engineers were held responsible, with penalties from five to eight years imprisonment. A law of October 19, 1940, permitted the transfer of engineers, technicians, office employees and skilled workers to any enterprise anywhere they were needed.

The law of October 2, 1940, introduced the conscription of one million recruits, boys between the ages of fourteen and seventeen, for training in industry.[22]

Shock worker, *udarnik*, or shock work, *udarnyy trud*, were terms for work exceeding the prescribed norm: volume of work per unit of time. Since the abolition of food rationing, the price range of many products had been raised. Shock work became essential for a normal subsistence. One had to fulfill the prescribed norm by 150 percent to 250 percent to attain a decent income. The general rule was to fill in a job order with false data to assure a decent pay check. This was called *tufta* in camp language. It is called *pripiska* in official language today.

## 1941

By the turn of the year Irina's parents arrived unexpectedly in Moscow on their way to a new assignment, the construction of a highway along the Caspian Sea from Baku to the Iranian border. With German armies moving eastward into Yugoslavia and Greece there was a noticeable change in the tone of reporting from abroad. In February 1941 a call came from Ramenskoye: I was to report at the military commissariat. On the way to Ramenskoye I wondered what it was about.

---

[22] Leonard E. Hubbard. *Soviet Labour and Industry.* Macmillan and Co., Ltd., 1942, pp. 93-104.

After some waiting at the military board, I was called in. Two officers sat behind the desk. They were military officers, not the police, and were friendly. They looked through my papers.

"You are a truck driver, specialty 26."

"Yes."

"Your nationality is German. Why aren't you in Germany?"

I laughed. "I am a Soviet citizen, comrade chief."

"Do you speak German? Read and write it?"

"Yes, a bit. I do."

There were a few more questions: Where did I work? Was I married? What did my wife do?

"Well, thank you. You may go."

Back in Moscow I dropped in at Aunt Nina's to tell her what had happened.

"I don't like it. There is something going on upstairs. Couldn't you change your nationality? Exchange your passport? Isn't yours running out this year? Report that you lost it. Get a new one and change your nationality."

"With my name? What? Estonian? "

"That's no good either," said Aunt Nina. "But you could be Jewish."

We talked over the pros and cons. For a lost passport, a temporary certificate would be issued. Police would check in Tashkent before issuing a new five-year passport. In Tashkent the passport had been issued in exchange for a temporary certificate from Kalinin; there was a chance of getting a new passport from the Moscow region. In March I decided to go to the Ramenskoye police station and report the loss of my passport.

A few days later I received a summons from the police and reported there. I handed the summons to a girl at the window. There was a score of people waiting, the usual crowd, mostly women in kerchiefs and felt boots holding house registers, books in which all residents of the house were listed. Arrivals and departures required official changes in the book and had to be presented at the local police station.

Most visitors sat silently, wrapped in their heavy winter coats although the room was well-heated. Some conversed in low whispering voices. It will take some time, I thought, and prepared for a cat nap until my turn came. But it wasn't long before a girl called my name. "Follow me, citizen," she said and led me out of the building across the yard to an adjoining building. A car and wagon were parked in front and I knew that this was the secret police. Past the door a guard sat at a small desk with a telephone. He waved us by; the girl opened a door slightly and pushed her head through the opening; then she swung the door open and let me in. Two officers were in the room. Just keep your cool, I thought, as my heartbeat quickened.

"Sit down, comrade."

I sat down on a chair somewhat removed from the desk behind which the officers were sitting. They both looked over some papers. Then one of them asked questions while the other looked on.

"Tell me, how did it happen? How did you lose your papers?"

"I really don't know; maybe someone pulled them out of my pocket in the streetcar."

He looked through the papers again. "Not recovered," he said to the other officer. "You work in Moscow? Moscow Soviet?"

"Yes, in construction."

"You are married?"

"Yes. My wife is a student."

"What year?"

"She graduates this year."

"How long have you been married?"

"We married in 1936." Should I say that it was in Tash-kent? A thought flashed. This would explain why I got my passport there before he asks why; or should I wait?

"In Tashkent," I said.

"You were born in Leningrad?"

Keep cool, I thought. If I get nervous, it's all over: Camp, Article 58, paragraph 10-11. In the best of circumstances they'll let me sign an obligation to leave Moscow province within 24 hours.

"Yes, in 1912."

"Do you have your military papers, or did you lose them too?" asked the other officer.

"No." I stood up and reached in my pocket and handed over my military booklet. At least a respite. The officer flipped through the pages.

"Mobilized in 1939," he said. Then he pointed out some-thing to the other officer. "Nationality German."

"Well, I am a Soviet citizen."

The phone rang. The interrogator picked it up. "All right... no...right away." He turned to the other officer.

"They brought them in." He turned to me. "Well, citizen, your papers were not recovered here. You have to report the loss to the Main Administration in Moscow. They will give you a certificate stating whether or not the passport was found there which you bring back here."

Again my heartbeat quickened; all right, just out of here, but calm, stay calm. The officer wrote something on the pa-pers in the folder. The other officer left for an adjoining room.

"Well, you may go." And, standing in the doorway, he called to the guard. "It's all right, pass him."

The air outside was brisk and I felt like a balloon. The waiting room in the other building was nearly empty; every-thing looked friendlier now. Even the girl in the window

# 10

## Turn of the Wheel

Sunday, June 22, 1941, was a warm summer morning. Irina left for the library and I gathered implements for my art class. It was still too early to go there and I dropped by the room of an acquaintance, an employee of the State Bank, amateur actor, and former friend and dance partner of the daughter of Morozov, the famous collector of modern art. My friend's room in Moscow's old Arbat district had a cozy, somewhat old-maid atmosphere with its bric-a-brac, old photographs, china, linen, and silver. He liked to serve tea with cherry jam and zwieback or sweet buns and went to prepare it in the communal kitchen. He returned looking pale and shaken.

"They just announced on the radio we are at war again."

"What war? Did the Finns attack us again?"

"No, it's serious. It's Germany."

Germany! Was that why the military board had summoned me last February? Was that why there was all that talk at work after Germany occupied Belgrade in April? But the harvest had not been brought in yet....

"Germany?" he repeated. "They attacked us, declared war or something. Molotov will be speaking on the radio."

We sat silently for a while looking at one another and

197

thinking what this meant for us. This was not 1940, not the lie that little Finland had attacked the Soviet Union. This was for real. The wall by which we had been surrounded for years had broken down. The winds of war and of change swept over us as once the air had swept in our Petersburg windows in spring. The sound of cannons replaced the noise made by the barrage of lies our ears had become accustomed to hearing. Pasternak wrote in *Doctor Zhivago:*

> And when the war broke out, its real horrors, its real dangers, its menace of real death, were a blessing compared with the inhuman power of the lie, a relief because it broke the spell of the dead letter. Not only [people]…in concentration camps, but everybody without exception, at home and at the front…took a deep breath….[23]

Clearly I would not go to my class. We turned on the radio and listened to Molotov. I decided to run down to the library and tell Irina the news. She was in the main reading room, took the news calmly, and said that I was much too excited and there was nothing we could do about it; she would stay at the library but come home early. I went to see Orest; he had heard the news, realized the precariousness of my situation, and suggested that if I didn't want to stay at Irina's I could use a room at the dacha he had rented for his pregnant wife. I accepted.

During the coming week I worked the day shift. At sunset darkness fell over the city; there was a curfew at night and patrols walked the streets. Anti-aircraft preparations were organized in the housing complexes.

At work everyone was subdued, waiting for events to unfold. Will there be a general mobilization? Perhaps a truce

---

[23] Boris Pasternak. *Doctor Zhivago.* London: Wm. Collins Sons & Co., Ltd., 1958, p. 507.

would be concluded or the Germans defeated. The front was still far away. But in the middle of the week anti-aircraft artillery could be heard during the night. There were rumors that German aircraft had been flying over the city. The party secretary was agitated. This was enemy propaganda spread by spies and saboteurs and those who repeated such rumors would be dealt with severely.

In the middle of the week I walked along the embankment with our surveyor, who handed me a folded piece of paper, a printed proclamation by the Orthodox Church declaring holy war and pronouncing an anathema on Hitler and the fascists. Where did he find it, I asked? He had gotten it in church the night before. In church? But he was our Komsomol organizer. He smiled. I had known him for years; still I didn't know whether to believe him. It was clearly typographical print which needed a government permit. God and war linked again: "With God for King and Fatherland;" "Praise the Lord and pass the ammunition." I thought of Alexander Blok's poem "The Twelve" — the Red Guards marching through the blizzard behind the flag, blood red:

> and with the wreath of roses white
> ahead of them goes Jesus Christ.

I read part of the proclamation and handed it back to him.

A week passed. The news from the front was uninformative; successful battles were fought in this and that "direction;" the enemy had suffered great losses. We did not know that by June 28 the Germans were already in Minsk.

On Monday morning, June 30, all employees were told to assemble at the office of the completed lock and dam for a short meeting. We were told to go home to pack clothes and other items needed for field work. We would leave the city to carry out defense work. I found Irina again in the library and we went home together to pack my things. She was optimistic; for her, the glass looked half full; for me, it was half empty. She was sure I would return with some medals and, the war over, I could study architecture or cinematographic arts. Everything would turn out for the best.

Returning to the assembly point we found everyone there, from our chief engineer to office girls with their spouses or families. Everyone was talking about family matters. Some of the young workers had brought guitars and there was singing and drinking under the trees.

Irina's optimistic mood had vanished. We were now seriously considering what might happen and whether she should join her parents in the south. Aside from all the exigencies of war, there was a possibility of my being arrested again. My temporary personal identity paper was going to expire the beginning of July. I would have to report to the police and, if they conducted a thorough check, it was impossible to predict what would happen to me. I told Irina that, should she not hear from me for a protracted length of time, she must file for divorce. She agreed. At dusk she left and I saw her waving from the streetcar which passed by on the opposite bank of the Yauza River. I would not see her again for forty-eight years.

It got dark, but nothing happened; some went into offices to sleep on desks and floors. Early in the morning trucks came and brought us to a passenger train at a railroad switching yard. There were about five hundred of us from various offices of our Department of River Embankments. While we were waiting for departure, a train stopped on the adjacent track with a boxcar filled with soldiers. It looked as if they were coming from the front; there was talk back and forth from train to train, some soldiers asking for cigarettes. When their train was about to leave, someone from our train shouted: "Hooray for Stalin!"

"Fuck your Stalin!" came the reply from the departing

train followed by loud laughter. In our car everyone was stunned; no one said a word. Then our train began to move. We were going west in the direction of Smolensk.

## BUILDING FORTIFICATIONS

On July 4, 1941, the train stopped on a side line near the town of Dorogobuzh on the same day my temporary personal identification certificate expired. But I was in the country and no one here, I hoped, cared about documentation.

We unloaded the equipment and went to work digging escarpments on the high eastern bank of a small river. We didn't have any maps to consult. Maps were secret materials in the Soviet Union except for those used for geography lessons in schools.

The first few nights we camped in the woods; I joined our surveyor and his helper, a Tatar girl. For a surveyor living outdoors was nothing new and, before the first night came, he had built a tent for the three of us out of bark cut from trees.

The Smolenshchina — the area between Smolensk and the Moscow region — is Russian heartland and the Dnieper River is an ancient trade route between Scandinavia and Byzantium. Down-river is Kiev, the cradle of Russian Christendom. We were about fifty kilometers east of Smolensk. Rural life was new for me; in the Far East it had been just wilderness, unpopulated and unspoiled nature. Here for the first time I saw the way peasants lived, glimpsed the brilliant yellow fields of flax, saw clouds of starlings over the horizon. At first I took them for explosions, since one could hear rumblings of artillery fire beyond the horizon.

The weeks and months that followed were times for me of inner calm. I knew Irina had left Moscow for the south. Information from the world outside was sparse; occasionally one saw a newspaper but reporting was vague and largely strident propaganda. There was no radio; all receivers had been surrendered to the authorities during the first days of war.

High school students arrived for work in our area and were assigned to me; my old workers were transferred elsewhere. The students camped in the woods and in the morning it was difficult to wake them and get them to work.

I was reminded of the precariousness of my situation and that my peace of mind could not last long when Golodov, the head of our agency, arrived from Moscow in a car on an inspection tour. (He was the "editor" who had cashed in on my safety posters in 1937; after the war he became Mayor of Moscow.) A general meeting was held in the field where Golodov criticized our work. I remarked that one couldn't expect the same results from high-school students as one could from construction workers. This was counterrevolutionary talk, Golodov declared menacingly. My colleagues immediately brought up other issues for discussion and our chief engineer whispered to me to get lost in the crowd. Fortunately Golodov was in a hurry to drive back to Moscow after the meeting.

My tenuous situation was brought home to me again when the secretary of the personnel department came from Moscow with the payroll. She said that my file was incomplete, that I was still listed as a student on temporary employment. On her next visit she would bring the questionnaire for me to fill out. Luckily she did not come again.

After a few days on the river's bank, some of us were transferred to build anti-tank fortifications. We took up quarters in a village on the *bolshak* (highway), the old road between Vyazma and Smolensk. We slept in the hayloft; during the night we heard German airplanes flying towards Moscow and coming back. Everyone thought quietly of his loved ones back in Moscow.

Before we came to the village a German bomber had crash-landed nearby. The sight of the dark gray machine with the iron cross and swastika was a strange, uncomfortable one, just as it had been two years ago at the Hotel Moskva. Someone asked the village women — most men had been mobilized — what had happened to the German crew. "Well, the Germans came to the village and asked us to call the authorities: 'Telephone, telephone' they said. Then our *sokoly* came with an interpreter and they all drove away in a car. They were all quite friendly," one woman told us. *Sokoly*, meaning falcons, was a name commonly used for Soviet air force men.

Off and on, horse-drawn peasant carts passed by the village carrying wounded soldiers from the front line. Usually they stopped in the village and the women brought out milk and bread. The soldiers looked pitiful in their dust-covered, sand-colored overcoats, as if they were dug out from the earth. The clean white bandages contrasted sharply with their earthen faces and figures.

One day when a few of us were waiting for trucks to deliver materials, a group of wounded soldiers and carts passed by. Our new young Party secretary made critical remarks about how poorly the wounded were taken care of; the rest of us said nothing.

"You keep mum," he said, "but I was in the Finnish war and have seen it all before — the disorganization, the unnecessary losses." He praised the fighting spirit of the Finns. We listened, but no one said a word and we were relieved to see the trucks coming.

In mid-August I moved with a group of workers into a forest to build fortifications along some byroads. The forest abounded in berries — wild strawberries, raspberries, blueberries — a welcome addition to our rations. Mushrooms were gathered and fried in the evening on open fires. It was quiet in the woods, no artillery to be heard. Sometimes there was activity in the air. Once we saw a Soviet plane shot down by a Messerschmitt and the Soviet pilot descending on his parachute. Work stopped and everyone ran through the woods searching for the pilot. We found him hanging in a tree. Some workers climbed the tree, freed him from the entanglement, and lowered him to the ground. He was only slightly wounded and the truck which brought us our provisions took him back to the village.

In September our scattered work groups were gathered together in a village on a hill overlooking a vast expanse of fields and forests to the west. A village to the north housed an army command post; to the south on a clear day one could see the railroad going west from Spas-Demensk. Fifty kilometers to the west was the town of Yelnya which was very much in the news. The town had been a German salient from which they were recently forced out and this was hailed as the first victory over German forces.

Our village was quite prosperous. Across the harvested fields on the western slope of the hill we were building machine-gun and artillery emplacements. The September weather was excellent, our kitchen served a good hot meal daily, and milk and eggs could be purchased from the peasants.

A postcard arrived from Irina in Tbilisi; she had visited her parents at Salyany and was to continue her studies at Tbilisi University.

## THE FRONT COMES CLOSER

Late September newspapers reported the fall of Kiev. One morning, as I was descending through the bushes towards an artillery position under construction, I overheard talk among the members of a Tatar brigade expressing satisfaction about the fall of Kiev. I waited in the bushes so as not to get involved in such conversation or for anyone to know what I had overheard. Eventually I came down to go over the daily assignments and wondered about the strong national bond among these men. They feared no informer in their midst; if there were one, he probably would have been dealt with the same way criminals in camp dealt with those who didn't tow their line — with a knife in the back. Early on the morning of October 1, I was in the fields when two German Heinkels flew over my head. It was unusual to see bombers flying during daytime. For a moment I wondered whether our village would get hit. Horse-drawn artillery had stopped at our village the evening before and were still there, the canons parked under big trees in the village center. But the planes flew by and continued east and my anxiety subsided. Then the bombers made a U-turn and flew back on a parallel course a few kilometers to the north dropping their bombs on the village housing army headquarters. There were explosions and fire; when I returned to our village it was in an uproar. Peasants were carrying their belongings from the houses, loading them on wagons, and some were already camping in the fields. However, nothing more happened during the day and our work continued as usual. Later in the day a girl from the office came looking for me. I was needed there; our chief engineer and Party secretary were waiting for me.

"I have an urgent assignment for you," said the chief engineer. "Four trucks will be coming soon. You'll need some workers to go by night to Yelnya. Concrete tubes have been unloaded at the rail station. Bring them here."

The Party secretary warned: "Be careful with lights; also, you'll have to cross a few bridges. Check them out before crossing; saboteurs could have wrecked them. Try to be back as soon as possible. The truck drivers know the way."

The trucks came and by dusk we were on our way. There were a couple of bridges and I checked them out. Under one of them two soldiers were smoking. They were guarding the bridge they said. We reached Yelnya in the middle of the night. To the west, artillery fire was rumbling and the horizon was lit by fires. Yelnya looked empty; many houses had been burned down, only the brick chimneys still standing, but even the remaining buildings seemed lifeless. Artillery was parked in a street near the station, some soldiers sleeping on the ground, some feeding the horses.

At the rail station everything was dark, the building locked. Eventually an old man appeared out of nowhere; he wore a railroad uniform. I asked him where the station master was.

"At home, I guess, sleeping. What do you want?"

I told him and asked whether he knew where to find the tubes I was looking for. "Yes, there are some at the road crossing, dropped there a few days ago."

"We have to load them on trucks."

"The night is dark," he said. "Better wait until morning, son. They are scattered along the embankment." He told me how to get there.

When we got to the embankment behind a road crossing it took us a while to find out where to park the trucks; daylight broke by the time we began to load the first truck. Then on the road out of the nearby woods a group of civilian men and women appeared. They were in a panic, asked where we were heading, and whether they could get a lift.

"The Germans broke through. We have been working on the defense line but orders came to leave and we were told to walk in the direction of Vyazma."

They could get a lift if they helped with the loading, I told them. From here on the work went quickly and, by the time the sun was up, we were on our way back. We took on as many stragglers as we could but there were now hundreds coming down the road.

It was afternoon by the time we unloaded the rings at our various encampments and I went home to catch up on sleep. The ringing of bells woke me. I looked out the window; smoke was rising from the center of the village and people were running down the street in the direction of the kolkhoz barns and sheds. I ran out too; the barn where the grain was stored was on fire. Everyone was there — peasants, soldiers, workers, — some trying to extinguish the fire, others protecting adjacent animal sheds.

By night the fire was subdued but people were still milling around when someone shouted that the village to our south was on fire. We ran to the school building from where one could see very far. The fire in the next village looked worse than ours had been. Word spread that German saboteurs were setting kolkhozes on fire. We had missed the Stalin speech of July 3, 1941, when he said: "The enemy must not be left a single engine or a single railway car and not a pound of bread nor a pint of oil. The *kolkhozniki* must drive away all their livestock, hand their grain reserves to the State organs...All valuable property, whether grain, fuel or non-ferrous metals, which cannot be evacuated must be destroyed."[24]

The next morning while in the fields I heard explosions which seemed to come from our village. The artillery unit was leaving the village at high speed. The village was under artillery fire I was told; shells came from the east but exploded in the field short of the village. At our office everything was being loaded on a truck. The workers were to be called back to assemble for further orders. Most of them had already stopped working when they heard the shells bursting and were on their way to the village.

I sat down on the steps of the school building overlooking the western horizon. A small airplane was slowly criss-crossing the autumn sky. The villages on the plain and the trees and bushes along the field roads and ditches were still cushioned in the morning haze. In the distance a dark smoke column rose into the sky; once in a while an orange flame licked it at the bottom. Far away one could hear short bursts of machine-gun fire; then it was quiet again. A light breeze carried the dis-

---

[24] Alexander Werth. *Russia at War 1941-1945*. New York: Avon Books, 1964, p. 172.

tant roar of engines; here and there dark objects glistening in the sun crawled like big bugs across the landscape. They were tanks.

What was I to do now? Stay in the village? I could find shelter and food and work too. Irina was on my mind. If I stayed here and the Germans came we would be separated. For how long? I took out her last postcard from my pocket and read it once more. "Darling, all is well. Just came by sleeping car from the Black Sea coast where I teach at a Navy school. Was accepted for postgraduate studies at Tbilisi University. Met some people there I know. Hope you are well and we will be together soon. Best wishes from mother and father. No news from Moscow since Uncle Alyosha died. Love and kisses, I."

"Well, there are the Germans," said the Party secretary just turning the school corner. "And what are you doing? Sitting like Pierre watching the Battle of Borodino?"[25]

"I am waiting for my workers to return." The secretary made a waving gesture with his arm as if to say "what's the use." Then he pointed at the small plane which was pacing back and forth in the distance.

"An observation plane," he said and sat down; we smoked a cigarette. "That's the end of the defense line. Let's have a look whether they loaded the rifles on the truck."

"What rifles?"

"Two boxes we got some days ago — to defend the village I guess."

We went to the office; it was empty and everyone was gone. Then we went to a shack behind the office. There were two boxes of rifles.

"I thought so," the secretary laughed. "Now let's go and

---

[25] Pierre Bezukhov watched the famous Battle of Borodino in Leo Tolstoy's *War and Peace*.

fight, defend the motherland in your encampments. At least I hope you know how to take rifles apart. We don't want the Germans to shoot at us with our own rifles."

"How do you take them apart?" I asked.

"What kind of a soldier are you?"

"I am a driver. MOS 26, Ryazan Auto Battalion."

He showed me how to do it, and after we took the rifles apart we threw the smaller parts into a well nearby.

"We have done our duty for today. Now let's go," he said.

We turned on to the main street and went past the kolkhoz yard. There was much commotion in the yard, screaming and cursing. Men and women were dragging horses and cows out of the stables. "That's my cow," an old man was shouting, trying to hang on to the rope pulled by a woman.

"We firemen did a good job last night," the secretary said. "We saved the socialist property. Now they can divvy it up and I hope they won't kill one another."

Once more women and children everywhere carried their belongings out of their homes to camp in the fields.

## RETREAT

We left the village and crossed a harvested field towards the main road. From an elevation we could see the road and the stream of humanity moving slowly eastward. Here and there in the midst of the crowd a horse or truck tried to make headway with little success. Back to the west behind a forest the dry sound of gunfire erupted at intervals but it was still far away.

When an airplane appeared some people ran off the road to take cover in the adjoining forest. But it was only an observation plane which passed over our heads and came flying back after a while.

"Counting the cattle," my companion said.

We marched all afternoon until we reached a large village stretched out along the road. At the entrance were men with signs, one of which was for us: "Office of Embankment Construction report at house No. 24." It seemed things were getting organized.

We found our house in the middle of the village. The workers were camping outside, the supervisors and foremen assembled inside where it was warm and crowded. A big samovar stood on a table; tea, bread, and sugar were distributed. Later I saw through the window an army officer descending from his horse. In his long greatcoat with belt and shoulder straps, pistol and map case, he reminded me of the officer in charge of our prisoners' transport in 1933. The romantic vision of a soldier. He came inside the house and I was called to the table where our chief engineer and the officer were examining a map. The road we were to follow was marked in red pencil. I was told to sketch a copy of the route and mark essential points and villages on the way. We were to get off the main road and continue north through a forest trail. The village where we had stayed in July was on our way. There we were to turn east and cross a rail line and a highway to the south of Vyazma. Once we had crossed the highway we would be informed about our next assembly point.

I was to lead the way. We started out at dusk on the forest trail, caught up with our truck which was stuck in the mud trying to cross a brook, and pushed and pulled it out of the ditch. As darkness fell, walking became more tiring on the uneven roadway. One had to watch one's step and look out for crossings where trails went off in different directions. When dawn finally came our column had spread out over a long distance and, by the time the sun was up, we had reached the village where once before we had had our lodgings. I stopped there to wait for the last stragglers. Everyone rested for a while; bread and sugar were distributed from the truck. By evening, according to our calculations, we would reach the designated area east of a railroad and highway.

I felt tired and wanted to rest. Our chief engineer agreed to lead the way from here on; I would be the rear guard to look out for stragglers. Nikonov, our economist, joined me and the two of us took a nap in the hayloft. In the afternoon we continued our retreat; the road led mostly through woods with meadows here and there but no plowed fields, no villages. Not long before sunset we reached a clearing, a wide low-lying meadow stretching east and south; towards the eastern horizon a dark line of forests framed the meadow. On the left off the road stood a house with barns and a garden. As we were considering turning off towards the house, planes flew south to north over the distant forest. We heard explosions where, according to our calculations, the city of Vyazma was located.

As we approached the lone house on the left an old man came out of the door and waited for us there. Could we buy something to eat, we asked?

"Ask the mistress," he said. "Workers passed by earlier; they asked for food too." We sat down on a bench in front of the house; the woman came out. Yes, we could have some bread and milk and butter too. We talked about the airplanes. They had been bombing Vyazma all day, the old man said. We asked how far it was to the rail line and highway.

"The rail line passes through the forest where the planes are flying; the *bol'shak* is five kilometers farther east." Nikonov and I tried to figure out how long it would take us.

"What's the hurry?" our host said. "It will be dark soon. *Utro vechera mudreney* (the morning is wiser than the evening). Stay here overnight. And then, by morning, with God's help." We looked at each other and nodded.

"Well, thank you, if it's possible."

"In war everything is possible," said the old man. "I was a

soldier in the World War, saw fighting and was taken prisoner. Lived with the Germans for years." He talked for a while about the World War but it was getting cold and we finally went inside; the woman gave us some pillows and we stretched out on the floor of the warm kitchen. In the morning we left after tea and bread and a final word from the old man at his doorstep. "Well, go with God. And watch out for the *zagradotryady.*"

Special NKVD detachments posted in rear areas to arrest stragglers and those retreating without orders were known as *zagradotryady.* Lone officers retreating could be executed by these detachments. Early in the war the State Defense Committee had issued Order No. 066: "Commanders of units at the western front are affected by defeatist reasoning and are unconcerned about a retreat from Smolensk and surrendering the city to the enemy. Such an attitude among the commanding personnel is considered criminal bordering on treason. The Committee orders that such an attitude be dealt with an iron hand."

Approaching the forest we saw the first war victims — a woman, two soldiers, and horse and wagon were strewn by the side of the road as if swept off by a storm. On the other side of the road was a crater. Was it a shell? A bomb? Had there been more soldiers with them? Were there some who were wounded and went away? Who will take care of the dead with no one around to know about it? Maybe the next village will not be too far away and we can tell them. As we entered the woods and crossed the rail line, the planes were flying again. They were *Stuckas* which we had only read about, dive bombers which made an awful whistling noise while diving and screamed when rising again. In the forest we could not see them, only hear them. Deeper in the woods, past the railroad, the forest was full of civilians and soldiers who had lost their units and were still carrying rifles.

Proceeding east we soon heard the noise of engines and were told that there was a big highway on which German troops were moving north; the noises we heard were German tanks. From a clearing we could see a stretch of the highway. Against the sky, behind the rising fields maybe a thousand yards away, tanks and trucks were moving as if on parade, engines covered with red cloth, but we could not see the swastika on the cloth. The column moved north slowly but without interruption. At the northern end of a village black smoke was rising in the sky; one could hear artillery fire rumbling far away to the north.

We left the trail which led to the village and walked south along the rim of the forest, well-protected by underbrush. There were people everywhere in the forest, walking or camping. We found a dell which offered cover and from which we could see the road. It was a good place to rest.

Here we had time to think what to do next. We could not stay in the woods forever — we would need food. Now we were behind German lines and the Germans were moving east with deliberate speed. The forest, filled with thousands of workers and soldiers milling around, could become a target for bombing.

Where could one wait for the end of the war? Kiev, Odessa, and Kharkov were in German hands; Leningrad and Moscow could fall soon. This would bring an end to the war; maybe a new government would be constituted. A year ago France and Germany were at war but it ended in a few weeks. No millions perished as in World War I and France had a new government. For us it was the third war in two years. First there was the Polish War, the easy one; then the Finnish War with many more casualties but it, like the war in France, was over in a few weeks.

Although we didn't know that two million Red Army troops had already surrendered, taken prisoner by the Germans, we had certainly sensed that the population at large — the rural people in particular — and the soldiers we saw had no stake in this war. How many kilometers had the Germans advanced in three months? The best in a war was the end of a war when one could go home in one piece. After all, did I have to defend those who killed my father and my best friend? But at that time I did not confront this quandary. This rationale came later when my sister questioned my decision to change sides. Never, not even during the siege of Leningrad, did she ever believe the Germans would win the war. I did. And did it matter?

Andrey Sakharov's wife, Elena Bonner, a patriot and then a Soviet lieutenant, observed in retrospect:

> I sat one day mending my stockings. We were in a kind of railroad car, everyone was sitting around talking. And one young guy said, "When the war ends, you won't have to do that kind of work."
>
> I answered: "So quickly?"
>
> "Well, not right away of course, but soon."
>
> Yes, the war will end, I thought. We'll win after all. Fascism won't exist.... And look now: thirty-seven more years of Soviet fascism. And so the question arises, a very strange question for me: should we really have won the war after all? ...I don't know....[26]

Then in the ditch Nikonov and I contemplated our options and watched the troops pass by on the highway. When I saw soldiers being posted on the highway with machine guns targeted at the forest I told Nikonov: "I'll get out now and walk towards the soldiers posted at the village entrance. I speak German. Better to get out of here now than later, or never."

---

[26] Kevin Klose. *Russia and the Russians: Inside the Closed Society.* New York: W.W. Norton & Co., 1984, pp. 176-177.

I did. I raised my arms and walked across the field towards the post. The Germans waved me on. I did not hear what they shouted but, when I was in hearing distance, I answered them in German — to their great surprise. When I reached them they asked whether there were soldiers in the forest; I told them what I had seen. They sent me back to tell the soldiers to come out slowly, arms raised, rifles in the air. Back in the forest the people had been watching and now gathered to hear what I had to say.

"How do you know they will not shoot at us?" they asked. I told them to stay in line and I would go first. Those who didn't want to go should stay and watch. After a while a group gathered, soldiers and civilians, and we marched out. When we reached the highway, the Red Army soldiers who still carried rifles dropped them in front of the German post.

German traffic on the road had resumed, more German soldiers had posted themselves along the highway, and more people came streaming out of the forest. I asked the Germans what we should do.

"Keep walking south along the highway on the trail next to the road," they advised. "There will be a POW assembly point somewhere. They will take care of you."

\* \* \*

We walked south the rest of the day, always on the trail off the road on the right side. There were many of us, civilians, soldiers, a never-ending line. On the highway German trucks and artillery passed by sporadically paying no attention to us. It was still light when we reached a village. Nikonov and I decided to look for night quarters there.

There were no German troops in the village. We chose a large house near a crossroads a few houses away from the highway which looked like a substantial household. When we entered we found it crowded inside. The master of the house, an old man, and the women there didn't mind people coming to seek shelter in their house. Some soldiers had their own rations, others wanted to buy food. The peasant women did their best to provide some food. As it was getting dark inside, everyone settled down for a night in the warm house. There wasn't enough space for all to lie down; a corner of the room or a place at the wall was all we had; we dozed off sitting up. It was the third night that I had not taken off my clothes. For a while one heard low voices and whispering, but soon all was quiet and dark; only the old man passed by a few times with a lantern to check on the stalls.

A cold draft woke me up. The door was open and Red Army soldiers were coming inside flashing battery lights. I dozed off again until loud voices woke me up again. The old peasant stood in the middle of the room with his lantern facing a sergeant who held a gun in his hand.

"It is an order," the sergeant was shouting but there was laughter in the dark and plenty of dirty language.

"Put away your revolver," the peasant said. "Otherwise I'll go and wake up the entire village. This is my house. Who wants to go — go; the door is open, the road is clear. Who wants to stay — stay. Now, you get out and wait outside for the others but don't make trouble here." And he pushed the sergeant gently towards the door. Everyone was awake by now.

Some soldiers left the house and joined the newcomers. Others remained in the house and soon it was quiet again; only snoring disturbed the calm.

In the morning I told Nikonov that I would continue to look for the camp the German soldiers had told us about. Maybe there would be food and an opportunity to get away from this area. I had talked with our peasant host and he told me that a big village — Znamenka — was not far away to the south. Nikonov wanted to stay with me and we set out once more on the trail next to the highway. German units were again passing us in the opposite direction. A few planes were in the air. Here and there in the distance one could hear artillery fire.

As we passed by some trucks which had stopped for the German soldiers to relieve themselves, I asked whether they had seen a prisoner assembly point. The soldiers on the truck became curious.

"Hey, here is one who speaks German. How far is it still to Moscow?" In the back of the truck a soldier looked over the shoulders of the others and shouted "What kind of German is that? It's probably Yiddish. *Bist wohl ein Jid?* (Are you a Jew?)," and he lifted his rifle menacingly.

"Shut up," shouted the others and pushed him back. "Let's hear what he has to say." Would they come to a "decent place" soon? They cursed the roads, they cursed the land, the poverty, and this war. But "it will soon be over," they said.

We parted and it wasn't long before we came to the big village spread along the highway. Old trees lined the road and shaded the houses. To the right was a harvested field filled with Soviet soldiers camping. At the entrance to the village two German soldiers in shorts were getting a shower; a peasant girl was pouring water out of a bucket over them while they stood in a ditch. I approached the soldiers and asked, "Is this the assembly point for prisoners of war?"

# 11

## The Germans

### SWITCHING SIDES

The soldiers and the girl looked at us with surprise. "Are you German?" asked one of the soldiers.

"I am," I replied. The soldiers, picking up the towels and drying themselves, turned towards the first house on the road where a motorcycle with sidecar was parked.

"Wait here, we'll be right back," one of them said.

Nikonov and I found a place in the sun at the village entrance, took our backpacks off, and sat down. The morning was crisp and sunny, the sky blue and clean, the trees touched by autumn gold. It was quiet except for occasional rumbles far away. Down the road in the village German soldiers were carrying out their duties and one heard the noise of motors running. In the field behind the village the human ant heap was stirring; Soviet soldiers, the POWs who had spent a night camping in the field, went about their daily needs; some were at the creek washing, others cooking something over small fires, and all waiting for things to come. For them the war was over; now food and shelter would be their main concern, and this was our concern too. Nikonov wanted to get away from here, from the front line, go back as far as possible.

It seemed the war should soon be over, a different kind of war than one had read about or seen in the movies: no front lines with trenches full of soldiers, no artillery incessantly pounding the trenches, but a fast moving war as the year before in France. How long was it until Paris fell?

Our ruminations were interrupted by the two Germans, now in uniform. "Don't you want to wash up and shave yourselves? There is hot water in the house."

We certainly needed a shave and started to unpack our bags. The corporal — he was the company medic — watched us and asked the usual questions: Where was I from? What was I doing here? Where had I learned German? When he saw me putting my safety razor together he asked whether I wanted a new blade. He gave me a pack of Rotbart blades, the same kind I had used years ago at home when Herr Wegerer brought them from Finland. After we were through shaving he asked whether we had eaten and sent the soldier to the kitchen for coffee; he returned accompanied by more soldiers. The word spread that there was a "Russki" who spoke German; soon the master sergeant came with two corporals.

While we were all standing on the roadside talking, two Russian soldiers approached our group. I had noticed them earlier when Nikonov and I were sitting not far away from their group which, all wearing new blue overalls, looked different from the other Russian soldiers in their sand-colored garb. They had been watching us when we had first arrived and I had spoken with the German soldiers. Now two of them wanted to tell me something.

"Comrade interpreter," said one of them.

"He isn't a comrade of yours," said the other.

"Never mind," I said.

"Well, *gospodin perevodchik* — mister interpreter — tell

the German officer that we left our trucks not far from here in the woods. New trucks just out of the factory — GAZiki and ZISY — and loaded with uniforms and foodstuffs. We could bring them here if it's all right with the Germans and help fight the Bolsheviks." The Gorki Automobile Plant (GAZ) built light Ford trucks; the Moscow Stalin Plant (ZIS) built heavier trucks.

"What does he say?" the master sergeant wanted to know and I told him. The roly-poly good-humored Saxon looked at the two Russians and the small group standing aside in the field, then turned to a corporal. "How about it *Shirrmeister*. Need a Russian column?" *Shirrmeister*, formerly the man who took care of the horses, was used now for the chief mechanic in motorized units who took charge of the trucks. His truck was always the last one in a motorized column and was equipped for repairs or to haul disabled vehicles.

"Well, why not; on these roads the Russian trucks aren't bad. I can also use good mechanics. How many are there anyhow — trucks I mean?"

I did not know if the Germans were only joking but asked the Russians how many trucks they had left in the woods.

"They seem to be clean fellows," the sergeant said. "I'll ask the company commander." He was getting serious and turned to me. "Tell them to stick around." And he returned to the village with the corporals.

Later the master sergeant came with a senior lieutenant, a tall stern man with dueling scars on his face and a softened-up uniform cap sitting slanted on his head. I thought of Eric von Stroheim in a World War I movie.

"Who is the one who speaks German?" The others pointed to me. "Are you a German?" he asked, and I explained who I was. Then he wanted to see the Russian truck drivers. They lined up in front of the lieutenant just as they would have in front of their own officer. The lieutenant looked them over, didn't say a word, saluted casually, then turned around and walked away. Everyone went back to his own business. The Russians talked for a while with me, explaining where the trucks were. The day took its course; prisoners were loaded on trucks and driven away; a German motorized infantry unit passed through the village.

Nikonov had found a house where we could stay. The rest of the day I spent in the company of the medic, a soft-spoken young man from Vienna, an orphan who had been studying medicine before he was drafted and who looked forward to continuing his studies as soon as the war was over. He asked me about my life, about Russia. He liked the people here, he said; they had been friendly everywhere, poor and friendly. He told me that his company was part of a Viennese division — the Second Tank Division — and most of the soldiers were Austrians. But the officers and sergeants were German.

We sat long into the night by the light of a candle listening to radio reports. The battle of Vyazma-Bryansk had just ended; half a million Soviet troops were cut off and trapped inside the encirclement. Here it was strangely quiet for such a great battle being fought. One heard sounds of war, but they were always far away. I thought of my colleagues, of the workers who had walked ahead of us and must have reached the highway just when German tanks were closing in on Vyazma. What had happened to them?

In the morning I watched the lineup and, as the company was being dismissed, a car arrived in front of the lieutenant's quarters. A short time later a messenger came looking for me. "The colonel wants to talk with you," he told me. As I approached the commander's house, two officers were standing outside and the lieutenant pointed to me: "That is the man."

The colonel wanted to hear my story. When I mentioned that I had been in Göttingen in 1923 visiting my grandmother, he became very interested. He wanted to know the names of my relatives. I mentioned Otto Schuetze and he asked me who he was. A store owner, I said, game and fish store. The colonel laughed, turned to the lieutenant and said, "Indeed, it's a small world. I know him. He is our game warden; we hunt together."

At this point the tone of our conversation became less official. The colonel offered cigarettes; we smoked and I talked about my family. Then he came to the subject of his visit. Where were those Russian drivers and their trucks? We drove down to the village entrance and I called the Russian drivers. The colonel unfolded a detailed Soviet General Staff map. One of the Russian drivers came forward to pinpoint where the trucks had been left and winked at me. "Nice map," he said and soon found the location.

The colonel turned to me. "Would you trust the boys and go with them to get the trucks?" I said I would. He told the lieutenant to get a truck ready with a few men and machine guns, load up the Russians, and go get their trucks.

"You go with them," he told me, "and good luck." He drove away and I told the Russians to get ready.

They picked up their belongings and we waited at the village entrance. Two of the drivers seemed to take charge of the crew; one was a quiet young man from Leningrad, a high school graduate, the one who had looked at the colonel's map. The other was a Muscovite, a big fellow, a real truck driver, brash but good-humored, and a born spokesman for the group. The rest of them came from farms.

A German diesel truck came with the chief mechanic at the wheel, five soldiers, and two machine guns. The Russians climbed in the back; I joined the chief mechanic in the cabin. He had a map and we rode north. The road was empty. At the next crossroads a German platoon was securing the road. In the woods to the west was scattered fire. "They tried to break out," the soldiers at the machine gun said. We continued farther north a few miles to where Nikonov and I had stayed two nights before. Here we turned west onto a field road.

"Is it quiet around here?" I asked some villagers.

"A few German cars passed by," they said. "But thank God it's calm here. Hope the front moves fast now and they wring Stalin's neck soon."

We approached the forest; cars were parked at the roadside and German Air Force officers were inspecting abandoned Russian trucks in a ravine. Our trucks were farther up under the trees. In a few minutes the Russian drivers had the engines running, five Ford trucks and one bigger ZIS.

It was getting dark when we came back to Znamenka, our village. The master sergeant instructed me to find quarters for myself and the drivers. The Russians tried to tell him as best they could that they wanted to stay with the company. "You — us — together drive Moscow. War kaput."

The POWs in the field were gone. Nikonov didn't know what to do; he was a civilian, free to do whatever he wanted. He decided he wanted a lift to take him westward and I promised to arrange this. The next day he left on a truck which went back for supplies; I never saw him again.

That evening I was called to the company commander. The lieutenant, master sergeant, bursar, and chief mechanic were playing cards. Would I take responsibility for the Russian drivers, the company commander wanted to know? They could stay for the time being in the village; perhaps there would be work for them to do. They should be fed by the villagers and get themselves new uniforms from the trucks we brought in. And I should get one for myself. If I needed anything I should tell the master sergeant. No one should leave the village.

"Sargeant, let them line up for formation in the morning at the left wing. Show them tomorrow how it's done," the lieutenant decided.

"Which house are you in?" the mechanic wanted to know.

The next morning he would inspect the Russian trucks; they should be parked under trees, front end towards the street. I should get my food from the company kitchen, the sargeant said, and get some money from the bursar for the canteen out of company funds. We all should stay in the house in case of an alarm.

The Russian drivers were quick to learn the ropes and pick up a few German words. In a short while, formation dismissed, the German corporals were shouting "Sasha, Ivan, Anton, you devil, on the double." "Jawohl," shouted back Ivan or Sasha or Anton.

The company stayed in Znamenka through most of October, and the Russian drivers continually asked: "Why don't we move ahead? Why are the Germans procrastinating? It's only two hundred kilometers to Moscow." Everyone hoped for the war to end and to go home. The company was advancing supply stores for the division from Smolensk which was two hundred kilometers to the rear and where the retreaded rail line ended. Soon the Soviet light Ford trucks with a Russian driver next to a German soldier were the *Schirrmeister's* preferred means of transportation; they saved fuel and wear on his heavy diesels.

Division and company logos were painted on the Russian trucks. Like the small metal flags placed along the roads and at crossroads to indicate the location of units, these logos were the subject of much discussion among us Russians. To us such disclosure of "military secrets" seemed unbelievable, unless, of course, it was a ruse designed to mislead the enemy. I talked about it with the medic. He laughed. "How could it be otherwise in a fast-moving war? How else could one find one's way to the right unit or office?"

I stayed in the village with the heavier ZIS truck and an older Russian driver; there was enough work for us too. An interpreter is advantageous to both occupier and occupied for information provided and confusion and conflict avoided.

The German soldiers occupied most of the village houses, usually about six men to a house in the front room facing the street. There were all kinds of minor issues to be settled between them and the house owners who were usually women, the men having been mobilized earlier in the war. The issues were mostly about sauna and laundry, about eggs, milk, and an occasional chicken to be bought or traded. With my ZIS truck I was able to help the "village elder" with some of his needs like hauling lumber from the woods or potatoes from the fields and, in exchange, get a pig slaughtered for the company's kitchen.

In the evenings I visited my new friend, the medic, who had a radio and so I was able to tell the Russians what was happening at the front. Leningrad had been surrounded, the Don River reached; in our area the front had reached Mozhaysk, halfway to Moscow from where we were. When would we start moving again, the Russians asked? As with all soldiers, they wanted to get home; it was not "win or lose," it was "let's get it over with as quickly as possible." This was true particularly among the Austrians; they often talked about the campaign in France, how quickly it was over, and that everyone, German and French, had been able to return to their families and business.

While I had always hated things military — uniforms and subordination — I was now happy to get a Soviet officer's greatcoat from the captured supplies to cover my civvies and keep me warm. It was nippy in the evenings when Sasha, the Muscovite with a newly acquired accordion, played on the porch to a gathering of villagers, mostly girls and women and some off-duty German soldiers. Slowly I acquiesced to the need for discipline and the unchallenged authority of orders in the same way one adjusts to the weather.

Here I was at least free from the constant drumbeat of propaganda, of Party Line, Party cells, and Party secretaries. But most of all I suddenly felt safe after five years of conscious or subliminal deceptions, subterfuge, and insecurity. I no longer needed to lie or conceal anything. Talking to soldiers, I heard different opinions, critical remarks about many things, particularly the war. For me, political criticism was of course *terra incognita* and wars, like stormy weather, were "inevitable historical events" and — as Clausewitz, the German general of Napoleonic times, had said — a "continuation of politics by other means," just as class warfare was in peacetime. I knew about that and had no concept of "just" or "unjust" wars. Every soldier had the "just cause" of defending his life without hating the soldiers across the front line. I had read Erich Maria Remarque.

Before we left Znamenka, a group of young officers arrived to travel with us as "Officers' Reserve." They had nothing to do except to be at the company's lineup to hear the orders of the day. They were mostly Austrian reservists, college graduates in their late twenties. Once they learned who I was, they invited me to their quarters for drinks and to ask questions. Most of them were appalled by the coarseness of the land, the poverty and lack of any amenities, but some showed an interest in Russia.

They had not yet experienced war and from their conversations it seemed to me that for them war was a kind of game, a deadly one, but played by the rules. They had been briefed about partisans who had lately appeared behind German lines. Well, partisans were outlaws. Why didn't the Soviet Union sign the Convention on Prisoners of War, they asked? I told them that Soviet soldiers were not allowed to surrender, that there were no rules of war, only fighting for victory by all means. They shook their heads. What would happen to them if they were taken prisoner? I didn't know.

The subjects of communism and the role of Jews in the Soviet leadership were brought up. The officers were well-informed about the political left in Central Europe which I knew little about. I tried as best I could to answer their questions. One day the company commander asked me about these meetings and told me not to get involved in discussions of "the Jewish question." In the weeks to come the young reserve officers gradually left to replace casualties.

## To Moscow

When orders came for us to move, the rains came with them. We advanced northeast past Vyazma and Gzhatsk, towns partly destroyed by fires. If the roads had been paved at all, by now the rains, tanks, and artillery had made them nearly impassable. Low-lying swampy areas had to be covered by lumber pavements for which young trees were cut. Time and again the heavy diesels had to be pulled and pushed out of the mud. Infantry units overtook us, marching over the fields through heavy sticky ground, the soldiers tired, wet, and cold, the officers on horseback, and horse-drawn light artillery in tow.

Once in a while a column of Russian prisoners on foot, accompanied by a few German soldiers, stomped through the heavy earth going in the opposite direction. Their condition was pitiful; you could see that some of them would not make it to their destination. Stories and pictures of the Napoleonic War came to my mind.

"If the Germans gave every Russian prisoner a rifle we would soon be in Moscow," declared our Russian drivers.

Gray day by gray day we moved ahead across the undulating landscape, the road winding toward the horizon under heavy purple skies past villages and forests. I rode often in the company commander's car leading the column to assist him in reading Russian maps with Cyrillic texts. During the day our column stopped along the road for a hot meal from the field kitchen; overnight we stayed in villages where the Russian drivers and myself arranged sleeping quarters for the company.

The news at morning lineup did not enhance the company's mood. A German field hospital had been overrun by Mongolian cavalry and both patients and medical staff had been killed. Counterattacks, raids behind our front line, and the weather were slowing the advance. We passed freshly established German cemeteries with neat white birch crosses, tablets with names and dates, and a steel helmet. Our German soldiers looked at them with increased concern while the Russians wondered at the care given to temporary burial grounds. We also wondered where Soviet casualties had disappeared. Only once in a while did a lone primitive cross made of two sticks over a small mound of fresh earth indicate that a Russian had been buried there.

Halfway between Vyazma and Moscow the frosts came. The earth froze, heavy snow came down; the blinding whiteness of the land under a cloudless blue sky would have brought some cheer but for the fact that the German soldiers were in their summer uniforms. We made quarters on the outskirts of a town at one of the old estates which had escaped destruction during the revolution. Since then it had been an orphanage which was hurriedly evacuated as the front approached. The white building with columns and pediments stood in a wooded area, once parkland in the English manner. Downhill a river passed through the grounds and an abandoned mill stood nearby. In the house, iron bedsteads, tables, and benches had been left intact. The tiled Dutch ovens were still in good order and there was plenty of firewood. With food supplies low, our Russians discovered a closed bakery, not yet pilfered, in the nearby town. The men who had worked at the bakery were mobilized and, overnight, fresh bread was delivered to our company.

Sasha, the Muscovite, told me that the area was known for its *valenki* (Russian felt boots) crafted by the peasants. We drove out to the surrounding villages and, in a few days, our company acquired *valenki* for soldiers on guard duty. Temperatures were dropping and permission was granted to wear any gear to protect hands, feet, heads, and ears. Only our lieutenant appeared at the lineups in his prescribed uniform, his military cap cocked above freezing red ears. Time spent at morning lineup got shorter.

On the radio we heard about the German advance to Kalinin, Volokolamsk, and Mozhaysk. The front passed Klin and our division reached the Moscow-Volga Canal at Yakhroma where I had worked in 1936. Our company advanced to Solnechnogorsk on the Moscow-Leningrad rail line fifty kilometers north of my home. We arrived at Solnechnogorsk on December 1. The temperature had dropped to below 40° Celsius. Truck engines were to be kept warm at all times but gasoline was in short supply. Our drivers who had delivered ammunition to the front line told us that tanks at the front had been dug in and used as artillery pieces. A few Junkers planes landed at a nearby field with only urgently needed ammunition. The Russian drivers told me that a local woman, a schoolteacher, was arrested and executed. She had been operating a radio transmitter.

Now, so close to Moscow, my thoughts were back at home. Whom would I find there? I knew Irina was in the Caucasus, Uncle Alyosha dead. And what was I to do once I was there? I thought of possibilities for a publishing business, of translating books and magazines. Behind the collapsed wall there was a big world we knew little or nothing about.

## Retreat Again

On December 5 we saw Soviet planes for the first time and in the evening orders came to be ready to move next morning. When we left Solnechnogorsk and reached the highway, we didn't turn south towards Moscow but north towards Klin, and we were not the only ones on the road moving in that direction; the traffic was heavy. In Klin we stopped on a street under big old trees; there was much activity in the air. An orderly came running: "Platoon commanders to the chief!" I was to come too. The lieutenant waited for us with a map and pointed out a village.

"We now proceed west 120 kilometers on the road to Rzhev. We are not going in a column but leave individually at intervals. The Russian trucks leave after the first platoon. I'll be leaving last. Be wary of Soviet airplanes. When approaching wooded areas, look out for small weapons fire. Soviet detachments may have the road under fire. Proceed immediately." I conveyed the orders to our Russian drivers and left with the last Russian truck. It was a gray day with low clouds. The frozen road was in good condition and we maintained a reasonable speed. Intermittently Soviet fighter planes flew over the road spreading machine-gun fire and we passed a few burning trucks. German anti-aircraft artillery had taken up positions on the way and Soviet fighter planes seemed to be wary of them. At dusk we reached the assigned village; in the evening the entire company assembled there except for one truck with two Russian drivers. "Don't worry," Sasha said. "They were homesick and went home."

We stayed in this village until Christmas. The situation at the front seemed stabilized. Soviet planes occasionally crossed our skies; at night the low winter clouds were lit red east and north. Temperatures were unusually low. Engines had to be kept warm all the time and small fires were lit under them during the night. We were under constant alert but, except for guard duty, had nothing to do but listen to the radio. We heard that winter clothing was on the way and that Hitler had visited the front; for the first time I heard Hitler speak on the radio. After all the advance praise by some of the soldiers, his speech was a disappointment, just a lot of screaming. Hitler's denunciation of Communists, Jews, and plutocrats was like the Communist litany against capitalists, imperialists, and "enemies of the people." It sounded like a performance by a provincial actor. I thought of Bamlag's Bel'skiy, the great actor who could uplift the spirits of even a gathering of prisoners.

On the radio we heard about Pearl Harbor and that Germany had declared war on the United States. The news was not well-received. Why would Germany fight the United States when Japan had just signed a non-aggression pact with the Soviet Union?

## WINTER QUARTERS

After Christmas we relocated to a village near Karmanovo. It was to be our quarters for the winter. The weather continued to be unusually cold. It was open country, brush-lined creeks cris-crossing a heaving landscape; here and there was a stand of trees or a small forest. Our village was a bare lineup of wooden houses along an unpaved street. A big white brick church stood at one end of the village surrounded by old trees and a cemetery.

We learned that a few miles to the east the HKL — the main battle line — stretched south to Orel, Kharkov, and the Sea of Azov. To the north, winter battles were reported between Kalinin and Leningrad. Twenty miles to the west the Vyazma-Rzhev rail line had been rebuilt to the German gauge; our company's task was to run supplies from there to the front.

A soldier knows little about the course of events except for what he sees with his own eyes and what official reports convey. Our drivers reported that it was now a trench war much like World War I. "The Russkis attack in human waves; there are hundreds of Russkis lying dead in no man's land but new unarmed waves rise from the trenches and attack with rifles taken from the dead."

Besides running supplies to the front line, the company was responsible for maintaining security in nearby villages. For the first time we were told about the "partisan threat" — Soviet resistance fighters. With a German corporal, I regularly visited our villages either on horseback or by sleigh. I appointed village elders to inform me about any problems and we discussed land redistribution, spring planting, and the possibility of getting horses for field work. New winter uniforms arrived and our Russian sand-colored uniforms were now exchanged for the German olive green, albeit without eagle and shoulder pieces. Of course we kept our warm Russian coats.

Our company had to keep a stretch of the supply road clear of snow. After a heavy snowfall the lieutenant called me. "We have to get the snow off the road. The men from the villages must be mobilized; they should be housed in the church here and a kitchen organized to feed them."

News of the mobilization caused anxiety among the peasants since the male population had already been reduced by earlier Soviet mobilization and evacuation. Eventually about sixty older men and teenagers arrived at our village and became my responsibility. They were promised days off and visits from their women after work. One of the village saunas was converted to a "Russian kitchen" run by some of our Russian drivers. From an army depot we picked up horses, artillery horses having been replaced by motorized vehicles. Once in a while a horse was sacrificed for the Russian kitchen. The village elders supplied potatoes, cabbage, and bread.

I also accompanied the medic on his visits to the villages to watch out for contagious diseases, but he was mainly concerned about the children. We usually used his motorcycle with the sidecar made into a moveable apothecary and were always well-received by the women. They were thankful for any small help and rewarded us with a few eggs.

Our villages were not affected by partisan activity but sev-

eral partisans were caught with a cache of arms in a village occupied by a neighboring infantry division. On one of my
rides through their territory I saw three partisans hanging
from a village tree.

Once a group of drunken German soldiers accompanied
by a Russian invaded one of our villages in search of booze,
geese, and girls. The Russian was known locally as a criminal
released from prison before the Soviets retreated. The village
elder was instructed to send the Russian to our village if he
appeared again. He came and was arrested; later the locals
told me that he had been executed by the military police —
"good riddance" they said.

"We must do something for your teeth," the medic told
me one day. "There is a well-known Berlin dentist at the army
hospital in Vyazma. I'll take you there." I had been losing my
teeth ever since I had scurvy in Bamlag and, in the spring of
1941 in Moscow, the roots of six molars had been pulled. The
medic took me to Vyazma on several occasions on his motorcycle over incredibly muddy spring roads and I received my
first denture.

When the snow melted, the men who had been mobilized
for snow removal returned to their villages to prepare for
spring planting and I had plenty of time on my hands. From
a closed school library I collected some books, paper, and In-
dia ink, and started to draw again. The wide landscape, big
heavy skies, spring storms, and wartime scenes lent themselves to black and white ink drawings; a few of them are still
in my possession.

* * *

At the suggestion of my company commander I had written a field postcard to my aunt in Bremen, an address I still
remembered from years long past. In reply, I was surprised by

a letter from my mother. She wrote that last summer she had stayed at Professor Schaak's dacha near Luga; my sister Ira had been with her but had to return to Leningrad to complete her medical studies. In August the German Army passed through Luga. Mother stayed in Luga for a while as an interpreter for the German town commandant but was evacuated to Germany before winter set in. She was never to see Ira again.

## THE BATTLE OF BELYY

In May our company was ordered to relocate. For weeks there was talk of a much-hoped-for pullout of our division to France, an ever recurring daydream among our Viennese contingent. We did move west on the Moscow-Minsk superhighway but only to Yartsevo, east of Smolensk; then we turned north on the road towards Belyy. France was not in the cards.

During our quiet winter near Karmanovo two Soviet armies and a Cavalry Corps had invaded a large area of about 5,000 square miles behind the German Ninth Army. In the large forests of this area Soviet partisan activities were organized by communist party officials who had been evacuated earlier and were now parachuted back into their native villages.

When the roads dried, "Operation Seydlitz" was launched to cut off these Soviet forces from their supply lines. Our Second Tank Division was advancing north on the road to Belyy; one of our company's tasks was to secure the road against partisan assaults.

On the way to our destination the company commander fell ill and was replaced by a young lieutenant, a newcomer to the front just out of law school in Vienna. Day-to-day decisions were now made mainly by the master sergeant and our platoon commanders and my assignment was to gather intelligence about partisan activity.

Our new quarters were halfway between the highway and a tributary of the Dnieper River. Across the river was partisan territory. The local populace often disliked their activities which resulted in German punitive actions. Besides the "Red" partisans, there were also "Green" partisans, former Red Army soldiers who had escaped German imprisonment and maintained "neutrality." The Greens wanted neither to fight the Germans nor be taken prisoners by them.

From a village on the other bank women often passed our place on the way to the market in Dukhovshchina, the nearest town. Occasionally our Russian drivers gave them a lift and learned from them that the forests of the region harbored Red as well as Green partisans. It was clear that the local populace — mainly women — wanted to be left in peace by everyone.

One night our village was assaulted by mortar fire which came from woods on "our" side of the river. We had no casualties and little damage was done to the village. It was decided to clear the woods by cutting off the partisans' retreat across the river. Machine guns were the only heavy weapons we had. It was a kind of Wild West operation. We had no casualties, nor did we catch any partisans. It was my only combat action during the entire war; I expended about a dozen bullets lying flat in the bushes listening carefully for sounds of enemy movements.

After this incident we came to an agreement with the villagers across the river. They would signal us the arrival of any partisans by closing or opening window curtains in a house facing the river; in return, we promised not to assault the village and to provide free passage for them to the market.

With the approval of the German commandant at Dukhovshchina, I sent word to the Green partisans that they were welcome to come and settle in the villages along the road to Belyy in exchange for protecting the villagers from Red partisans. A meeting was arranged with the Green commanders at the river's edge and a deal was struck. On the day our company was ordered to move north, several hundred Greens came out of the woods. It was a strange looking crowd carrying a variety of weapons including hunting rifles.

While we were still staying in the village we had heard about the capture of a General Vlasov, defender of Leningrad and Moscow. Rumors spread about a Russian Liberation Army (ROA) to be organized under Vlasov's command; some of our Russian drivers were eager to enlist. But, for the time being, our company had no intention of letting them go.

One day in June, when we were again on the road towards Belyy, I was called to the lieutenant's car. A car with two military police sergeants was parked next to it.

"I have received orders for your transfer," the lieutenant said. "I'm sorry to let you go but those are orders. Get your things. The sergeants will take you to Ninth Army Headquarters." I went to my truck, packed my belongings, said short goodbyes, and got into the car with the military police.

We made quarters for the night in Prechistoye at the house of the local commandant, an old captain who had seen World War I. On learning that I spoke Russian, he asked me to help him with the interrogation of a peasant who had been brought in by the Russian police for sheltering partisans. A scared elderly peasant was brought in for an interrogation; he did not deny that partisans had spent a night in his hut which was in a remote area. It was a common story. I knew also that the German-appointed police often settled old scores from prewar times. Clearly the old man had acted under duress, but was harmless.

The captain agreed to release the man but led him first into the adjoining shed, took off his officer's belt and ordered the poor man to drop his pants. He hit his bare buttocks several times but not very hard. Then the man was told to put on his pants and go home. At first he didn't believe it; then he fell on his knees and tried to kiss the captain's hand, much to the latter's embarrassment.

After this Gogolian scene I took leave of the captain and departed with the sergeants to Sychevka about 150 miles away to the east.

## SYCHEVKA

Sychevka, a town on the rail line halfway between Vyazma and Rzhev, had seen action and damage in 1941. Now headquarters of the German Ninth Army, it had been cleaned up and some buildings repaired.

I was dropped off at the old store arcades which housed a *Geheime Feld Polizei* (GFP) unit, an army counterintelligence unit. My arrival was obviously expected and I was shown to a cot at one end of the store where I was surprised to meet two Soviet colonels in full uniform. They occupied cots next to mine and were also surprised by my appearance, i.e., in a German uniform without insignia and a Soviet officer's belt with shoulder straps. It didn't take long for us to get acquainted. One of the colonels had been Chief of Artillery of the 39th Army; the other one — wearing a karacul hat and black sheepskin cape — Chief of Staff of the Eleventh Cavalry Corps. They had been taken prisoner at the Battle of Belyy and were here to be debriefed by officers of Ninth Army Headquarters. I was to act as interpreter.

The next day we were escorted to a nearby house for the debriefing which lasted several days with intervals for food and drink. The atmosphere was businesslike and friendly, the Soviet colonels cooperative. They had suffered heavy losses, left behind German lines without supplies during the long winter, and accused the High Command of having sacrificed them for no good reason.

Often the discussion drifted from military to political issues, from General Vlasov and the ROA to a Russian provisional government in Smolensk. With debriefings concluded, the officers departed for Smolensk and Central Front Headquarters.

In August 1942, during the Soviet Rzhev offensive, the sounds of battle could be heard at Sychevka. It was a tense situation and I was called to assist Captain v. Schlippe, a Russian-speaking officer and aide-de-camp to the army's staff intelligence officer. During sleepless nights, with telephones ringing and dire battlefield reports coming in, I learned to admire the calm reasoning of officers under stress, their quick perception and resolve, as well as their realism and professionalism.

After the crisis passed, my life in Sychevka was agreeable. I knew some of the local people in town and was invited to their homes. They had gardens with fruits and vegetables in abundance, while tobacco, sugar, salt, and soap were in short supply. Although I received no army pay, I did get free PX goods and always had cigarettes.

It was also my first opportunity to see German movies. The big church, already converted by the Soviets to a movie theater, now showed German films. I remember once watching "Wedding at Baerenhof" while a Soviet small plane known as the "sewing machine" dropped a bomb which hit the corner of the bell tower. No great damage was done to the building, but the lights went out and I never saw the end of the movie.

My pleasant situation changed when I was called to report to Commissar Gramsch, the officer in charge of the GFP, the counter intelligence unit. I disliked him on first sight.

The GFP unit had two interrogators, both Volksdeutsche from Poland who spoke some Ukrainian but barely understood Russian, and I was ordered to interrogate a girl with a GFP sergeant present.

The girl's story was a familiar one: evacuated in 1941 before the Germans came, she had later returned to her native region, now more or less a no-man's land northwest of Rzhev. During the winter she had been in Moscow working in a cafeteria. It was not difficult to unravel her cover story. In fact her father had been appointed village elder during the German occupation. After the Germans retreated the Soviets arrested the family; the daughter was promised her parents' release if she completed an intelligence assignment. She was trained in Moscow, dropped by parachute, but got separated from her leader who had the radio transmitter.

I was glad for her sake that her activities had caused no harm and that, a few days later, I saw her again cleaning field police billets; at least she received good food.

One day one of the "interpreters" came to me and asked me to take a look at a prisoner in the church. "He lies his head off. Maybe you can pin him down. You know these sons of bitches. They must have dropped him but he won't confess." I went into the church and saw the prisoner, a lieutenant, lying on a bed of straw. He had been badly beaten and asked for water. Eventually we talked; I asked where he was taken prisoner, got a map, and checked everything out. Everything he said was correct. There are many villages in Russia with identical names and the first interrogator had used the wrong map.

In late August, while riding with GFP soldiers to pick up a suspect, I asked about the girl and the lieutenant I had interrogated earlier. One of the soldiers laughed and made a sign of pulling the trigger. I could not believe it. On my return I asked other soldiers whether this was true. When they confirmed the story I was furious and went to v. Schlippe, and told him what I had learned. Earlier, he had suggested that I take care of my legal status. Since I had not been drafted, I was not a German soldier; but under German law I was a

German citizen. Now I asked him to help me get travel papers for Germany. After a telephone call, he sent me to the Quartermaster's Office.

When I reported there the colonel was irritated with my appearance. "I am not a soldier," I told him.

"Who is your officer in charge?"

"Commissar Gramsch."

He ordered me to wait outside. After a while I was called in and told that what I wanted could not be done; I was not a soldier and therefore not entitled to travel papers.

I went back to v. Schlippe resolved to leave unless I got my papers.

"Where will you go?" he asked me.

"Never mind, I know people here. I'll find a place."

"Now calm down," v. Schlippe said. "Go to your quarters. Report tomorrow morning at the office of the Army Chief of Staff. You will get your papers." He also asked for my mother's address and promised to send a cable about my arrival.

## ON THE WAY TO BERLIN

I left Sychevka the next day on the train from Rzhev to Berlin, a daily train for soldiers on leave with clean passenger cars, some for officers and others for enlisted men.

Near Minsk, women with yellow stars sewn on their clothes were working on the tracks; they watched our slow-moving train. Some soldiers threw cigarettes to them, a few made nasty remarks. It was a disturbing sight and reminded me of Bamlag when I was on a train watching prisoners begging and listening to passengers making similar nasty remarks. I had already heard that Jews in Germany had been ordered to wear yellow stars.

After Minsk it was slow going, with flat cars being pushed in front of the locomotive in case tracks were mined by partisans. We crossed the former Polish border and soon the train stopped at a siding in the midst of a forest, next to neat new barracks in a landscaped plot with gravel walkways and flower beds. Red Cross nurses waited for us, young women dressed in ironed striped dresses and white starched headgear.

"Ah! German girls at last!" the soldiers shouted as we were welcomed to a delousing. We disembarked at the shower house and got clean new uniforms and haircuts, then went to a cafeteria for good hot food, beer, and our "leave packages" with canned food, toiletries, and cigarettes. In the evening we boarded our train again and waved goodbye to the nurses.

Poland. Still a Russian landscape but neater, more habitable. We passed Warsaw by night and it was light when we crossed the German border. The eastern landscape ended abruptly. Paved roads lined by trees ran towards the horizon; brick rail stations with tiled roofs, swept platforms, washed windows, flowers on the window sills. In his book, "August 1914," Solzhenitsyn would later write: "Poland, poor and ragged as it was, had seemed familiar enough to them, but when they crossed the German frontier, it was as though they had passed through some magic barrier. The crops, the roads, and the buildings — everything was eerily different."[27] For me, too, it was a strange feeling to enter this new world. But I had come only as a visitor; I meant to go back where I had come from, to my own life, to Irina, to my friends, to my home.

East Prussia, Allenstein, the Mazur Lakes, names familiar from the history of World War I. The train sped through the new landscape, discarding soldiers on the way at towns and stations. A day, a night; ever faster the train sped towards Berlin. I stared out the window full of anticipation.

I knew Berlin only as I knew Paris, from books and maga-

---

[27] Alexander Solzhenitsyn. *August 1914*. New York: Farrar, Straus and Giroux, 1972, p. 131.

zines, maps and films, and accounts of those who had been there. I had read what Ilya Ehrenburg had recently written about Paris and Berlin; I had read Kellermann's "The Brothers Schellenberg" about postwar Berlin. I knew the Berlin of Zille and Kollwitz, Koepenick and Red Wedding, Grunewald and Wannsee; the Avus where Opel had raced his car propelled by a rocket; the radio tower photographed by Moholy Nagy. There was the traffic tower at Potsdamer Platz, the Mosse House and Einstein Tower by Mendelsohn; the Bauhaus; Babelsberg and the UFA studios. And the movies: "Berlin, the Symphony of a Metropolis" and "Variété," the film with Emil Jannings, Warwick Ward, and Pola Negri.

The train sped now past the multitude of little garden plots with weekend sheds, vegetable beds, berry bushes, and fruit trees. Miles of them. Then came red-tiled roofs, villas on tree-lined streets; yellow streetcars, cars, busy pedestrians, people on bicycles; then apartment houses, city blocks, the elevated train cutting through their back yards past rows and rows of windows and wall advertisements, passing over more city streets with more cars, streetcars, and people. Bahnhof Friedrichstrasse. I saw mother standing there with Ernst Holl, who twelve years ago, when I had last seen him, was not yet in his teens. Now he stood there in uniform, a sergeant. I was in Berlin.

# 12

## Soldiering

### DAYS IN BERLIN

The three of us — laughing and talking — walked from the station down into the street.

"How are you? "

"How long were you on the train? Is this all the luggage?"

"Ernst also just came home on leave from the eastern front."

"Where are we going?"

"To the Holls — it isn't far." And more talk holding on to mother's arm while going down the stairs.

Friedrichstrasse. Now there was no time to talk, only to look at the bustling street under a faded blue-green sky, its spotless pavements, buildings, sparkling shop windows and glistening cars, buses, and yellow trams; to breathe the autumn air, the "Berliner Luft;" to watch the fast-moving crowd, its faces, attires, gestures, colors and movements of elegant women. I had never seen such a crowd.

Unter den Linden; the Brandenburg Gate at one end. Hotels, cafés, porters, waiters, a marching band. One could almost forget the war but that there were only a few men in the

245

streets, mostly officers in gray-blue uniforms. I had to salute all the time though most officers tried to look the other way.

We turned into quieter streets to Anhalter Strasse and Hotel-Pension Gessler, the Holls' place they had bought in the 1930s when Uncle Albrecht retired and they had left the Soviet Union. We went in and found Aunt Martha, unflappable as always, placing some ironed laundry on a chair in the hall.

"There you are finally. Your mother has been waiting for you. Your bed is upstairs. Uncle Albrecht and Roderich are out but they will be back soon. Meet Emmchen, our help. And here come Gudrun and Katya. Katya belongs to the family and you can talk Russian with her too."

Gudrun when I had last seen her 12 years ago was a child; now she was a university student. Katya, the daughter of Russian emigres whose mother lived in Paris, was Gudrun's friend.

Later the younger generation assembled in Gudrun's room to chat and play records. Their friends were from Berlin's Russian School and everyone spoke Russian. In Leningrad we used to converse in German; here in Berlin we were speaking Russian. We played French, Russian and German records: *Parlez-moi d'amour,* the Don Cossacks Choir, and Sarah Leander singing in her hoarse voice, "*es muss einmal ein Wunder geschehen* (I know a miracle must happen)." We talked about Russia. Ernst, on leave from the Stalingrad front, served with a radio listening post. Roderich, waiting to be drafted, would certainly be sent east too. Gudrun, trying to avoid Labor Service, hoped to get an assignment to work in Russia the following summer; she loved Russia and everything Russian, particularly the memory of Baldina, her Leningrad nurse.

For meals we assembled in the dining room, sometimes with other hotel guests or Russian-speaking visitors: Herr Strecker from the Foreign Service and Blumental-Tamarin from the Anti-Comintern Radio Station, an actor whose name in years past I had seen printed in large letters on Leningrad Theatre posters. Hotel-Pension Gessler was like being in Petersburg again: pieces of furniture, a portrait of Bismarck the Iron Chancellor, and a fireplace screen brought back memories of the Grand Hotel.

Ernst Holl took me around town. We saw the deep sea wonders of his favorite aquarium, walked through the zoo, sat at the Kranzler Café on Kurfürsten-Damm, got tickets to the "Scala." For soldiers on leave it was easy to get tickets. After the show our small crowd walked home through the darkened but still lively streets of Berlin.

I asked Martha Holl about Alfred, remembering that back in 1930 or 1931 he had taught the children of Martha's relatives on a farm in Pomerania. No, Martha had no knowledge of the Blumenfelds' whereabouts. But there was one Berliner from old Petersburg's Litseyskaya Street — Erica Nicol, née Eilers, once Mrs. Salome. She had a house in fashionable Wannsee. I went to see her; she lived alone in the house while Captain Nicol was away at sea.

On the S-Bahn to Wannsee I was sitting next to the compartment door when an old lady came in and she looked tired. I offered her my seat. A yellow star was sewn on her overcoat. Somewhat reluctantly she accepted. A man in the compartment asked me whether I had noticed the yellow star; he objected to my giving a seat to a Jewess.

"I don't need advice from a civilian," I said and felt my temper boiling. "Put on a uniform first — damn it — have your ass frozen in the Russian snow before telling a soldier what to do."

The man looked about for some support but none came from the other passengers. At a stop the compartment door flung open. "Your tickets please."

The old lady showed her ticket and the conductor clipped it; she slipped out of the compartment on to the platform and disappeared in the crowd. I took my seat again and everyone sat in silence; at the next stop the man left.

At Erica's, the first thing I had to do was take off my boots in the hall. A row of slippers stood there ready for anyone who entered. Her polished floors reflected like mirrors. When Erica went downstairs to shovel coke into the furnace she put on white gloves. I was there again in 1945 when Aunt Vera stopped over on her escape from Posen; there was still heat in the house but I did not take off my boots that time.

## AT THE DRAFT BOARD

My orders for Berlin were to report at the "Draft Board, Foreign Countries." There were no problems. I was a German citizen as attested to by the Foreign Service; my Aryan descent established when mother and Aunt Vera, my father's sister, had gone through refugee procedures. When questioned about my residence and future plans I asked for reenlistment. I wanted to get back to the front. It was September 1942; German armies had advanced into the North Caucasus to 100 miles from Tbilisi. I wanted to be there to get as close to Irina as possible.

After a three-week home leave, I was told to report to the Reserve Battalion, Altenburg. Before leaving Berlin I was sent to Supreme Command Headquarters for a debriefing, a lengthy conversation with a colonel whose questions covered many subjects but whose main interest was the Soviet transportation system. How did automotive transport function in the absence of roads and service stations? I did my best to explain the abundance of time, of manpower, and of patience inherent in people of a vast country.

Then mother and I set out to visit relatives, first Aunt Vera Schmiedeberg, her daughter Edith and sister-in-law Erna, in Posen — now Polish Poznan as it was also between 1918 and

1939. Vera, father's only sister, was closest and dearest to me. I remembered her from my visits in Tallinn in 1924 and 1925; in the 1930's, family communications were nearly severed but we had learned about Uncle Rolf's and grandfather's deaths. Left on her own, Aunt Vera went through hard times, boarding school girls from Sweden and giving foreign language lessons. Following the Stalin-Hitler Pact, Aunt Vera, Edith, and Erna left Estonia as did most Estonians and Latvians of German ancestry and were resettled in Posen. There they were given a furnished apartment from which the Polish residents had been evicted, as probably were its German residents in 1919.

Vera was now working at an office of the Siemens Corporation, Erna attended to the household, and Edith went to high school. They had enough to live on, never complained, always searched for the lighter side of things. Vera did not like having to live among things which were not hers. But eventually they had to abandon these anyway when they fled for the third time in 1945 with only the possessions they could carry.

From Posen we traveled to Bremen, Soest, Gottingen, and finally to Eisenach where mother had settled. I met all of my six aunts and uncles and sixteen cousins except for one who was with the army in northern Finland.

When I arrived in Altenburg the basic training course was nearly over. I still learned the proper care of boots and how to make bunk beds but, coming from the front, I was treated kindly by my corporals and sergeants. Then five of us, all Russian-speaking soldiers, were ordered to report at Suleyovek, near Warsaw, where we would be assigned to various frontline intelligence units. My companions were all Balts resettled from Riga now living in Posen. We stopped in Posen for goodbyes and a farewell party at the house of a wine and spirits merchant from our group.

## SULEYOVEK

After a night on the train, we arrived in Warsaw in the morning and decided to tour the city before continuing to our destination. The city looked drab; only the historic buildings of the old market had been beautifully restored. I made some drawings while we wandered about town; my companions took photographs. The streets were lively; trams and sidewalks filled with people looking for what there was to buy in stores or in open markets; the younger women seemed determined to remain stylish and enlivened the sounds of the streets with the click-clack of their wooden soles and high heels. Men in black garb and round hats, always a threesome walking together, were a frequent sight; I was told they were members of the Society of Jesus. On a main street soldiers stood in line at a building entrance; I wondered what they were waiting for and my companions laughingly explained that it was a bordello maintained by the army.

Not far from the railroad station we saw an entrance to the inaccessible ghetto. We talked about why Jews were considered alien enemies and about the history of ghettoes, subjects unknown to me but familiar to the Balts. There was also talk about concentration camps, a term familiar to me since childhood, because it preceded the term "Corrective Labor Camps," and meant places to keep alien civilians in wartime, or class enemies in peacetime.

Toward day's end we took the suburban train to Suleyovek. The cars "for Germans only" were rather empty, the rest crowded with older women in kerchiefs carrying heavy loads of something somewhere, minding the unfriendly military police.

The office to which we reported was not far from the train stop. A large sparsely wooded area was enclosed by a barbed wire fence. Near the gate were two brick buildings which could have been a school or office at one time. A car and truck were parked there with a pair of dice as the logo. Farther away in the woods one could see widely spaced two-story country houses.

At the office the soldier on duty collected our papers, gave us tickets for the mess hall, showed us our night quarters — a room with a dozen bunk beds — and told us to report to the office the next morning for assignments and travel papers. After breakfast at a canteen, a corporal carrying folders told us to line up outside. A one-armed lieutenant with decorations on his tunic looked us over, asked our names, checked the folders, and went with the corporal into his office. When the corporal returned he told a private to prepare marching orders for everyone except me.

"What about me, corporal?" I asked.

"You are staying here."

"But I don't want to stay here," I said. "I have been at the front for a year and I want to be sent to the North Caucasus."

"It doesn't matter what you want; here you follow orders."

I was upset and asked to speak to the lieutenant but the corporal shouted "Attention!" A captain had entered the office and the corporal made his report to the "Rittmeister" — the old rank description for a cavalry captain. It was an occasion for me to ask for my transfer.

"Herr Rittmeister, I'm told that I have to remain here. I request an assignment to the South Front." The captain looked at the corporal.

"The lieutenant has his folder," the corporal said. The Rittmeister went into the lieutenant's office. When he returned, he told me to follow him to his office where he sat down behind his desk and looked through my papers.

"Why do you want to be assigned to the South Front?" he asked me in Russian. He spoke with a light accent as people from the Volga region do.

"My wife lives in Tbilisi, Herr Rittmeister, and I want to be there by the time we are in Tbilisi."

"We are not there yet and we can send you there when the time comes. Now, for the time being, you will remain here." Then he switched back to German. "You will have to change your name; take your time and think of a name. It is for your own protection."

I was surprised and stood there for a while confused while the captain looked through some papers.

"Mattern," I said, remembering the American pilot who passed over my head in 1934 when I was walking along the tracks of the Trans-Siberian Railroad.

"A good East Prussian name." The captain nodded, "Now choose a birthplace in Germany instead of Petersburg."

"Soest, my mother's birthplace." The captain filled in a form, spelling my new name "Matern," picked up the phone, called in the corporal, and gave him the form.

"Issue Matern new identity papers. He will be staying here for the time being. And you," turning to me, "wait for me outside in the office."

It took a while until my papers were prepared, mess hall tickets issued, and the papers taken for signature to the captain's office. After some time the Rittmeister came in accompanied by another captain.

"Herr Auferman," the Rittmeister said to the captain, "this is Matern. You can take him to his quarters now."

"Yes, Herr Rittmeister. Come on Matern; take your belongings."

## I-G Detachment

I followed the captain along a footpath to a two-story building some distance away near the fence. We entered a small hallway where the captain told me to leave my pack and proceeded upstairs to an office, a room with a window, three desks, and filing cabinets. A man in civilian clothes was sitting at one of the desks.

"Mr. Zorin, this is Matern," the captain introduced me in perfect Russian. "He will work here with us."

Mr. Zorin looked me over; he was short, well-built, his black hair parted and covering part of his forehead over dark piercing eyes. He wore a civilian suit with slacks tucked into Russian officer's boots. "Welcome," he said to me in Russian.

"Before we go further, Matern has to sign this paper. Nothing that you see, read, or do here is to be disclosed to any person outside this building. Your living quarters are downstairs." The captain opened the door to an adjacent room and called in a sergeant. "Klughart, this is Matern. Take him down to your quarters later and instruct him about rules and regulations." The sergeant, an older man, looked at me inquisitively. "I'll pick you up later when we go to the mess hall," he said.

Presently the telephone rang and the captain picked it up. "Jawohl, Herr Rittmeister, immediately. Yes, of course." He stood at attention while talking on the phone. One could see that he was a nervous man, constantly puffing his cheeks and blowing air through his lips. "I have to leave," he said. "Mr. Zorin, please show Matern around."

"Well now, sit down," said Zorin. "Let's get acquainted; what is your first name and patronymic. Between us we'll do it in the civilian manner. Have you been a soldier for a long time? Where did you learn Russian?" We began to get to know one another.

Then he took me next door into a big room occupying the rest of the upper floor. There were five men and a boy in the room; two were in uniform, the others in civilian clothes. At a long table in front of a window Sergeant Klughart, a private, an old man with a white beard, and a teenager were working at engravings. In a distant corner of the room a middle-aged civilian sat at a desk next to several filing cabinets. The rest of the room was occupied by a small printing press, letter-cases, and a composition table. A young man in an old, blackened

French or Belgian uniform was busy at the press. I was first introduced to the German private. "Walter Goebel, Private First Class, " he said with a smile. To the rest of the crew I was introduced in Russian.

I had arrived, and I would remain with this unit until the end of the war. It was I-G Detachment, Staff Walli I, Strategic Reconnaissance East, Abwehr I.[28]

Sergeant Klughart took me downstairs to the room I was to share with him and Private First Class Walter Goebel. It had three beds, a table, chairs, and lockers. Klughart, a veteran of World War I, gave me instructions like an old sergeant would instruct a soldier of the lowest rank and sent me to pick up blankets and straw for the mattress.

After work we didn't go to the mess hall. Goebel brought the food to our quarters; later he asked me to take a walk through the compound. He joked about Klughart. "He likes to boss you around a bit but he is a first class engraver. He worked twenty years at the Rosenthal porcelain factory." Goebel was a businessman from Nuremberg where he owned a stamp and engraving business, a jolly fellow who with his businessman's sense had already realized before I did the situation in which I found myself — the lowest-ranking soldier but, besides the captain, the only bilingual man in the office. He gave me a short account of the staff.

"Our captain was born in Russia. He came to Germany after World War I and studied agriculture, then went back to Russia and worked for Krupp selling agricultural machines to the Soviet Union. A decent man but very nervous. He hasn't

---

[28] Abwehr I, literally "defense," was the German Intelligence Service under the Supreme Command of the German Armed Services (OKW). Staff Wall I stood for Strategic Reconnaissance East and I-G was the Department of Technical Support Services within the Abwehr.

much authority around here. Zorin is more the one in charge; he is a Soviet major taken prisoner early in the war. There are many more Soviet officers on the training staff. As far as our Russians are concerned, they are all fine people. The old man with the beard is from Kiev, a good carver and photographer, and quite an artist. The boy is his nephew and our apprentice. The other civilian was a policeman, also from Kiev; and Sasha, the printer, was a sailor. He is our most recent acquisition and was taken prisoner at Sevastopol."

On our walk Goebel wanted me to meet some people I should know. We met Lachman, a German colonist from the Ukraine who had lost a leg in the war and was in charge of the warehouse of Soviet uniforms and equipment. He shared quarters with Karl, a German colonist from the North Caucasus taken prisoner in the first days of war and already a private first class who had seen action and been decorated with an Iron Cross. We also met Corporal Mueller, a German from Poland and a radio technician on the communications staff.

During my first days in the office Zorin introduced me to the tasks, files, and procedures. The office was attached to a training school for agents, volunteers recruited at POW camps. The instructors were former Soviet officers of various ranks teaching reconnaissance techniques, Soviet counterintelligence methods, radio communication, and camouflage.

Our mission was to support strategic intelligence operations. Agents selected for an operation came to us to consider their cover stories and to be issued appropriate documentation.

Step by step I learned my new trade. Zorin showed me a recent Soviet document: "Top Secret. To be destroyed in case of danger of capture by the enemy. Memorandum for field agents of the counterintelligence section SMERSH (Death to Spies) of the 46th Army. On Detecting Parachutists, Radio Operators, Saboteurs and Other Agents of German Intelligence." The memorandum listed German forgeries: Internal passports, military identity documents, travel orders, employment, and party documents. It drew attention to the high gloss of German photographic paper, the absence of rust on split pins in stitched documents, and went on for many pages to describe defective letter types, too sharp contours of water marks and other items, noting that "very often the distinguishing marks are so imperceptible that they are hardly visible by the naked eye."

"You see," Zorin told me, "Berlin makes all the forgeries and also gets the bulk of captured documents, though we manage to get some of the latter directly from the front. Here we print only travel orders; our engravers copy the seals and stamps from the most recent originals. When we use forgeries from Berlin we exchange the staples for rusty ones from captured documents. Recently we got some Soviet photographic paper, but we need all kinds of Soviet paper. German paper is of too high quality; it raises suspicion at any check point. It is silly for us to depend on Berlin but our poor captain is too timid to ask for what we need."

Zorin bragged about two agents dropped behind the front who had travelled by train all the way to East Siberia carrying their radio equipment as a "top secret" package which Zorin had assembled. He had been Chief of Staff of a Soviet regiment and was well-versed in military staff procedures and documentation. I had no knowledge of Soviet military life but knew the issues of civilian documentation.

A few weeks after my arrival at Suleyovek our captain departed on a trip to the front; the Rittmeister called me to his office before the captain left.

"Matern, how are you getting along with Zorin and the others?"

"Fine."

"Good. You know that Captain Auferman will be gone for

a while. You are the only Russian-speaking soldier in your detachment. So you will be in charge. It's a bit awkward as far as ranks are concerned. If you have any problems come to me." There were no problems, although Sergeant Klughart didn't quite know what to make of the situation.

The first case I was involved in was the deployment of two agents to observe traffic on the Arkhangelsk-Vologda railroad where the U.S. lend-lease supplies came in. Most of the documentation work was handled by Zorin while I coordinated work in the shop. Goebel took this opportunity to instruct me on all its technical aspects. He was in his forties with an alert mind and not much education, but he knew his business.

"Only the military can afford such inefficiency," he told me. "At home I would soon be out of business; my employees would complain to the Arbeitsfront." Goebel was a party member and very proud of his employer-employee relations. "Here we sit and carve wood as if it were for the Germanisches Museum." His disdain for the military he showed also after work by addressing Sergeant Klughart in jest. "Request to be excused Sergeant." Then he left the house and compound through a nearby hole cut in the wire fence and went to a Polish woman he knew to buy "bimber" he said, the name for local moonshine. Although dissatisfied with the ways of the army, he was always in good spirits.

During his visit to the southern front Captain Auferman became ill and was transferred to a hospital in Berlin. He didn't return to his duties until early in the new year.

One day the Rittmeister called me to his office and spread on his desk a pile of photographs of German officers, mug shots used in military identity records.

"Can you alter these for use in Soviet documents?" he asked.

"We can try."

"Try your best. It's urgent."

We set to work altering the photographs, replacing the German uniforms with Soviet ones. Then we used the photographs to complete Soviet military documents issued by units we knew were on the Stalingrad front. Zorin and I worked for several days filling out the documents. We never learned the purpose of it all but, in any case, the operation was cancelled and the documents returned to us for destruction.

When I delivered the fruits of our labor to the commander, I used the occasion to report the inadequacies of our equipment and our dependence on Berlin. The Rittmeister listened and promised to give it some consideration. A few days later he told me that Major Baun, Chief, Staff Walli I, had authorized my travel to Berlin to procure needed equipment. Walter Goebel rejoiced and together we made a list: a big reproduction camera, dark room and etching equipment, and type fonts. Sergeant Klughart expressed doubts that our captain would approve of our initiative.

In accordance with my orders I reported at I-G Headquarters in Berlin. Colonel Mueller, the department chief, was out and his secretary suggested that in the meantime I consult with the staff technicians who would provide me with information and folders of companies where the equipment could be procured. I also visited a Russian-speaking lieutenant in charge of Soviet document archives which were stacked up in cartons by the hundreds of thousands for evaluation. The lieutenant complained bitterly that he only had two helpers and it would take the rest of his life to complete the task.

Eventually I was called to report to the colonel who was visibly irritated. "Return to your unit," he ordered. "Tell Major Baun that if he needs anything he should follow proper channels and procedures." I saluted and left, taking with me

the catalogues and folders I had collected. Upon return to Suleyovek I submitted my report and the collected materials to
the Rittmeister.

In Berlin I stayed with the Holls, where the mood was
somber. They had not heard from Ernst in Stalingrad and
knew that the situation there was critical if not hopeless. Only
Martha, the eternal optimist, was sure that Ernst would be all
right; she was proven wrong.

Early in 1943 I was dispatched to Warsaw to a hotel to
meet a Major Mayer-Mader. At the hotel desk I was given the
major's room number. When I knocked, the door was opened
by a lieutenant in a smart new uniform. I noticed on his
sleeve a St. Andrew's shield, the emblem of General Vlasov's
ROA. A middle-aged man in a pullover sat behind a desk.
There were three more ROA lieutenants who all had Muslim
names; one of them had an artificial leg. During our meeting
I learned that the major, the man behind the desk, was Commander of the Turkestan Legion, consisting of former POWs.
With a few selected men, he intended to land by plane in Soviet Turkestan in order to organize a muslim movement. He
needed technical support and advice, and wanted me to come
to his farm near Berlin.

I received my travel orders and spent a week at the farm
discussing the issues involved. I also learned that the major
and his wife had spent many years in China where he was a
military adviser to a warlord and knew Singkiang well. The
officer with the artificial leg, a former Soviet fighter pilot,
would be the plane's pilot. He had lost his leg when parachut-
ing behind German lines and was shot at by another Soviet
pilot; according to Stalin's orders: Soviet soldiers should not
be captured alive.

I spent some weeks both at the farm and in Berlin until orders came to abandon the project after the German defeat at

Stalingrad. Later I learned that, upon return to his Turkestan Legion, the major committed suicide.

## EAST PRUSSIA

While I was at Mayer-Mader's farm our school and unit were transferred from Suleyovek to East Prussia. Grossraum, a small rail station, was located in a forest halfway between Koenigsberg and the Baltic beaches. It was a mile's walk through the forest to the compound, commonly referred to as "the forestry." A villa and several brick buildings housed officers' quarters, a kitchen, mess hall, garage, and warehouse. Military-type wooden barracks were scattered around the woods housing the school, its Russian staff, and our I-G offices and living quarters. Our commander, the Rittmeister, just promoted to major, occupied the forester's villa with his new assistant, Miss Morgenstern. She came from Danzig and was an old Abwehr hand.

It was still winter when a moving van arrived in front of our barrack. I was returning from the mess hall and saw an excited Captain Auferman wave a bill of lading in his hand and talk to a lieutenant who had arrived with the transport.

"Who ordered all this stuff?" the captain shouted as I saluted. I told him that, in a way, I had.

"God damn! What got into you? What good is it? The more one has, the more one is responsible for." The upset captain and the lieutenant departed to see the commander. Our men came out to inspect the load. After a while the officers returned, the captain looking dejected. He told us to unload the van. Walter, smiling happily, ran to the mess hall to mobilize some help.

We unloaded a big reproduction camera, dark room equipment, etching materials, and complete sets of printing types from "Berthold," the company which, in the past, had supplied Soviet printing establishments. Now our outfit needed more personnel, and it wasn't long before graphic artists and technicians arrived.

One evening in our room Walter Goebel told me, "You should meet the new girl who arrived at officers' quarters. Her name is Maria. She is beautiful, a real lady. She is Russian and came from Staff Regenau in Warsaw." Staff Regenau was an intelligence unit consisting of old-time Russian émigrés, mostly officers.

I didn't have an opportunity to meet her until one day a group of us went to see Schiller's "Maria Stuart" at the Koenigsberg theatre. Because of an air raid warning the performance started late and, when it was over, we caught the last train which took us only halfway to our station. We had to walk a good stretch to the compound. It was a starry night and a good chance to get acquainted with Maria; we enjoyed flirting for the two hours it took us to get home, but after that we had little opportunity to meet again.

Maria was staying in the transit officers' quarters where I had no business and I was surprised one day when she appeared in our barrack to say goodbye. She had been ordered back to Warsaw; there had been some unpleasantness among the officers caused by her presence and the commander deemed it best for her to return to Staff Regenau where her father worked.

It was an abrupt ending of what had been just a beginning. The bond between us was our native tongue. I loved her melodious accent of old Russia. She loved me for coming from the phantom homeland the émigrés could not forget. War is a fertile time for fantasy, without concern for dreams. It was a sad goodbye. We had no expectation of meeting again.

One day a few weeks later the phone rang and Captain Auferman picked it up. "Yes, Miss Morgenstern. Of course,

Miss Morgenstern. In Warsaw? Well, Miss, I don't know. Of course, if you say so, Miss Morgenstern. I'll send Matern over right away.

"Matern, go over to the chief. There is some typographical equipment in Warsaw. Find out what the story is."

At the office the major told me that our procurement officer from Suleyovek had called. There was typographical equipment for sale by a local Russian newspaper in Warsaw. I was to go there and see if it would be of use to us. With the usual travel papers — *im Auftrag des Geheimen Meldedienstes* (on behalf of the secret information service) — I left for Warsaw.

The supply officer occupied a country house surrounded by a high wooden fence. Several Tatars served him as caretakers, bodyguards, and cooks. When they let me in I found the lieutenant with another officer drinking wine and target shooting in an enclosed veranda. I was welcomed and asked to join in; my business had to wait until the next day. Late in the evening, after supper and more drinking, the Tatars helped us to our beds.

The next morning I was introduced to a young Russian-speaking woman. She took me to Warsaw; on the train she told me that she had been married to a Soviet officer stationed in Lithuania. Her husband retreated with the Soviet Army but she stayed on; later she went west to Warsaw and now lived there with a new "Polish husband."

In Warsaw she escorted me to an apartment building, told me the apartment number, and we parted. When I rang there the door was opened by Maria. The surprise was mutual. She introduced me to her father who arranged for a car to take me to the print shop in town.

It was dark by the time the car arrived. The shop was in an old part of the city; the driver stopped at a main intersection and pointed out the dark street where I would find the shop.

When I was ready he would come to load my purchases. I found the shop; there was light inside. Two men were waiting for me. They spoke Russian, had printed samples of the typefaces for sale, and asked me to write down what I wanted. With my list one of the men went back into the shop to have my purchases packed. Meanwhile the other one engaged me in conversation.

Despite my uniform he didn't quite believe that I was a German soldier; I also didn't speak Russian like an old Russian immigrant and my handwriting conformed to the new Soviet orthography. Maybe I was a Soviet? But, no matter; even if I had come down on a Soviet parachute, a deal was a deal. Typefaces are heavy; they had prepared four packages, each one light enough to be lifted with one arm. I went back to my car; we drove to the shop and loaded my purchase.

In the evening I went with Maria, her sister, and a Waffen SS officer to the Hotel Bristol for supper, with entertainment and dancing. Late in the evening I became concerned about the midnight curfew for soldiers but the officer told me not to worry. We stayed until the music stopped. When we were leaving the hotel, a military police patrol stopped me. My companion intervened, I showed my travel orders and, after a written report was made out, the patrol let me go.

We walked a long way back through the city under starry skies as at our first encounter. Tomorrow it was goodbye again with little hope of a third chance.

The next morning Maria brought me to the railroad station. As we were kissing goodbye, planes flew over the city and we heard explosions. It was April 19, 1943. Back at headquarters I learned that there had been an uprising in the Warsaw ghetto.

Soon after my return from Warsaw a telephone call came in. The captain picked it up. He rose to attention and I gathered that it was Major Baun. When the conversation ended the captain told me that I was under house arrest for five days.

"What the devil were you doing in Warsaw? The military police reported you to Staff Wall I." He called in Sergeant Klughart.

"Klughart, Matern is to be kept under arrest. Take him to his room and lock him in. You'll bring him his daily ration and take him out for half an hour's walk after work. Goebel will have to move to another room for the time being."

A day later I could hear our captain on the telephone asking whether it was permissible for me to work while under arrest.

"Yes, here at my office. Good. Thank you ma'am."

A few days later Miss Morgenstern told me, laughing: "I released you from your cell. When you're in Warsaw next time try wearing civilian clothes." Only Klughart was unhappy; it was just more work for him.

## IN RUSSIA AGAIN

In the spring of 1943 our Russian instructors became officers of the ROA, Zorin with the rank of major. He never bought himself a uniform and continued to wear his black civilian suit and boots. By now he had been on the job a year and a half and had issued hundreds of documents with thousands of entries: residence and employment, promotions and transfers, assignments and salaries, equipment and decorations. Zorin wanted help; he also wanted to get out of the office for a while and travel to occupied Russia.

It was decided that Zorin and I would undertake a trip to the central front at Smolensk. We traveled by train to Army Group Center, visited the I-G Detachment there, and conferred with its Russian staff, also former Soviet officers. We also examined the most recent information and captured documents, interviewed recent prisoners, looked over their documents, and searched among them for a new assistant to Zorin, preferably an NCO familiar with up-to-date staff procedures. Zorin found a man to his liking.

In April 1943, the German Army discovered a mass grave of Polish officers who had been executed by the Soviets in 1940 in the Katyn forest. Zorin insisted on visiting Katyn. The mass graves were open for inspection by representatives from neutral countries. At Katyn a large crowd was looking at the graves; Zorin examined the place in detail and talked with various people working there, on the slight hope that he could get information from them about the remains of his former colleagues, Soviet officers, who had been executed during the 1938 purges.

Zorin returned to Königsberg. My assignment was to visit frontline intelligence units in Orel, Akhtyrka, and Kharkov; my route skirted the Kursk salient, the stage for a coming battle.

While originally our task was to support agents dropped in the hinterland who then reported by radio, the situation after Stalingrad changed. Now most agents were sent closer to the front to report on the deployment of Soviet forces. These agents had no radio and returned to the German side by crossing the front line. Soviet security measures in these areas became of paramount importance to us, and my purpose for visiting our front line reconnaissance commandos and prisoner assembly points was to collect up-to-date information and materials relevant to these issues.

I flew from Smolensk to Orel on my first flight ever in a Heinkel plane of the Special Air Squadron which deployed our agents behind enemy lines. Gustav, a young Russian-speaking corporal from Berlin, met me at the airfield. He was one of the few who had left the Soviet Union with his family in the thirties.

The intelligence unit occupied a former estate, more recently a Soviet state farm. The old mansion was beautifully located on the high bank of the Oka River. Across the river was a picturesque village with a white church tower topped by its onion-shaped dome. One could see the tower gleaming in the moonlight as we had supper on the veranda overlooking the river. The cooking was Russian, the bread fresh from the oven, all prepared by a village woman and served by young village girls; afterwards they sang Russian folk songs to the accompaniment of a guitar. It was a vision of times gone by.

"Have you shown our guest your establishment, Gustav?" asked the lieutenant.

"Not yet."

"When you see it don't talk about it to anyone here," the lieutenant told me.

The next day Gustav and I drove to his office, a cluster of small buildings in a remote area of the farm enclosed by a barbed-wire fence. It housed four engravers, Jewish watchmakers whom Gustav had brought from Orel. (A year later during the German retreat Gustav hid them in the forest to await the arrival of Soviet troops.)

Gustav was preparing a "drop" and we did some work together. In the evening we drove to a safe house, picked up two Russians with their equipment, and drove together to the airfield. The plane which had brought me the evening before stood ready for departure. The two agents boarded the plane with their equipment and took off. We waited at the airfield for the plane's return to get a report on the drop from the crew. Papers were signed and we went back to the farm.

From Orel I traveled by freight trains to the commandos in Akhtyrka and Kharkov about 300 miles to the south. Kharkov, the largest industrial city of the Ukraine, had changed hands three times. There I looked for materials of use to us such as newsprint, photographic paper, cloth, and typeface.

On my way back I stopped in Kiev to see Mr. John whom I knew from my 1925 visit to Tallinn where he had been a representataive of Renault cars and had given me a bicycle to use during my visit there. Now he headed the Kiev office of a German corporation. We had lunch together and he complained about the difficulties of doing business in occupied Ukraine, the fiefdom of Reichskommissar Koch.

"Koch's sole concern is to dispatch young men and women for work in Germany. Any effort to do constructive work in Kiev runs against the wall of bureaucracy in Rovno where Koch reigns like a czar."

After some sightseeing, including its famous cloister, I stopped at a mess for military personnel. It was empty at this time of day; two waitresses were chatting in a corner and paid little attention to a low-ranking customer. Finally one of them came and — in broken German — asked what I wanted; I asked her in Russian what was available. She was surprised but tried not to show it. When she brought my order I engaged her in a conversation. Her name was Marina and her attitude became much friendlier. I asked her whether she would be working the next day. She said it was her day off. What did she do on a free day? She would go with her son to the beach across the river to spend a day in the sun.

The next day I went to the beach which Marina had described. It was a big sandy area nearly empty of people; I spotted a female figure and a child in the distance. Marina didn't seem surprised when she saw me. It was a sunny day but rather windy and, after a while, we agreed to go back into town. On the way she asked whether I would like to meet some of her friends. We could have supper at their place. She bought food at the market and I stopped at the PX for cigarettes and travel rations.

Marina's friends, a middle-aged couple, lived in a big apartment complex of recent vintage. They were educated people who had worked at an agricultural research institution and spoke some German and French. They were eager to hear news from Kharkov and the situation at the front, fearing a German retreat and the return of the Soviets. They knew that the population in recovered areas was always under suspicion of having collaborated with the enemy and faced persecution.

We had supper and vodka; it was getting dark when we left our hosts. Marina asked me to accompany her and her son to their home. We walked to a different part of town and, when we came to a street with older, smaller houses, she asked me to wait; she went ahead to take care of her boy and showed me a place where she would meet me. Obviously she didn't want to be seen entering the house with a soldier. It was as if I were back in Moscow trying not to be seen while entering and leaving Irina's apartment.

After walking around for a while and returning to our meeting place, I found Marina waiting for me; we entered her room through a small garden. The room was sparsely furnished: bed, chest of drawers, bookshelf, and a low small table with cushions spread around it on the floor. A candle was burning. Marina left the room and returned with a kettle of hot water. We sat down on the cushions and had tea.

"Now tell me, where do you come from?" Marina asked.

"From Kharkov."

"Do you know my husband?"

"No, how should I?"

"Do you know that he was arrested?"

"No, I am not with the police."

Marina smiled. "Don't tell me you are a German."

"I am from Leningrad. My wife lives in Moscow," I said, "but I am a German soldier."

She looked straight into my eyes, seemed to believe me and to feel relieved. We sat silent for a while.

"Whoever you are, it doesn't matter now."

We talked long into the night, two orphans of the war, occupier and occupied, for better or for worse. Our sleep was short. Marina told me about her husband, an athlete with the "Dynamo Club," who left the city shortly before it fell. Some months ago he returned but did not stay; he was on assignment and hiding somewhere. But something went wrong; he was arrested and had let her know that he was in a nearby camp. She brought him a "peredacha" but soon he was transferred. From the first moment Marina did not believe I was a German soldier; she assumed I was a follow-up Soviet agent in German uniform.

Early in the morning, as I was leaving through the garden, she asked, "Will I see you again?" She touched my forehead, chest, and shoulders, making the sign of the cross. "May God protect you." As I turned again to go, she called out to me.

"Wait where you did yesterday. I'll come with you to the rail station."

I saw Marina once more when I came to Kiev a few months later. This time it was a very short stopover. I looked her up at the mess hall. She took off from work to write a letter to relatives in Poland and asked me to mail it. She had decided to leave and make it somehow to Poland. I never heard from her again.

On that trip I had come to Kiev from Zaporozhye where the apricots were ripe. It was August 1943, and my last trip to Russia. I had left Grossraum with Rautenberg, one of our draftsmen from Hamburg. Hamburg had just been bombed for several days with tens of thousands dead and hundreds of thousands homeless; Rautenberg went on home leave. I took off from Königsberg for Lemberg (now Russian Lvov) with an air force lieutenant in his small private plane. There I boarded a Junkers-52 for Zaporozhye. It was loaded with spare engines and parts. The pilots had girlfriends at the airport and flew a low goodbye loop over the terminal during which the heavy load where I was sitting began to shift. It did not seem to bother the pilot and we landed safely at Dnepropetrovsk near Zaporozhye, site of the great Dnieper River Dam and a region where early German colonists had settled.

There the I-G Detachment South had its quarters in a former German settlement with comfortable houses and big orchards. I remember this trip mainly for the deliciously sweet apricots which we picked from trees just outside the office. My travel through the bleak Donets industrial region, soon the theater of a new Soviet offensive, was short. I returned to Kiev on a small courier plane sitting in back among bags of mail. Between my legs I could watch the passing landscape through a hole in the floor like a live geographic map. The plane was of canvas construction and the hole, the pilot told me with a laugh, was just a lucky hole from a shell.

After meeting Marina I boarded an Army Supreme Command Junkers passenger plane which flew to Rastenburg, the airfield where later Stauffenberg landed to deliver a bomb to Hitler's headquarters.

We flew low just above the trees over the endless forests of the region encompassing parts of Ukraine, Belorussia, and Poland, and harboring Ukrainian, Russian, and Polish partisans. Sometime later the pilot of this plane was shot down over these forests.

# 13

## Dark Clouds

**1943**

The year 1943 had begun with the German defeat at Stalingrad, followed by the retreat from the North Caucasus. Thus my hope to see Irina vanished.

The *Sondermeldungen* (victory reports) continued on the radio from the Atlantic Front; great amounts of tonnage had been sunk by German U-boats. Our supply and accounting clerks, Corporal Frenkel and Private Niekirch, listened regularly to the BBC in their quarters. Frenkel, once a buyer for KdW, the great Berlin department store, had traveled abroad, including to the United States. One evening when a few of us were sitting together talking about the war he asserted: "Germany has lost the war. It doesn't matter how many ships we sink; what matters is how many come through to England and Russia. American industrial capacity is enormous; it is only a matter of time."

In the fall Rzhev, Sychevka, and Vyazma fell. Orel was abandoned and, by November 1943, Kiev as well. I thought of all the people I knew there and wondered how they were faring. A retreat always means destruction; the Germans could be more thorough at that than the Soviets.

With the German retreat, a flow of refugees from the Caucasus, Crimea, and Ukraine moved west: Chechens, Kalmuks, Tatars, Armenians, Ukrainians. In June, mother wrote me of the news she had from Martha Holl. Professor Schaak, our neighbor on Litseyskaya Street, and his wife were in Berlin. Mother was going there to see them; I was able to arrange a trip to Berlin too. Professor Schaak and his wife, also a doctor, were working at a Berlin hospital for Russian patients. We saw them there and they told us that my sister had survived the terrible Leningrad winter of 1941-42 and was evacuated in April 1942. The Schaaks were evacuated later with the medical school and ended up in the North Caucasus. When the German army occupied the region they were evacuated to Germany. What happened to Ira after she left Leningrad, they didn't know.

German cities were now bombed with increased ferocity. Total war had been officially declared. But there were still horse races at Berlin's Karlshorst. I did some drawings there which I still have. I always carried a sketch book on my travels and back at the shop had the opportunity to make my first etchings. Soldiers whose families were affected by bombings went on short home leaves. Walter Goebel was one of them. His business and his parents' home in Nuremberg's old city center were destroyed; the house where his wife and two children lived was damaged but they were all alive.

Daily tasks kept us busy at the office. With changes at the front, tactical reconnaissance became ever more important. We had successes and failures. Some agents disappeared — either caught or giving up. However, we were now better equipped to cope with contingencies. For every operation a new set of documents was printed to prevent SMERSH from discovering and recording distinguishing marks.

Zorin and I often talked about the situation on the eastern front, the U.S. Lend-Lease supplies arriving in the Soviet Union, and the "Fortress Europe" concept in the west. Zorin's concern was the second front on which Stalin constantly insisted. If the Americans and British secured a foothold in France and were not thrown back decisively, his conclusion as a professional military officer was that Germany would lose the war. But, for both of us, the situation on the eastern front was of much greater emotional concern. Although Russian prisoners of war and *ost* workers — those mobilized for work in Germany — now were treated reasonably, the foolishness of *ostpolitik*, Germany's policy in the east, had passed the point of no return: the possibility of establishing a Russian government, a political arm for the ROA and a liberation movement, had now passed. The situation on other fronts in Africa, Italy, or Greece, and later even in France, had little emotional impact on me. How the war would end in the west was irrelevant.

Among the German staff, the concern was predominantly about their families back home and the bombing of German cities. The most discouraged among us seemed to be the few who had been Party members, Goebel among them.

Shortly before Christmas 1943, I was in Königsberg meeting one of our occasional visitors sent to us for training and deployment to front line detachments. His appearance was unusual. He was in his forties, and over a civilian suit he wore the green poncho of a Soviet officer. From the way he spoke German I knew immediately that he was from my home town. It didn't take long to establish that he was also a graduate of the Petri School, ahead of me by eleven years, and a geometry professor at the Leningrad Polytechnical Institute. We often talked about people and places we both knew and he told me his own war story. His name was Misha Vogt.[29]

## 1944

Misha stayed with us until the New Year and was then deployed to the Intelligence Command in Pskov. There was another curious coincidence in that Misha's cousin in Berlin was also a Petri School graduate and a good friend of my Aunt Vera's; they had played tennis together in Petersburg before World War I.

The year 1944 began uneventfully. Except for a few British night air raids over Königsberg, East Prussia was still a quiet corner of the country. After air raids we were sent out into the woods and fields to look for Allied airmen who parachuted from shotdown bombers and to protect them from possible assaults by civilians.

In the spring I was sent to NCO school in Kalisch in preparation for officer's training. It was a welcome diversion and I even enjoyed it. Most of the training was outdoors. The weather was fine, the landscape pleasant, the exercise healthy, and food pretty good. After the training I went on home leave. Eisenach was not bombed although there was a BMW plant nearby, but nights were often spent in the basement listening to the air armadas flying over our heads.

Upon my return and, as the weeks went by, the character of our work changed. With the retreat of German armies from Russian territory, the deployment of Russian agents decreased; there were fewer volunteers and, among those who did volunteer, questions of reliability were raised. Eventually our training camp became deserted and the Russian instructors spent many days in Kranz, a sea resort half an hour away

---

[29] For Misha's story see Appendix Five.

by train. A cousin of mine came to Kranz with her little daughter both to avoid nights in bomb shelters and to enjoy the beach.

Agents were now recruited among Estonians, Latvians, and Lithuanians and were trained by front line commandos. We supplied them technical support based on our current files and *Fremde Heere Ost* (FHO) — Foreign Armies East — maps showing the deployment of Soviet armed forces.

For me there was more travel to Berlin and Jüterbog to assist an SS sabotage staff. Ever since Admiral Canaris, Chief of the Abwehr, had been removed from office, we were increasingly called upon for support of the SS intelligence service. The assignment was to retrieve a unit of German and Russian Waffen SS men from behind Soviet lines where they had been deployed to destroy Soviet communications and supply lines. The unit was to be brought back across the front lines. I suggested equipping it as a Soviet front broadcast propaganda unit; German POWs had been used at the front to broadcast anti-Nazi propaganda.

We went to the Oranienburg concentration camp where uniforms for this operation were being made. I didn't enter the camp itself but conferred at the front office with various men, some in SS uniforms, some in striped prisoners' garb. Everybody was very businesslike and it all reminded me of Bamlag. Sometimes it seemed to me that the difference between soldier and prisoner was mainly the uniform worn, and that a prisoner had a better chance of survival than a front line soldier. Back in Berlin we went to a Grünewald villa occupied by the SS Technical Assistance Staff. To my surprise I met there the Tatar pilot of Meyer-Mader's crew who was now in an SS uniform. On my travels I had met Waffen-SS men of many nationalities: Spaniards, Danes, Belgians, Norwegians, Dutch, and recently French of the Charlemagne Division.

The Allied landing in France Zorin had feared came on

June 6, D-Day. For days he was preoccupied with listening to the radio together with his friend, the radio communications instructor.

In July I went by train to Riga to assist Commando Zeppelin in an operation to penetrate Soviet Supreme Command Headquarters. I didn't think much of the plan, nor of the Soviet major and his female companion who were the agents. But this was not for me to judge. We supplied them with what they requested, including front pages of Pravda with a portrait of the major decorated with the Golden Star as a Hero of the Soviet Union. Twenty years later I came across an article in the Soviet newspaper *Izvestia* headlined "Duels with the Fascist Reconnaissance:"[30]

> In September 1944 two fascist agents were apprehended by security organs in the Smolensk region. One of them had documents of a Red Army major. The woman pretended to be his wife. These agents landed by German airplane; they had a motorcycle, a special weapon with nine shells capable of penetrating armor of 35 to 44 mm at a distance of 300 meters; they had 7 different pistols, a radio-triggered mine, a portable radio sender as well as codes and invisible inks. The man had several medals and orders including a Golden Star of a Hero of the Soviet Union. He also had false newspaper clippings referring to the granting of these awards. Their objective was to penetrate the headquarters of the Supreme Commander of the Soviet Army.

It was on my return trip from Riga that I learned about the events of July 20, the last failed attempt on Hitler's life. The mood of the staff was subdued and ambivalent; some were stunned that this could happen, others that it failed. But the war went on, and failure has no champions.

---

[30] *Izvestia*, issue No. 78, 1965.

Later Misha told me his recollection of that day: on the retreat from Estonia they were getting a delousing before crossing the German border. They were in the bathhouse cleaning themselves with the gray ointment when the water stopped. Then the door flung open and an SS officer in black uniform with a red arm band shouted, "There was an attempt on the Fuehrer's life. The Fuehrer lives. Heil Hitler!" There they stood itching and with no water; eventually the water was restored and they were deloused.

To keep Zorin occupied, a trip was arranged for us to go to the POW camp in Burg near Magdeburg to debrief Soviet officers recently taken prisoner and to win them for the ROA cause. It was, of course, a futile attempt; certain now of their victory, the officers were no longer interested in Vlasov. Whenever Zorin brought up the subject of the 1938 army purges, the officers replied that now Stalin would have to listen to the soldiers, the true victors. Zorin laughed. "When you go home on leave you are not even permitted to carry your pistol."

On the way back we stopped over in Berlin at the Holls and went to "Medved" (The Bear), a Russian restaurant; as in Petersburg, a stuffed upright bear guarded the entrance and there were the familiar Gypsy songs and guitar music.

Among the agents in training this fall was a beautiful young girl from Tallinn, the daughter of a prominent Estonian deported by the Soviets in 1940; she had lodgings at a Königsberg hotel. From our Russian staff, only the counterintelligence instructor met her; Niekirch accompanied her back to Tallinn. When everything was settled there she asked Niekirch to thank everyone, but not to bother establishing radio contact. She intended to take up communication with Sweden and England. Our major was not very surprised about her defection.

In September 1944 one of the last boats from Tallinn was

docking in Danzig. Among its evacuees was a young Estonian couple with a baby; the father had been our resident agent in Estonia and I was to meet them at the boat's landing. Danzig, known for its beautiful ancient brick architecture, had not yet sustained any damage and when I arrived, the ship had not yet come in. There was time to walk around town to see the beautiful old residences, the famous brick cathedral, and ancient warehouses along the harbour.

The Estonian family disembarked amid hundreds of passengers, mostly civilians, and all assembled at a big restaurant for processing and evacuation. I waited there with my charges for a train to Königsberg due late that night; the other arrivals were waiting for an earlier train west to Berlin. At a nearby table I noticed an attractive girl whom the Estonian couple knew and I asked to be introduced. I learned that Agnes — that was the girl's name — was going to Potsdam to join her married sister who had left Tallinn earlier. At the station, before her train left, Agnes gave me her Potsdam address.

Soon after returning to Grossraum, orders came to relocate to Harnekop, an old estate east of Berlin which belonged to an Abwehr officer. I was dispatched to several estates in East Prussia which belonged to Abwehr officers to inform their families of the dates for their evacuation. It was a secret assignment because any evacuation of civilians was prohibited by Government and Party authorities.

When my detachment left for Harnekop, I remained in Grossraum where our quarters had been taken over by a Lithuanian intelligence staff under Colonel Vilkutaitis. I was to assist this staff and traveled with the colonel by car to Lithuania where a network of agents was organized to be left behind Soviet lines. For the first time I would be in direct radio communication with agents to instruct them in the use of documents and to receive from them new documentation intelligence.

However, in November I was ordered to join my staff in Harnekop. The train ride from Königsberg to Berlin was a long one and followed the Baltic coast rather than the usual way via Posen. As the train proceeded west we stopped several times on account of air raids. There were frequent controls by military police which were of much concern to other ranks. Field Marshal Schoerner, known as "Heldenklau" (hero grabber), had issued orders to apprehend soldiers on nonessential duty and send them to the front. My travel orders proved sufficient, however, to proceed to my destination.

At Harnekop our staff was idle. Only the shop was busy supplying front detachments with new documents, stamps, and seals. I was dispatched to Cracow and units along the Vistula River where a big Soviet offensive was expected. Cracow, a beautiful ancient city and meeting place of many cultures, had escaped destruction.

Upon return to Harnekop I had an opportunity to travel to Potsdam where I found out that Agnes was living and working at the Potsdam Officers School. I met Agnes for a walk and lunch at a local restaurant. The simple meal contrasted with the ambiance of its patrician setting, more a Victorian sitting room than a public place. Until the last days of war, Potsdam escaped destruction and retained much of its stolid, semi-feudal character.

When Agnes failed to appear at a rendez-vous later that year I returned to Berlin distraught and went to a movie theatre at the Zoo Station. The movie was preceded by a newsreel which showed the beginning of the German Ardennes offensive, the Battle of the Bulge, the tremendous artillery barrages and Panzer columns roaring into Belgium. It was incomprehensible to me that German forces were engaged in such an offensive on the western front while Soviet forces with a five to one preponderance in men and arms stood in the east at Berlin's doorstep.

I left the movie theatre upset and, staying overnight at Corporal Frenkel's apartment near Tempelhof Airport, listened to the radio and tried to imagine reasons why Agnes had missed our rendezvous. It was a night without bombing.

Christmas 1944 came. It was the third Christmas with my staff, who now seemed like family. Home was wherever they were. Agnes came to Harnekop for a holiday and I arranged quarters for her in the village where our Russian officers stayed. There we had a small Christmas party with plenty of food and wine. No one talked about the future; everyone reminisced about the past, of Christmases in Riga, Nuremberg, or Hamburg or the Erzgebirge on the Bohemian border. Agnes tried to be brave. She was only 19; her mother was now in Soviet Tallinn; her married sister had left Potsdam, moving west. Agnes never told me about her father and I didn't ask. Had he been "taken" in 1940 by the Soviets? Or fled with them in 1941? Or was he dead? Or her parents divorced? One didn't ask such questions then. Agnes was now alone and I felt she leaned on me as on an older brother. I gave her my mother's address; whatever might happen in the future she could go there. We took a long walk through the snowed-in forest before I brought her to the train and she went back to Potsdam.

In 1945, when leaving Berlin for Dresden, I stopped over in Potsdam to learn that the Officers' School had been disbanded and Agnes had left, address unknown.

# 14

## Last Train to Nowhere

**1945**

By New Year's 1945 the Ardennes offensive had faltered but the bombing continued. Why didn't we use all our forces to defend the eastern borders? Let the Western powers come; at least the bombing would stop. Whatever the outcome, the danger for me was from the east. When Stalin declared that "Hitlers come and go but the German people and the German State go on," I had no illusions as to what kind of state he meant it to be.

During January we often were sent out on patrol to look for Soviet parachutists but found none. The Red Army reached the Oder River near Goeben and Oppeln, still 350 kilometers to the southeast. As the Soviets advanced through Prussia, Poland, Pomerania, and Silesia, millions of refugees were moving west. Among them were Aunt Vera, Edith, and Erna. They came to Berlin to Erica Nicol whose house in Wannsee was spared from bombing as were most of the suburbs west of Berlin.

Staff Walli left Harnekop in late January. For the third

time we loaded our equipment and archives on box cars. But I was not to go with my staff; instead I was to report at I-G headquarters in Berlin for an officer's training course in Dresden. To go to officers' school now was a surprising but not unappealing prospect. The future of our staff seemed uncertain; there was no school, no agents, no need for our type of activity. The war was coming to an end. Besides, I had no choice in the matter.

I-G headquarters had moved from central Berlin to the Dahlem suburb. On a sunny clear morning the truck I was riding in stopped short of the city because of an air raid. From a safe distance, we watched hundreds of bombers flying in formation, dropping their loads on the center of Berlin. After the raid, the truck took me to the edge of the city where the fires began. Dahlem was at the opposite end of Berlin. I decided to go first to Hotel Pension Gessler to see how its inhabitants had fared. A group of us, mostly soldiers, set out to walk through the burning center, avoiding the worst fires and protecting ourselves with blankets against the wind and debris flying from the firestorm. I reached the Holls by late afternoon and found them unhurt but blackened from soot and dirt and the building still standing. Located only half a block from Anhalter Rail Station, the house had burned on various occasions but its residents always had been able to extinguish the fires.

I left them at dusk. In the vicinity of Tauentzien Street field kitchens were dispensing food. From there I was directed to a subway station still in operation; Dahlem is on the subway line.

The big old villa now housing I-G Headquarters was dark. I rang the bell and was met by an old sergeant; no officers were there. Several sergeants, all older men, were sitting in a big basement kitchen and there was food, light, and even hot water. I was dirty and was offered a bath before the meal, a bath fit for kings. To my amazement, an old sergeant picked up my dirty uniform for cleaning and brought me big bath towels and a fancy bathrobe. After the meal I expressed my astonishment to one of the sergeants about the treatment I had received.

"The old man was a valet before the war; it brings back old memories of gracious living in a rich household," he said.

The next day I reported to an officer upstairs and was told that it would take some time until I got my travel papers for Dresden. Meanwhile it was all right for me to go to Wannsee to see my relatives: Erica Nicol, Aunt Vera, Edith, and Erna. Eventually I got my travel orders for Dresden where I was to report first to Baun's staff.

## DRESDEN

Dresden before February 12, 1945, was untouched by the war. It was a strange feeling to arrive at its famous rail station, walk intact city streets, sit in a cafe, watch the girls, and walk along the river past the beautiful sights of Dresden's baroque architecture.

Baun's staff was located in an old hotel on the market plaza not far from the great cupola of Notre Dame Cathedral. The hotel was owned by the family of Mrs. Baun. The baroque building, with an inner court, on the upper floors surrounded by enclosed glass galleries, exuded the atmosphere of times long past. Looking down from the galleries onto the paved courtyard, one could imagine horse-drawn carriages clattering in to unload their elegant passengers.

The first person I met in the hotel lobby was Misha Vogt.

"What are you doing here, Misha?"

"If you want to know the truth, polishing princely boots. I am the last German soldier without rank, so I am polishing Prince Kudashev's boots. Suits me fine; there isn't much else to do here except eat and sleep. Everyone seems to be in transit to somewhere else."

Misha told me that in August while stationed in Silesia he was sent to Litzmanstadt (now Lodz) to become a German citizen. "The SS doctors looked me over in case I had two left feet; they checked head, ears, and so on. I was fit and received a blue certificate; there were also green and red ones but blue was tops; I had to volunteer for the army."

When I reported to the staff officer upstairs I was told that all officer training courses were abolished and the school transferred to the front.

During my few days in Dresden, meals at the hotel were served in the top floor dining hall; well-prepared food was served on Meissen china, the famous blue onion pattern. I waited for new orders; my staff was somewhere in transit.

On February 12, I received orders to take the train to the Bavarian town of Eschenbach and report there to Staff Foreign Armies West (FAW). With their help I was to prepare quarters both for our staff and for refugees, families of officers evacuated from the east.

In the evening, when my train passed Chemnitz, an air armada flew overhead; it was the first wave of Allied planes to bomb Dresden. At a small station we passed a transport and I saw our Russian training staff instructors occupying several box cars. I never saw them again.

## ESCHENBACH

Eschenbach, a small ancient town at the end of a rail sideline, was a quiet place located between Bayreuth and Bohemia. The town hall, a beautiful baroque building, was now in part occupied by the FAW staff. With the German retreat on all fronts, staffs from the eastern and western fronts met in Eschenbach. Quarters were arranged for the expected refugees and our staff was billeted at the local school, part of it an old medieval building with a tower, the rest a modern structure well-suited for our workshops. I established myself in the old tower reached by a spiral stone staircase. The tower had a beautiful view over the town and enough space for a mattress, table, and chair. It was my refuge during the last weeks of the war, where I spent much time reading and drawing.

Our staff and the families of evacuees arrived together. Among the latter was our captain's family and the Estonians I had met in Danzig. A tragedy struck the Estonian family a few days after their arrival; their baby pulled a kettle of boiling water over himself. We buried the little boy at the old Eschenbach cemetery.

After unloading the equipment our staff was idle; the training school had been relocated elsewhere. There were rumors that Colonel Baun was under house arrest in Bad Elster. Our captain spent most of the time with his family. Towards the end of the month old friends reported for reassignment; the first one was Misha Vogt.

"You left Dresden just on time," he told me. "At ten that night the bombs fell. I wasn't at the hotel and ran into a shelter. When it was over and I came out there was a sea of fire."

An officer ordered him and other soldiers to bring the injured to a first-aid station. It took them two hours to reach the station but when they got there the place was on fire. By that time a second alarm sounded. City Hall was nearby but a guard there didn't want to let them in. Misha drew his pistol and they went down into the vaulted basement shelter. There were no doctors or nurses, only Party bureaucrats.

During the second raid the basement filled with fumes. Towards morning an exit was cleared through the rubble. Looking out, one saw only an ocean of flames; once in a while some shadows, figures, rushed past. Misha crawled out with his overcoat over his head for protection against the heat. In the street were burned-out fire trucks and bodies of firemen. Misha set out towards the river passing what he thought was a bombed out department store with mannequins strewn about — female bodies with no hair clad only in underwear. When he saw a female body holding a boy by the hand he realized that these were human bodies. Their hair and clothing had burned off, but then the flames went out for lack of oxygen. Small blue flames and black smoke rose from their intestines. The city smelled of burned flesh. He reached the Podchapel Rail Station to get to Mohorn where his staff was. The rail station was not damaged at all.

"I tried to get on a train but had to buy a ticket first and left my purse at the ticket counter; by the time I returned it was gone. Thus life went on as usual."

From the train he saw American planes coming; it was about noon and they came to work over Dresden one more time. Though he was by now far away, the smell of burned flesh stayed with him for quite a while.

That evening he went back to Dresden with some officers and men from Staff Regenau. The hotel had been destroyed, but Baun and most of his staffers were alive. Mrs. Baun and her family, however, were buried in the basement; an attempt to dig into the basement was futile.

After a few days at Eschenbach, Misha left to join an intelligence detachment in Czechoslovakia. "Until we meet again," he said. And so we did at war's end.

Roderich Holl and Gustav Hoffman also came for reassignments and resupply with updated materials. Roderich went to Army Group North near Stettin, Gustav to Army Group South in Hungary.

One afternoon I was sitting in my tower drawing and reading Rainer Maria Rilke's "The Lay of the Love and Death of Cornet Christopher Rilke." I had collected a small library on my travels, mostly small Insel Editions or Russian books from abandoned village libraries. Goebel always complained: "Books, books, books. Others come back with Ukrainian bacon or lard; you bring only books."

This time Goebel came up the tower stairway. "The captain needs you in his office," he said.

Down in the captain's office was a young SS man.

"Matern, this is Mr. Saar, that is...." he looked at the unfamiliar insignia.

"Oberscharfuehrer, Herr Hauptmann," Saar said. A corporal like myself, I thought.

"Show him around, Matern, and help him in whatever he needs."

It didn't take long for me to find out about Saar; I recognized his Baltic accent. He was younger than I and had grown up in Tallinn. In 1939 the family was resettled and he was drafted into the SS; he came to us from a Berlin office. We established a good relationship and I acquainted him with our work and procedures.

In mid-March Saar and I left for Schneekoppe, today called Sniezka, a mountain straddling the Czech-German border. We carried with us document blanks, stamps, and the latest data on the location of enemy troops. On the train, there were only soldiers. I read Rilke:

Riding, riding, riding, through the day, through the night, through the day.
Riding, riding, riding...

And courage is grown so weary, and longing so great...And always the same picture. One has two eyes too many. Only in the night sometime one seems to know the road. Perhaps we always retrace by night the stretch we have won laboriously in the foreign sun?...

Someone is telling of his mother. A German evidently. Loud
and slow he sets his words. As a girl, binding flowers,
thoughtfully tests flower after flower, not yet knowing what
the whole will come to—: so he fits his words. For joy? For
sorrow? All listen. Even the spitting stops...

Now are they all close to one another, these gentlemen that
come out of France and out of Burgundy, out of the Nether-
lands, out of Carinthia's valleys, from the castles of Bohemia
and from the Emperor Leopold. For what this one tells they
too have experienced, and just as he has. As though there
were but one mother....[31]

We changed trains in Prague, passed the beautiful castle of
Hradec Kralove, and continued on to Trutnov in the moun-
tainous Sudetenland. A cable car took us up Schneekoppe
Mountain to 5,000 feet. From there we had a great view over
the Silesian front. Beautiful fir trees and deep snow covered
the mountain. The big hotel was occupied by SS men and
women; there were horses and skis, food and wine, and the
atmosphere was *après moi le déluge*. We stayed only a few
days, working in a hotel room on the materials we brought.
After our work was done, Saar and I came down from the
mountain and stayed overnight at a farm with a German family; the farmer's two daughters walked with us the next day to
Trutnov and on the way I took a few snapshots which I still
have. Should they leave for Germany, they asked us? We did-
n't know what to say.

On our way back we again changed trains in Prague and I

---

[31] From *The Lay of the Love and Death of Cornet Christopher Rilke*,
Rainer Maria Rilke's story of a Rilke fallen in a campaign against
the Turks in Hungary in 1663. New York: W.W. Norton & Co.,
Inc., 1959, p. 23-27.

wanted to see this beautiful city. Saar didn't want to go with me and stayed at the Commandatur near the station. I rode the streetcars and walked up to Hradcin Castle and down to Charles Bridge, then sat at a cafe in Wenceslas Square which was still alive with people. I noticed the many young men in the streets; in Germany one didn't see young men any more, only their obituaries with Iron Crosses and dates of birth and death. It was late March 1945.

I met Saar at the Prague railroad station; the trains still ran on time and the next day we were back in Eschenbach.

After exchanging my travel rations at the Eschenbach Commandatur, I saw Zorin on the big landing, squatting against the wall as he used to do.

"What are you waiting here for?" I asked. He only waved his arm for me to go on. Then I noticed the soldier with a rifle standing next to Zorin who apparently was under guard. Back at the office I could not find the captain and nobody knew anything about Zorin. When the captain finally arrived he was very agitated. Yes, Zorin was under arrest; no, he didn't know why.

The next morning a call came and the captain asked me to go to Zorin's room, pack some of his belongings, and take them to the prison up the hill on the perimeter of town. It was an ancient building of thick stone walls with small windows and iron bars; it looked like an operatic stage set. I delivered my package. I never saw Zorin again. Years later I learned that some of our Russian staff officers had made use of their radio equipment to establish contact with Soviet forces. Zorin was a close friend of the radio communications instructor. Their communications were overheard by the SD; they were arrested and paid with their lives.

A letter from mother informed me that the Schmiedebergs had left Berlin and arrived in Eisenach, and had rented two rooms in the house where mother lived.

## LAST TRAIN TO NOWHERE

"Wheels must turn for victory" someone said sarcastically as we were loading our files and equipment on a train for the last time. This was a wartime slogan posted at railway installations along with "Enemy Listens In" and "Save Coal."

It was the third week of April. There was a boxcar for our files and equipment, one for our staff, one for a kitchen and supplies, and a platform car for a truck. There was also a sealed boxcar with the private belongings of evacuated families; the families, however, remained in Eschenbach. A passenger car came with personnel from Berlin with two officers and a Russian family of women from three generations. Our Captain Auferman was also accommodated in a compartment of the passenger car.

None of us, including the officers, yet knew our destination. We had heard rumors about a last stand — an Alpine redoubt in the Bavarian and Austrian Alps. We had heard also about the execution of Admiral Canaris, the former Abwehr Chief.

Our first stop was on a cloudless day at the big Regensburg rail yard. There was an air raid and the sky suddenly filled with Allied bombers. We dropped flat into nearby trenches dug by railroad workers. However, the bombs missed the yard and came down on the settlement nearby. We were lucky.

The next morning we skirted Munich; it was burning. We didn't stop there and continued west. At Kaufbeuren a few planes came and we ran out into the fields. Lying flat on my stomach among the young grasses I enjoyed nature's designs close up: a young cloverleaf, drops of morning dew, some tiny bugs crawling busily in the grassy forest. A bomb hit the rail depot and an army warehouse. Then we were rolling again and saw German airplanes landing on an autobahn. These were the first jets, yet unarmed; they took to the air whenever enemy bombers were approaching.

We listened to the radio, mostly to reports about which

cities were bombed. Walter Goebel's Nuremberg was already in American hands. Kienzl, our accountant, who was from Prague, lived in fear that, after the destruction of Dresden, Prague would also be bombed. Prague remained in German hands until the last days of the war but escaped destruction. Kienzl, however, did not survive.

## DESTINATION OBERSTDORF

At the small station of Oberguenzburg our train was moved to a siding. A lieutenant arrived by car with instructions. Our destination was Oberstdorf, fifty kilometers away, a famous ski resort in a valley near the Austrian Alps.

We were to unload our train there. The station master promised us a locomotive the next day. In the morning while shaving in my boxcar, I heard the noise of an airplane. People from other cars were running by towards the station's underpass shouting "air alarm." I looked out. There was a plane overhead with French markings but it had already passed our station. Only when I heard it coming back did I jump out of the car. It was coming low toward the station. I ducked under the car to the other side where the embankment offered protection. Then I was falling head over heels down the embankment and while rolling downhill saw roof tiles flying high through the air like birds; when I landed on even ground, I saw a big roofless warehouse and heard explosions coming from the rail station. Debris was flying through the air.

The captain and some of our men emerged from a road underpass and together we worked ourselves slowly towards the station, taking shelter behind buildings from the exploding munitions. On the embankment our boxcars at the end of the train stood undamaged but, once the station came into view, we saw that everything was gone. No building, no train cars, only a heap of rubble.

When the explosions subsided we heard cries coming from

the station's underpass. We cleared an opening to it and crawled down. At the far end, thrown against the wall, were the dead and injured. The lieutenant from Berlin and his secretary were bleeding from nose and ears; we helped them get out. Our accountant Kienzl from Prague, the cook, and the Russian family were dead.

In time, more help came from the nearby village: soldiers, officials, and firemen. A car came to take the wounded to a nearby cloister. We found a handcart and brought the dead bodies to the village chapel. The captain went with the local authorities to attend to formalities.

Returning to our boxcar late in the afternoon, I saw our Russians carrying cartons from the roofless warehouse.

"Another army warehouse thrown open," they shouted.

"What's in it?"

"Wine and schnapps."

For the rest of the day they carried carton upon carton into our rail car and stacked them up high against the wall.

The next day a railroad crew arrived to clear and repair the tracks. They told us that high explosives for V-2 rockets and munitions had been loaded in the front rail cars and they exploded when the airplane attacked the train.

We were busy the next day. A common grave was dug at a nearby cemetery, coffins were brought, and Rautenberg, our graphic artist, made markers for the dead we knew. From the nearby cloister a priest came for the burial and, except for the captain, everyone, including the priest, was high on the spirits provided by the bombing the day before. A crowd surrounded the grave site, the priest waved his sensor over the grave, and I stood behind him ready to grab him should he lose balance or step too far forward.

When the tracks were fixed, the first train came from the opposite direction. The passengers were Moroccan soldiers of the French Pétain-Laval government. Their train stopped, the

Russians brought cartons of French wine on the platform where French, Moroccans, Germans, and Russians continued to party until the train left. Later our locomotive arrived and we proceeded to Kempten. Sometimes French planes were in the air. Then the crew uncoupled the locomotive and sped away to some sheltered place to return when the danger had passed. At Immenstadt, where the main line continued to Lake Constance, we needed a locomotive to bring us on the dead-end spur to Oberstdorf. To arrange for one I brought bottles of liquor to the station master and locomotive crews.

At Sonthofen our captain went into town to see the local commandant and came back with orders for us to join in the local defense. Just as we were telling the captain that we already had our orders, a lieutenant from Baun arrived with further instructions on where to store the contents of our transport. Our equipment and files should be stored at a house in Oberstdorf; the private family treasures — clothing, porcelain, rugs, silver — at the Hotel Walzerschanz just across the Austrian border. Upon arrival in Oberstdorf it took us two days of loading and unloading the truck to deposit everything at the designated shelters.

Our work completed, the captain told me that our staff was to be divided, some of us to accompany him on our truck to Bavaria, the rest to remain in Oberstdorf. A lieutenant who had joined us at Sonthofen would travel with us to Innsbruck on his way to Italy. Cease fire negotiations between Alan Dulles in Switzerland and SS General Karl Wolf in Italy had been going on since March 1945; a local armistice was arranged on April 29 and scheduled for announcement on May 2.[32] I was to select those to go with our captain; we agreed that Goebel, Rautenberg, and myself would accompa-

---

[32] See also John Keegen. *The Second World War.* New York: Viking-Penguin, 1990, p. 533.

ny him. Goebel, who was already making postwar plans, wanted two of our Russians, the printer and his helper, to come with us to help eventually in rebuilding his business in Nuremberg. Corporal Weiss from our transport joined us to get closer to his home in Leipzig.

A hitch developed when Goebel told me that our truck driver refused to go anywhere except home to Saxony. I went to see the driver. The Soviets were in Saxony, I told him, and certainly he didn't want to go near the Red Army. This did not bother him, he said; he had nothing to fear from them since he had once been a member of the German Communist Party. I suggested it would be closer to home for him from where we were going, but he answered that he wasn't stupid and had heard about the "fortress in the Alps." I reported the situation to the captain who called in the driver. He promised him, on an officer's word of honor, that he would release him as soon as we arrived at our destination in Bavaria. The driver relented and we drove to fill up the tank and gas cans. We were to drive over the Austrian Alps as the crow flies more than two hundred miles east to Chiemsee.

## AUSTRIA

Early the next morning we climbed into the truck with our last carton of spirits and not much else. We drove toward Lake Constance and, via Bregenz, into the Alps to the St. Anton pass where we loaded our truck onto a railroad car in order to pass through the tunnel. The drive through the Alps to Innsbruck was beautiful. I made myself comfortable on the front fender to watch the snow-covered Tyrol mountains pass by. Near Innsbruck the lieutenant said good-bye and left to look for a lift to Italy.

Our destination was Chiemsee in Bavaria, but our captain never confided to us the purpose of the expedition. We had nothing of importance in our luggage. Goebel carried some bottles of spirits; the Russians had a bag of salt; and we had blank documents and travel orders which we could issue for ourselves when needed. Our route to Chiemsee was circuitous but scenic. Using secondary roads we passed St. Johann, stayed a night in Ruhpolding, and continued to Traunstein where some new instructions were obtained by the captain. We turned towards Rosenheim and back into the mountains.

On May 1, in Rosenheim, we heard on our radio that Hitler was dead. The news did not have much impact. One government had been replaced by another one under Admiral Doenitz. We knew that the war was lost and hoped only that the bombing and needless death would cease.

Meanwhile we had to drive on. We stopped in Kufstein where Goebel went to a cafe and exchanged a bottle of spirits for coffee and pastry. Then we drove on to Kitzbuehel and Zell-am-See, still not knowing our destination, but as long as we had provisions and gas it really did not matter. Time went by and the landscape was beautiful.

We made quarters in Zell-am-See. On May 4, the captain drove with the truck to the town commandant; we were out of gas. After a while he came back on foot looking dejected and told us that the truck had been requisitioned. This was now Austria, he was told; Germans must leave the country in short order. We should take off all uniform insignia and proceed north on foot.

The captain was the first to take off his jacket and, using his sewing kit, cut off all his signs of authority. We divided the rest of our rations equally and consulted our maps. Goebel put the last bottle of brandy into his backpack — he didn't mind the added weight — and the next morning we started out on the road north towards the Hochkönig Mountain range and Sea of Rocks.

Short of Saalfelden we took a road veering off east into the mountains. A sign saying "Army Field Bakery, Field Post Number. . ." pointed up the road to a village. The captain went to the bakery office but came back empty-handed. Goebel in the meantime tried the back door of the bakery and returned smiling. He had swiped a loaf of bread while no one watched.

Toward nightfall we reached an old mountain farm. Two women were running the place with the help of a demented young man. There were cows in the stall and milk; we could stay overnight in the barn. They made us *kaiserschmarren*, a dish of eggs, milk, and flour fried in a big pan; we all sat down at a large round table, each seat marked by two dents in the table surface — places where many elbows had rested over the centuries. Between the dents were small drawers under the table with wooden spoons. The big pan, about two feet in diameter, was placed at the center of the table and everyone, with elbows in the dents, dipped his spoon into the pan at regular intervals.

The next morning we continued our ascent. Soon the road ended in a trail and snow covered the ground. We sat down on stones and Goebel cut a good slice of army bread for everyone. While we were munching, a whistling sound came from up the trail. I knew the tune — "It's a long way to Tipperary." A man in a British uniform appeared on the trail with rolled-up sleeves and walking stick in hand. He halted when he saw us, then continued down through the snow.

"How do you do?" he said, sitting down on a stone next to us and lighting a cigarette. Goebel offered him a slice of bread which he took in exchange for cigarettes. I knew enough English, and so did Rautenberg, to strike up a conversation. He was a British officer taken prisoner in Yugoslavia and had been released a few days ago. Now he was going home to England. He told us that past the top of the range was a ski house. It was open and run by two Viennese ladies. We surely could find shelter there, but he warned us about SS men and women he had seen between here and the ski house, although he didn't think they posed any threat; they were also biding their time, waiting for the war to end.

After a short rest, the Englishman bid us good luck and proceeded downhill while we continued our climb up through the snow. We reached the ski house by nightfall. A German soldier met us; he was cutting firewood and took us to a hut. The main building was occupied by British officers, former POWs. He informed the ladies who owned the place of our arrival. After a while they came to us and we asked them for hot water. We could come and get it in the main house, they said.

Rautenberg and I did so and met the Brits, who invited us to join them for tea. I went back with the water and news but the captain declined; he felt despairing and beaten. After making excuses for the captain, I mentioned the soldier whom we had met cutting wood outside. "We don't want him here; he is a deserter," the British officer replied.

We had tea and cigarettes, kidded the ladies, and made small talk as much as our knowledge of English allowed. After tea everyone hit the sack.

The next morning was May 7, my birthday, and Goebel opened the last bottle of brandy in my honor. We had bread and brandy for breakfast, left the ski house early, and started on the trail downhill towards Bischofshofen and the Salzach River. Halfway down we reached the road and stopped to consider further action. Our travel orders read "on special assignment." They were of no use to us any more. We substituted them with new travel orders: releases from a military hospital. We disposed of our pistols and continued our march down the mountain until we reached a farmhouse above Bischofshofen. We were told that there were no Americans yet in the area, but in Bischofshofen there was a camp under German command to assemble scattered German military personnel.

We decided to stay overnight at the farm and to check out the situation in the morning. The captain was determined to continue the search for the elusive higher staff; I thought that what he really wanted was to get back to Eschenbach and his family. The next morning we parted; Corporal Weiss took off with the captain hoping to get home to Leipzig.

Rautenberg went down to Bischofshofen to reconnoiter and came back with the news that there was a Disarmed Wehrmacht Camp run by Germans. No Americans in sight. "Guess who was standing guard at the camp's gate armed with a rifle? Misha Vogt. He said that we should all come down and join the club." The war was finally over. It was May 8.

Everybody's thoughts turned towards home and getting there. We were now in Austria, and had to find a way to feed ourselves. The camp in Bischofshofen would provide us with food and shelter for the time being.. But would that mean we were POWs? In any case, we decided to follow Misha's advice and went down to the camp.

In camp some of the usual soldier's routine set in: lining up, standing guard, kitchen duty, getting grub, cleaning the premises and uniforms. But we had plenty of time to consider our future plans and to exchange our recent news with Misha.

When he left Eschenbach, Misha was assigned to an intelligence detachment of Army Group Schoerner in Czechoslovakia. There he met Gustav Hofman. It was April 24; two agents were waiting for Misha to be equipped and sent on a mission near Bystritz on the Czech-Silesian border where the SS was training soldiers for partisan warfare. When they arrived there, the lieutenant in charge of escorting agents across the front line told Misha that it was folly now to send men in harm's way. Of course, Misha agreed and left the men in the lieutenant's care. (Army Group Schoerner surrendered in Czechoslovakia in May 11 1945; it was the last German army group to surrender.)

In Prague he stopped at the military hospitality center; it was crowded with soldiers, officers, nurses, and women auxiliaries. A Czech band was still playing music and bottles of cognac were being passed around. Misha went to a movie house and saw a film about the exploits of Baron Muenchausen starring Hans Albers.

When he returned to his detachment, he learned that the commanding officer had left, leaving two German soldiers and a Cossack behind who didn't know what to do. Misha made out travel orders for all of them to proceed to Salzburg by train.

In Ceske Budejovice the rail station was under guard: "Heldenklau" was in action. They managed to get out because of confusion over an unexploded bomb. They passed several checkpoints with their travel orders "on assignment of the Secret Service." In Linz they were about equidistant between Soviet and American forces, then hurried to cross the Danube and walked south towards Salzburg. A truck loaded with munitions offered them a ride but they declined. A while later they heard explosions and came upon the burned-out truck which had been attacked by an airplane; they saw no bodies.

In Salzburg a Cossack unit occupied the military barracks; their Russian companion stayed there and the two German soldiers took off on their own. Misha went on to ASt (Intelligence Office) Salzburg where a lieutenant suggested that Misha continue to Gastein and gave him new travel orders. By train and truck Misha made it up to a mountain pass where the SS was building fortifications and checking all passersby. They detained the truck and soldiers but Misha was allowed to continue with his travel orders. In Gastein he stayed overnight in a cloister and learned about the cease fire.

The next day an officer in command at the rail station told Misha to take a train back to Bischofshofen where soldiers would be discharged. And that was how we came to meet again.

The campsite at Bischofshofen was on the road from Salzburg to the Gross Glockner Pass and Italy. The Salzach Valley is narrow here, just the river, a rail line, and a highway. On the highway going south Russian Vlasovites and Cossacks, on horses with wagons and kitchens passed by, coming from Salzburg. They were headed for Italy, our Russians told us. One morning when I woke up, our Russians were gone. They left behind a small bag of salt, half the amount they had carried with them. "You can't live without salt," Sasha used to say. The two had obviously joined the passing Russian units. Goebel was livid.

"Those idiots. I would have taken good care of them. They would have had a good life with me. They were good workers; I worked with Sasha for nearly four years. They can't go home anyway; and what is so great about Italy?" I was sure he was right.

There was no rail traffic any more and soldiers from our camp were posted to guard the rail station. I met my first Americans while standing guard at the entrance. Three soldiers in a jeep came swerving in front of the station and were stunned to face a German soldier with a gun. One of them approached and, mixing English with German, explained that they came from a hospital and that there were also German soldiers in the hospital. They had been told that at the station's restaurant eggs were stored in big jars which they wanted to take. "*Gut*, all right, o.k." I said. They went into the station, came back with the jars, and drove away waving.

A few days later a train arrived. All soldiers in the camp boarded the boxcars, twenty to a car and, with doors open on both sides, we enjoyed the scenic ride and beautiful weather on our way back to Rosenheim via Zell-am-See and Kufstein.

## MILITARY DISCHARGE

From Rosenheim we marched to Thal and were dispersed in groups of twenty to thirty men to a farm, occupying barns or haylofts. At a nearby school a German staff was ready to execute discharge procedures. I suggested that Misha come with me to Eisenach but he had other plans. In Dresden the wife of an officer had given Misha the address of their textile factory in Lindau on Lake Constance where he could find shelter at any time. Lindau was in the French zone of occupation; Misha spoke French well but his English was poor and he decided to go there.

At the end of May a call came for farmers and farm workers to report for discharge processing. We considered whether or not to report and decided against it, not knowing if we would be sent home or somewhere else to do field work. When the next call came for construction workers to register, I decided to go. Since I had disposed of my military identity document, a new one was made out for me, this time with my real name and birthplace. A few days later, I was called to be processed for discharge.

In a big tent we were told to strip to the skin. An American army doctor checked us out, signed the discharge certificates, and handed them out; he was the only American officer I met there. Army tractor trailers were waiting for us; the truck drivers were the first black Americans I saw. They drove us at high speed through fields and woods to a rail station where a long line of boxcars was waiting for us. Rations were distributed. By nightfall we had passed Munich; at Augsburg Station coffee was ready for us courtesy of the Red Cross. Standing there in line I saw Corporal Weiss, who had left us with the captain. He told me that they were stopped and put into a camp in Salzburg where he was discharged and the captain remained.

The destination of our train was Frankfurt. Weiss' home

was in Leipzig and he decided to stick with me until Eisenach, about halfway between Frankfurt and Leipzig. At Schweinfurt we got off the train; another corporal from Thuringia joined us. It is a good hundred kilometers from Schweinfurt to Eisenach. Off and on a peasant took us in his wagon for a short distance; there was no other traffic along our way. We met three men in striped prisoners' garb walking in the opposite direction and passed one another with a short "good evening." Somewhere we stopped at a town hall to get travel rations and overnight accommodations.

In the late afternoon of our last marching day we quickened our pace in order to reach Eisenach before curfew. It was a hilly wooded area. We marched in step and our spirits were high. We had just passed a village where American soldiers were quartered when a jeep came downhill with a GI at the wheel. We waved and continued marching.

The squeal of tires made us look back. The jeep had made a U-turn. "He'll give us a ride" one of us said just before a bullet hit the road. The GI was shooting; we went flat while two more bullets hit the pavement causing little swivels of dust. Then the jeep came a bit closer. The GI motioned for one of us to get up. I was the closest and stood up, walking towards the jeep until the GI rifle nearly touched my chest. "Documents!" I was ordered. I got the discharge certificate out of my pocket and put it on the rifle. The GI examined it, then gave it back and told me to turn around and walk away. Once I reached my companions the same procedure was repeated for the other two. Then he waved us on. It was an anxious moment — walking away with our backs to the jeep — but we heard it turn around and he drove off.

We left the road now and were walking on a side path when two American GIs on bicycles caught up with us on the uphill ride. They came from the village after having heard the shots; they wanted to see what was going on and whether we were all right. "Crazy man," they said, "crazy American soldier." I wondered what they meant. "Crazy" was not yet in my vocabulary. We were all right, we said, and in a hurry — "Eisenach, curfew." The two GIs offered us cigarettes and turned back downhill. We reached Eisenach before nightfall. It was June 17, 1945.

# 15

## Landscape of Freedom

### EISENACH

After 12 years I was together again with mother; for me the war was over. For the last 1,300 days I had been fed and sheltered by the army; the kitchen keeps an army going. There was no going back to Russia for me. I was a refugee, but a lucky one; others were herded under threat of arms back east to the Gulag or death.

Eisenach, a town both ancient and provincial, Bach's birthplace, with the famous Wartburg Castle where Luther saw the devil and threw the inkwell at him, was spared by the bombs and suffered no wartime damage. Its inhabitants knew only the discomfort of nightly hours in basements or shelters listening to the overhead roar of air armadas on their way to bigger targets. Nearby Kassel burned, but Eisenach was only a marker on the bombers' highway.

Now, the war over, there was general relief but no illusions, no "stab in the back" talk as there had been after World War I when German politicians had negotiated a humiliating truce while their army still stood on French soil. No regrets either, no joy, and no parades — just relief. Lost or won, it didn't matter; it was over. There would be occupation and displacement, *demontage* and internments. Later, far away, an atomic bomb exploded, perhaps the wonder weapon we had been promised; but the "progress" made from dropping one bomb instead of ten thousand did not sink in yet.

I had a roof over my head in a comfortable room on the top floor of a house owned by the Appelius family, and a couch to sleep on. Looking out the upper floor window in June, I saw gardens in bloom, tiled roofs, a white church tower, and the wooded hills of Thuringia. Was this my home now? I was 33 years old, my past in ruins like most of the land around me: cities, lives, families, the country itself gone. There was no return to Irina. Had she carried out our agreement to divorce if I did not return? Four years, four long years. Friends with whom I shared the war years were gone too. I was free, free of everything: no country, no property, no responsibilities, no profession.

Reading Pushkin's "Poltava," I mused about Peter's victory over the Swedes:

> He bids the lords beneath his scepter
> both Swede and Russian to his tent
> and gently mingling prey and captor
> lifts high his cup in compliment
> to the good health of his preceptors.

It was a different time then, a royal age. Stendhal wrote that when Czar Alexander drove along the boulevards of Paris, Napoleon's old supporters "waved white handkerchiefs from every window and appeared to be drunk of joy."[33] There

---

[33] *The Private Diaries of Stendhal*, W.W. Norton & Co., 1954, p. 525.

were no white handkerchiefs now and, while the territories occupied were to be converted "into a country primarily agricultural and pastoral in character,"[34] Eisenach was lucky to be occupied by the Americans, the "rich uncles." German burghers, whose earthly possessions had been spared by the bombs, could now retrieve them from basements or shelters; their fine linen, china, silverware, and clothing, were again stored in big armoires, chests, and china closets, though soon perhaps to be bartered for country produce.

My cousin Charlotte gave me a fine English tweed knickerbockers suit which had belonged to her doctor husband, killed in 1943 on the Eastern front when his field hospital came under fire. I was able to shed my army uniform. As one of Eisenach's new residents I received ration cards. Corporal Weiss collected travel rations, uncertain whether to continue home to Leipzig, now in Soviet hands. The landlord's daughters were glad to see him stay; there were not many young men left in town and, at the Appelius house, rations were pooled and supper prepared for all its inhabitants.

I went to work in nearby sugar beet fields, mostly with women and teenagers; some were Russian refugees who tried to escape repatriation, some German refugees. It was the only job around. But farm work did not appeal to me and I left after a few days.

*Frau* Appelius, who had seen some of my wartime drawings, found paper and pastels in the attic which had belonged to her brother Erbsloeh, once a member of the famous *Der Blaue Reiter* group of artists. She gave them to me and — since there wasn't much else for me to do — it was back to art.

Three weeks after our arrival in Eisenach the Appelius'

---

[34] According to the Morgenthau Plan agreed upon by Churchill and Roosevelt on September 14, 1944.

daughter, who worked at a U.S. Army Hospital, came home with unsettling news. "The Amis are packing in a hurry; the Russkis move in tomorrow."

Early the next morning I went into town and saw the news confirmed by big posters announcing the arrival of Soviet occupation forces. Persons who wanted to leave the city could do so that day at Wartha Crossroads several miles away.

We packed whatever we could carry; the Schmiedebergs, having abandoned their household already three times, traveled light. So did I. Most of mother's new possessions had to be left behind. We joined the exodus on the highway, an endless line of mostly women with their possessions on their backs or in hand carts. On nearby field roads Soviet soldiers on horse-drawn wagons took possession of their new territory.

At the border crossing point in Wartha a crowd had assembled where U.S. soldiers were examining documents of the new refugees. Mother and the Schmiedebergs passed examination but I was stopped.

"Born in Russia? Go back. Russians there," the American sergeant told me after examining my discharge certificate.

On the other side of the new border my relatives waved excitedly. I waved back and went off the road into a stand of nearby trees where mother could meet me unobserved. She showed me her identity card with the inscription in pencil: "Pass boundary, CIC" and a signature. Only that, no stamps. I copied it on my discharge certificate — one could not know what border controls might lie ahead — and we proceeded through the woods to where the Schmiedebergs were waiting. One more illegal border crossing for me, I thought, not knowing what its implications might be.

We parted ways with the Schmiedebergs, mother and I to go to Göttingen, the nearest town where we had relatives, the

Schmiedebergs to Heidelberg where Edith had just spent a university semester.

After a night in a farmer's house, mother and I got a lift on a milk truck to Bad Sooden, the closest rail station. However, there were no trains, only horse wagons for hire; we found one willing to take us to Göttingen about thirty kilometers away, a day-long trip along a road bordered by fruit trees ripe for picking. Near Friedland we crossed into the British zone without any "border controls." In late afternoon the spires of St. Johannes, the church where my parents were married, beckoned us on as they appeared and disappeared behind the horizon while we trotted up and down the hills and valleys.

"The town of Göttingen," wrote Heinrich Heine, "famous for its sausages and university, belongs to the King of Hanover." King and sausages were gone now but the university was still there, the town untouched by war, and the hostel where we stayed not changed much either since Heine's time. It accommodated horse and wagon and both of us for the night.

Göttingen in the British zone of occupation was less than 10 miles from the Soviet border and we were among a flood of refugees for whom it was a haven, a town not damaged by bombs. "Travel ration cards issued, Göttingen, July 10, 1945" was added to my discharge certificate.

The next day we were warmly welcomed by my Uncle Otto and his wife Lene. I had held fond memories of my uncle ever since our visit in 1923, the quiet, friendly man who provided me with a bicycle and took me with him on martial outings. He was in his sixties, a World War I veteran without much education, who had married late and now had five children ages four to fourteen. They occupied a small house near the airfield where my uncle had worked as an accountant. Among his seven siblings he was the only one who had joined the Nazi Party. Now retired, he tended his small plot raising vegetables and berries. I occasionally helped him along with his two sons. In crowded Göttingen there were no other opportunities for me to work and, as the house was definitely too small for all of us, I decided to try my luck in Bremen.

## BREMEN

Bremen, the U.S. port of supply, was an American enclave within the British zone. One didn't need a pass to enter it, and my relatives' house in the outskirts was still standing with only half of its roof gone. Their officer son was still in northern Finland, their son-in-law a prisoner of war in Russia. Two daughters also lived in the house but there was room for me too.

To get to Bremen one had to change trains three times; the trains were overcrowded, mostly with women and children. Past Hanover a band of young Russians and Poles — former *Ostarbeiter* and now DPs[35] — pushed their way through the cars, selecting pieces of luggage to their liking and throwing them out the windows for accomplices to pick up. No one could prevent their actions and, when at the next stop the women complained to the station master, he just shrugged his shoulders.

My relatives were glad to see me. With cousin Lilo I bicycled to the countryside to forage for food; there were also small repairs to do around the house. Eventually I signed up at the Labor Exchange Board to unload U.S. ships in Bremerhafen, a seaport sixty kilometers downriver.

The train for longshoremen left Bremen at six in the morn-

---

[35] *Ostarbeiter* were wartime foreign workers from Eastern Europe; DPs were "displaced persons," stateless foreigners then under the protection of the United Nations Relief and Rehabilitation Agency (UNRRA).

ing and departed for the return trip at five in the afternoon. For the nightly walk to the station through the city's ruins, I received a curfew pass. It was a long day, but the pay was good and working in the ship's hold had a special attraction — pilfering cigarettes and women's stockings from "broken" cartons which had been deliberately damaged. American guards watched us from the deck and checked us when we left ship but, as a rule, they were not thorough. Their main preoccupation was talk about going home; the Pacific war was now over.

In the downtown ruins I discovered a store which still sold art supplies and, on my free days, I went out to sketch and paint. When fall came and the weather turned foul I received a postcard from mother: we were in line for a place of our own on the Göttingen Town Hall housing list and I had to be back in Göttingen when our turn came.

On the return trip, while waiting in Hanover at the station, an empty coal train came by going to the Ruhr mines. On the spur of the moment I boarded it to find out the fate of Karl, one of our Russian-born staffers who had been sent to the Kurland bridgehead. In Essen I left the train, slept in the rail station's underground bomb shelter which now served as a free hotel, and continued the next morning by streetcar to Gelsenkirchen. I found the street among the ruins. No houses were standing, but here and there on a piece of wall were painted news and directions for searchers like me: "We are alive, moved to sister Annie's," or "I am back, went to Mueller's," etc. At Karl's address there were no walls, no directions; I never learned his fate.

## GÖTTINGEN

The last weeks of 1945 in Göttingen I remember as bleaker than the days of war. Four years ago I had been optimistic about my future when it seemed as though the war would soon end and whatever peace might follow couldn't be worse than the years preceding the war. In 1941 I had plans for the future; now I had none. What I had loved and cherished in the past was irretrievably lost. My days were filled with necessary boring tasks: fetching rations, having old razor blades resharpened, shoes and clothing repaired; getting coal or wood to heat our rooms, and soap to do the laundry. To "organize," as it was called, included buying, bartering, and obtaining things through connections.

Money was of little consequence; everyone had some and it was of little value. Whatever there was to sustain life was spread equally through ration cards and grey or black markets. We were sometimes hungry and often without heat or light, but there was no famine as there was in 1921 and 1932 in Russia.

During the first postwar year I covered over 3,000 miles on travels and errands through Germany, most of it by train. Travel by train was not as simple as it had been during the war; there were few trains, lines were interrupted, bridges blown out, and there were occupation-zone borders. Crossing the border between the British and American zones passengers had to exit the train and line up on the platform for document and luggage checks. Going south into the French zone, one arrived there in the evening and ended up staying overnight in the Karlsruhe bunker. For travel between zones one needed a permit or *laissez-passer* and, to obtain travel rations, one needed a good reason.

Although mother and I had nothing to barter, we could get potatoes and vegetables from uncle Walter who managed a sawmill in the countryside a couple of rail stops away. Going there was not always safe and one had to watch out for bands of *Ostarbeiter* who roamed the countryside looting. There were no occupation authorities, no police, and no curfews in the villages. The black market, maintained largely by DPs from the UNRRA camps, was an important source of additional food. Women and children bartered belongings of their dead kin for Canadian bacon or powdered milk and powdered eggs or for canned food.

On behalf of Uncle Schuetze, the former game warden, I traveled by truck to Hamburg for an allotment of fish to be distributed at his store; the wartime distribution system was still operating. I also travelled to a place close to the Belgian border to retrieve my relatives' possessions harbored there during the war when, ironically, the Ardennes seemed to be a more secure area.

With bridges blown up during the German retreat, trains were running only between the big rivers. Endless lines of mostly women were crossing the Weser and Rhine rivers over temporary military structures.

Across the nearby border of the Soviet zone, German refugees from as far as Königsberg, and other nationals from lands beyond, were fleeing west, the latter seeking food and shelter as DPs at UNRRA camps. They came with stories of postwar sufferings. For many of these civilians the end of war had brought more suffering than the days of war.

Wartime military death notices in newspapers were now replaced by search notices for relatives: "Who knows Heinz Mueller? Last seen in Budapest, 1st Company, Third Panzergrenadier Division." Or "Siegfried Schmidt? Last reported prisoner of war in Stalingrad" or "Have you seen Marlene Meier? Left Königsberg on foot in March 1945."

But there was no way for me to ask anywhere about my wife and sister in Russia. Had they had as much luck as I had had during the 46 months of war? I had experienced very little combat; it was only shortly before the war's end that I had close calls. How many saw combat, I wondered, except for the dead and maimed? And how many dead, how many maimed were there — soldiers or civilians — men, women, and children? No one knew.

I had survived before the war and now I had survived the

war. Was I lucky to have lost everything but my life? Life was now as real as death, but "rest in peace" was only for the latter.

For the living there were tales of plunder, rape, and revenge; there were women with shaved heads marching through Paris streets and stories of Russian POW survivors and Vlasovites herded under threat of British arms into Gulag captivity or death. The survivors waited for the POWs return, especially from Russia; it took ten more years for some of them to come home. Was the war really over or would the Leninist dictum of "transforming an imperialist war into a civil war" prevail?

The first gory news about concentration camps appeared in the local press, read mainly for its local news about food distribution and other daily needs. Reports of "lamp shades made of human skin" or pictures of mass graves had, at first, little credibility and seemed like wartime propaganda. The first concentration camps were liberated by the Soviet Army in Poland; a newsreel showed women with children leaving a camp with Soviet soldiers standing at the gate. In the Soviet Union children could never accompany their mothers to Gulag camps, I thought. It took time to accept the reality of human cruelty.

A German policeman in his old uniform regulated British traffic at the main intersection in Göttingen. Part of the university had been taken over by British armed forces and courses were offered to British troops. In town the British kept a low profile; mainly they occupied the big villas on the outskirts, where in the wide streets under old oak trees one could watch their "fall in" and other unusual marching orders — officers with riding sticks exuding upper class distinction.

My cousin, Elizabeth, was employed as a housekeeper in a villa occupied by NCOs. She had a room in the attic and collected butts of Player cigarettes and second brews of tea and coffee. Friends came to share in these treasures after work; often it was late, past curfew, and the attic provided enough space for all the guests to stay overnight.

The British did not observe the "non-fraternization" order. A pretty teenage girl in my uncle's neighborhood got engaged to a British officer and I made watercolor place cards for the festivities. A Welsh coal miner regularly came to my uncle's house and sat on a rocking chair in the dining room corner while we had our evening meal. He seldom spoke, smoked, offered cigarettes, left his butts — a treasure for the boys to barter — and went home to his barrack before curfew.

The mail was functioning; we received letters from Berlin forwarded from Eisenach. Martha, Gudrun, and Roderich Holl and Katya were alive, but Uncle Albrecht perished in a bunker during the last days of war. Misha wrote from Lindau on Bodensee where he was designing print patterns for a textile factory and interpreting for the town commandant, a French colonel, who protected Russian refugees from the Soviet repatriation commission.

Walter Goebel's wife wrote that Walter came home for a few days but was arrested again as a Nazi party member and was in a detention camp at Hanau. He was kept busy there engraving soldiers' war bounties — daggers and watches, rings and silverware, beer steins and medals — and was paid in cigarettes which he gave his wife on her occasional visits. In this way he was supporting the family and did better in camp than he would have working at home.

Agnes wrote from Bergen Belsen where she was working for the British Army. On one of my trips north I visited her; she promised to come to Göttingen but I waited in vain for her at the railroad station. Years later a postcard arrived from Scotland where she was working as a companion to a wealthy old lady. She asked if I still had the same feeling for her as before, and whether I would like her to come to Germany? But by then I had already married and had two children!

Mail came from Professor Schaak who was working at a Soviet Army hospital in Berlin. He continued to write until ordered back to Leningrad where his daughters were living. They gave our Göttingen address to Ira who was in Karaganda. Later mother received letters from Ira mailed by German communists — Ira's wartime friends — who were returning from Karaganda to East Germany. Eventually mother could send packages to Ira via East Berlin, but she never saw her daughter again. From Ira I learned that Irina had remarried.

Shortly after Christmas the housing authority assigned two small attic rooms to mother and me in a rooming house for students run by three sisters; we shared a kitchen and toilet with a young couple and their baby.

From my window I could see a tree-lined street and a school building behind which there was a theatre. The school was now a hospital and, in the schoolyard, Red Cross nurses exercised convalescing soldiers and officers, mostly amputees. The nurses drove them hard, showing little pity for the poor fellows. Pity and self-pity were of little use. Passing by the yard, I said to a lieutenant resting near the fence: "You get rough treatment here."

"Life ahead will be rough," he answered. "If we can't make it here, there is no future for us."

A room of one's own, even if shared with one's mother, does establish a *Lebensraum*; one can meet with people and make friends. For me one such person was twenty-one year old Peter Hansmann. His father and my mother knew one another from childhood. Peter grew up in Berlin where his father was a corporate executive; in 1944 they left the city for their villa in Göttingen which was now occupied by a British colonel. Peter was very interested in Russia and the Soviet Union; he had somehow avoided conscription. He told me that in Berlin he had close connections with members of the communist underground.

Peter was now working as an actor at the Göttingen theater; he also wrote poetry and was knowledgeable about contemporary literature and art, in particular German expressionism and Egon Schiele, whose self portraits he resembled. From Peter I learned much about contemporary art and literature. We met in my room or walked the hillside parks talking about Russia and art.

I was now actively painting and selling my work at a local bookstore. There was a good market for art in those years with money afloat and nothing to buy. Peter provided me with art supplies recovered from their villa; he spoke English and was on good terms with the caretaker of the colonel's quarters. He also introduced me to theater people and I got involved again in stage design for possible future productions. In the winter of 1946 such projects were tentative and futuresque.

Later Peter moved to Munich to join the famous Kammerspiele theatre. We remained friends until his untimely death from pneumonia in Munich in 1949.

I also met Thiele and Abich, two men who later became film and television producers; in 1946 they sought approval from the British authorities to set up a film studio at the Göttingen airfield. Their company — Filmaufbau — occupied a house next to the one in which we lived. We met there to discuss future film plans with occasional visitors, former celebrities of film and stage.

In the spring of 1946 an ad in the local paper attracted my attention: "Persons interested in drawing from a model report.... [time and address of a school were given]." I went there and met Hans Pistorius, a Weimar Bauhaus graduate who had placed the ad. He became my friend and mentor. Eventually I joined a group of artists who met regularly to draw or paint and my circle of acquaintances expanded. Gerda Winter, a young art teacher, and her husband Ernst, a postgraduate student of Indochinese art, lived in a big attic studio. Ernst had plans to publish a magazine of the arts and politics. A group of university students and professors met evenings at the studio for talks and games, fried potatoes, thin beer, and whatever the participants could contribute. Among them was Pasqual Jordan, the well-known physicist and Heisenberg collaborator; Aurelio, a philosophy lecturer; and Piet Linneman, a lecturer of Romance language and literature. There were also artists and musicians, mostly young people. Some were former soldiers; others had evaded conscription. There were foreigners: Aurelio was from Spain, Piet from Holland. The latter had completed his doctorate in Berlin and married the daughter of the university bookstore owner. He could not go back to Holland and taught at the British College for servicemen which was part of Göttingen University. Another young man, from Poland, had spent time in a concentration camp; he didn't talk about it. Nor did Claus, a young artist, talk about his year of service in a tank crew. He was lucky to have made it home from the Riga front with one of the last transports of the wounded and sick. I usually sketched while the others played games and discussed quantum theory, determinism and chance, Indochinese art, the music of Bartok and Hindemith, or the philosophies of Ortega y Gassett, Benedetto Croce, Berdyayev, and Heidegger. On some occasions the music of Bartok and Hindemith was played.

Together with a young woman artist I worked on a commission for the British officers' mess hall, painting murals depicting lands where British troops had fought during World War II.

In the spring of 1946 I traveled with a group of friends to Konstanz where an arts festival was organized by French occupation authorities. Filmaufbau helped us procure the necessary *laissez-passer*. Paintings from France were brought for an exhibit, among them the big "Figure décorative sur fond ornamental" by Matisse. French films were shown, Brecht's "Mother Courage" was performed by a theatre group, and there were endless lectures and discussions involving people of the most diverse convictions, from catholics to communists.

Johannes Becher, once a famous expressionist poet and the future Minister of Culture in Ulbricht's East German government, came from East Berlin. He tried to make converts and invited young people to the farm where he was staying and where food and wine were served in abundance. A wartime refugee in the Soviet Union, he had lived in Tashkent and praised socialist realism and the "simple life" there. When he learned that I came from Russia, he cut short his proselytizing efforts.

With Piet Linemann I traveled to Baden-Baden where we took advantage of the well-stocked French bookstore and I bought editions of works by Picasso, Braque, Bonnard, and Utrillo. I stayed with Piet in an hotel occupied by French Air Force officers to whom he introduced me as *mon ami Russe*. There was dinner dancing in the evening and, despite my sloppy appearance, I had an opportunity to dance with formerly German — now French — ladies from Strasbourg.

A Göttingen gallery owner asked me to travel to Munich to collect watercolors by Erich Heckel and Schmitt-Rottluf for an exhibit. In Munich I visited Peter Hansmann who took me to a theatre-in-the-round located on the top floor of a Schwabing apartment house spared by the bombs. I was reminded of the German Verein in Petersburg. The play being staged was Steinbeck's "Of Mice and Men" and we met Fritz Kortner, the famous movie star.

In February or March 1946 I had a visitor. A jeep parked in front of our house and a German civilian accompanied by an American soldier came upstairs and introduced himself as von Lossow. I had never met him but knew that he was the owner of the Harnekop estate, our staff quarters in 1944. He asked whether I was interested in coming to Frankfurt to see old friends and talk about working for the U.S. Army. I was definitely not interested but prepared tea; the visitors brought some rations: pork in apple sauce and Lucky Strikes. After tea they left; I met von Lossow again two years later.

I didn't tell mother anything about the visit; she had been out of town that day. I was somewhat suspicious about it. Harnekop was now in Soviet hands; maybe von Lossow was working for them. The Soviets were roaming all over Germany herding their people together for repatriation. Why Frankfurt? Eisenhower's orders were "non-fraternization"; there were still internment camps for officers and Waffen SS; certainly they were looking for Abwehr people too. For whom was von Lossow working? In any case I was not interested.

In December 1946 I met Rosemarie; a friend introduced me to her. She had grown up in Berlin, had just finished her dissertation at Freiburg University, and was visiting relatives before starting work at the *Badische Zeitung*, a daily newspaper. We took her to one of our "fried potatoes parties" and the next day I went with her to an exhibit of German expressionist painting. Afterwards we took a long walk, talking about art and life, the world revealed and a world destroyed; about Thomas Mann, his *bourgeois manqué* and "gypsies in green wagons." She gave me *Tonio Kroeger* by Thomas Mann to read. And of course we talked about ourselves. She had lost her father and a brother in the war.

We fell in love at our first encounter. In January 1947 I procured a *laissez-passer* for the French zone to meet Rosemarie's mother and her eleven-year-old sister. We went to the Freiburg Town Hall to register our marriage, only to find out that I didn't have the required documents — certificates of birth and divorce. (Eventually we were able to substitute sworn statements.) We sublet a room in a villa belonging to a colonel's wife; her husband was still a POW in France.

Early in April two telegrams arrived, forwarded by my mother from Göttingen.

"It must be your old club," my mother-in-law said, looking at the cables. "Signed with different names but having the same initials."

One telegram was signed Nikolay Savitskiy, the other Neil Sorensen. In the telegrams I was asked to come to Munich to discuss a business proposition. During the coming Easter holiday Rosemarie and I had planned a few "honeymoon" days on Lake Konstanz and a visit to Misha Vogt in Lindau. I cabled back and agreed to a meeting in Lindau.

There I met with a young man from Munich whom I didn't know; he mentioned names of persons I had known in wartime who wanted to see me. Rosemarie was adamant about my not going back to any intelligence activity. Misha's advice was his usual "maybe...or maybe not." We returned to Freiburg. Despite Rosemarie's objections, and because the food situation got even worse — if that were possible — I sent a telegram agreeing on a time and place for a meeting in Munich.

## MUNICH

At the Munich rail station I was met by a middle-aged man speaking German with a Baltic accent. "Sorensen," he introduced himself. He had an old car and we drove to a big farm in Tutzing overlooking Lake Starnberg where I was welcomed by Gunther Golly. I knew him from a 1944 visit to a front intelligence unit in the Carpathian region. He had grown up on an estate near the Polish-German border and had studied farm management. Now he was employed by U.S. authorities to manage the Tutzing farm requisitioned from an imprisoned Nazi Party member. I also met Golly's wife and mother. We had supper together and I was given a room for the night. The next day I would meet some people who wanted to talk with me.

In the morning I noticed the arrival of two big cars but couldn't see who was in them; it was clear that some sort of meeting was taking place. After the mid-day meal, one of the cars left and I was asked to come to the front room.

Two men were sitting at a large table. The one in civilian clothes, who introduced himself as Dr. Schneider, I recognized as former General Reinhard Gehlen whom I had seen once at Harnekop. The second man was in American uniform and introduced himself as Captain Erikson. Our conversation was in German; the American captain spoke with a Viennese accent. I was asked whether I would be willing to organize a technical support staff for a U.S. Army-sponsored intelligence organization.[36] I asked what rank I would be given, meaning American rank; in no case would I work as a "Hiwi."[37] I was told in reply that I would not be working for the U.S. Army, but for a German organization working in cooperation with U.S. authorities. Who was paying the piper, I asked? Dr. Schneider didn't like my question; his face turned red.

When I asked where and how my activities would proceed and the conditions of my employment, I was told that I would get a house in the vicinity of Lake Starnberg, a car, a

---

[36] The organization, which became known as the Gehlen Organization, was sponsored in Europe by U.S. Army Intelligence. With the creation of the Central Intelligence Agency (CIA) in late 1947, the activities were gradually shifted to the supervision of the CIA. Erikson was an alias for Captain Eric Waldman, an Austrian who had enlisted in the U.S. Army in 1942. See Mary Ellen Reese. *General Reinhard Gehlen: The CIA Connection.* Fairfax: George Mason University Press, 1990, p. 56.

[37] "Hiwi," abbreviation for "Hilfswilliger," the term for the first Soviet POW volunteers in the German Army before the Vlasov Army was organized, and roughly translated as "volunteer."

monthly salary of 400 marks, and a regular allotment of C-rations and cigarettes. Thinking back to Freiburg, it was an offer I could not refuse.

In any event I agreed to the task of setting up a technical staff which, under the existing circumstances, would take time; but I was not interested in extending my activities beyond that point. My interest was in art, not in intelligence.

We shook hands. Mr. Golly, our host, joined us and I was told that he would take care of all practical steps connected with my employment. Gehlen and the captain soon drove away in their car. From my host I learned that the earlier departure I witnessed had been that of Hermann Baun, the former Chief of Walli I. This had been the occasion when Baun was removed from his position as head of intelligence procurement by Gehlen and the Americans. Baun, who grew up in Odessa, came to Germany after World War I and joined the Abwehr; many General Staff officers considered him a "shadowy figure born and raised in Eastern Europe" and "not accountable for either his actions or his expenditures."[38] For better or worse, he was secretive about his sources of information; after 1945 his motto was: "You want information. I deliver. You pay what it is worth to you." Such a businesslike attitude was incompatible with and unacceptable to any bureaucracy.

During the next few days of April 1947 Golly and I visited U.S. offices in the Tegernsee area. A house was assigned to me on a hill overlooking the Tegernsee Lake as office and private quarters for my staff and I obtained an old car which had seen wartime service. Nikolay Savitskiy, alias Sorensen, moved in with me as an aide. Later I brought in Misha Vogt as my assistant.

---

[38] Reese, *op. cit.*, p. 74.

From Golly I learned that the farm he now managed had also been Baun's field office while Baun and his colleagues — and now Gehlen — were housed in a U.S. compound near Frankfurt. During the war Golly had collaborated with Ukrainian and Polish partisans who had first resisted German occupation but later, when the Soviets advanced to reoccupy the former Polish territories, had joined forces with the Germans. After the war Golly renewed some of his old contacts. Several of the Ukrainian leaders were now living as DPs in Bavaria, organizing support for their old resistance groups which were still active in what was now Soviet territory. However, in recent months the survival of these groups had become tenuous; they had called for assistance to facilitate their evacuation through Czechoslovakia to the West. They needed documents and Golly was asked whether he could be of any help. That was why he had contacted me and also Walter Goebel in Nüremberg.

A few days later I met an Ukrainian known as "the Colonel" and we discussed pertinent issues, but to begin my task I had to get hold of our old archives which we had deposited in what was now the French occupation zone. I couldn't go there without proper permits and went for assistance to Frankfurt. There I learned that the archives had been shipped to Washington, D.C. and, more importantly, that we were prohibited from operating on Soviet territory. The lands ceded to the Soviet Union by the Stalin-Hitler Pact were now secured Soviet territory according to the Yalta Accord. Our activities had to be limited to East Germany and the still independent Central European countries which, except for Yugoslavia, would soon become Soviet satellites. The 1948-49 events in Berlin, Warsaw, and Prague changed the political climate and the relations within the former Grand Alliance, but the restrictions on our activities remained intact for years to come.

Before I began working in Tegernsee on my assignments I

went back to Freiburg. Rosemarie continued to object to my going back to intelligence work. The only good argument in my favor was the food, cigarettes, and nylon stockings I brought with me. Finally we decided that Rosemarie would stay on her job until dismissed due to her pregnancy. I packed my few things and left for Tegernsee where she joined me in July; in October our first daughter was born.

Around New Year's, 1948, the Gehlen staff was moved from Frankfurt to Pullach near Munich, and I was ordered to move there too with my family and Misha Vogt. In the compound I met Hermann Baun again and also von Lossow who had visited me in Göttingen in 1946. With Baun I spent many evenings with talk and cognac, but he was soon relieved of all duties and remained inactive and unhappy until his death in December 1951. After he had to leave the compound, Golly and I were his only visitors. During his last months he asked me whether I could facilitate his move to Damascus. Why Damascus, I asked? Because oil and Islam will be the main issues in the years to come, he answered. Only a few people met at the cemetery for his burial: Baun's second wife and his son; Gehlen, Golly, and myself with our spouses. The minister, coached by Baun's wife, spoke about the injustices suffered by the deceased. Gehlen kept a steely face. I was reminded of the burial scene in the movie, "The Third Man."

I worked as Chief of the Technical Services Division in Pullach until 1953. The compound in Pullach grew fast in numbers as well as bureaucratic encumbrances. Intelligence concerns often gave way to internal political issues, i.e., the integration of the Gehlen organization into a future German government. Russian affairs, which were of interest to me and to Misha Vogt, were of only tangential interest to the Gehlen organization. Misha on occasion gave talks on Russia and Russian history to staff officers. My efforts to stimulate interest in the political consequences of Stalin's eventual demise were unsuccessful. It seemed to me that he was considered immortal.

In 1951, together with other colleagues, I visited the United States: Washington, New York, Chicago, Seattle, and San Francisco. I liked the wide spaces and open minds there. Upon my return I asked Rosemarie whether she would consider emigrating to the United States or Canada. We discussed it at length between ourselves and with our American friends. There was no hope for a return to our native cities, Berlin and Petersburg; no going home again.

In 1952 we applied for immigration visas at the U.S. consulate in Munich. There were no problems; we both had our denazification certificates and had not been members of the NSDAP (Nazi Party) or any of its affiliates. Our American counter-intelligence officer took me to an apartment in Munich for lie detector tests to ascertain that I had not been a member of the Communist Party either. Eventually we could collect our immigration visas at the U.S. consulate where we pledged to relinquish any allegiances to kings and potentates.

While we were preoccupied with our new plans, a momentous historic event took place on March 7th, 1953: Stalin died quite unexpectedly. No one was prepared for this eventuality. His death caught everyone by surprise and was followed by the June 17th uprising in East Berlin and other East German cities which brought about a turbulent time at my office. I was able to file my resignation by the end of July and, in early September, we took a train to Cherbourg. There we boarded the French ship "S.S. Liberté," the former German steamship "Europa." After leaving port we hit a sandbank but, with the help of the tide and several tugboats, we eventually proceeded out to the ocean and landed in New York with our, by then, three children, on September 14, 1953.

When we met in 1946, Rosemarie gave me a clipping of

an article she had written for a local paper on March 20, 1945, shortly before the war's end. It was about the Rhine Bridge at Konstanz:

> The bridge leads from one bank of the river to the other bank. On the bridge one stands between the shores; one doesn't belong to the one side any more and not yet to the other. I look down on the young river which runs west thinking about this and that and wonder about pros and cons. The realities drown in the rushing water and everything seems light and easy. The water runs uninterrupted westward and then north. But there no one is standing on a bridge because there are no bridges any more. Downriver the waters don't elicit dreams; there the river is a horrible barrier soaked with the blood of two continents.
>
> The bridge railing is hard and cold as is reality. I look down once more on the young river which leaves the lake rushing towards the sea, still spanned by the bridge on which I stand, half dreaming but facing the hard realities as I walk towards the other side.

# *Appendices*

## APPENDIX ONE

Excerpted from Nadine Wonlar-Larsky, *The Russia That I Loved.* (London: self-published, 1932), pp. 174-187.

[Wonlar-Larsky was the aunt of the well-known writer Vladimir Nabokov, the author of many titles including "Speak Memory" and "Lolita." One of the reasons for having chosen Wonlar-Larsky's memoirs for quotation here is that she wrote them in London while staying at the Aban Court Hotel. The hotel belonged to Rhoda Schotte whom she knew from earlier years in St. Petersburg when Rhoda Schotte and her husband Fritz owned the Grand Hotel and Hotel d'Angleterre. Wonlar-Larsky writes: "Chance which had already so often played a curious part in my life, led me to the Aban Court Hotel where I happened to meet Mrs. Shotte, daughter of the proprietors. She immediately recognized me from the old days in St. Petersburg where she and her husband had owned two large hotels. She generously offered me special terms; I have lived there for seventeen years."]

[After Uritskiy, the director of the Bolshevik police, was murdered by a young student]...in Gatchina there were nights when people were shot in batches of sixty, eighty, etc. at a time. The graves of the victims were dug by themselves and they were told the reason for the digging. An ex-nurse ...herself offered to carry out the killings one night. She shot eighty...but always to wound and not to kill. She looked on while they were buried alive.

In the summer of 1919 the white Russian Army was approaching Gatchina and I made arrangements for mama to be smuggled somehow out of the country.... Sophia, and I, traveling under assumed names, with the passports provided by our old manservant...managed to get by train to Petrograd. Having the little girl was a great responsibility.... I never could take her out in the daytime; the sights one saw in the streets every day were no sight for the eyes of a child.... We were commandeered nearly every day for clearing the streets ...hauling wood, clearing snow off the railway line... clearing the snow off the roofs with spades...hauling logs off the frozen barges on the river.... Harnessed to a heavy sledge of wood, women without help from the men had to drag it along, surrounded by fat sailors with whips.... By this time, our physique was so reduced owing to starvation, that the work was doubly hard.

During this winter [1919-20], we nearly died of cold, it being impossible to obtain a permit for fuel. After standing for hours in queues for many days, trying to get permits, a party of us was once given an order for fuel. Filled with joy — there were about ten of us — we arrived at the address given, where we found an empty and deserted house which we were told we could pull down. Tools of every kind had long ago been confiscated...but the terror of freezing to death is, like necessity, the mother of invention; one man somehow managed to get part of a wall loosened.... I was given a lovely beam of wood which I had no means of carrying home. Somehow, together, we managed to drag our precious wood along although it took the best part of two days...the party had to keep watch in shifts during the night....

There was a time when orders were...given that every house should be guarded at night.... The whole town was in complete darkness and I…found it a very nerve-wracking job. One night when I was on the shift from 2-4 a.m.…the figure of a tall man wearing felt shoes made his approach quite silently over the thick snow. He said to me, "Do you realize that I could easily strangle you and no one would be any the wiser?.. A few yards from here, on the quay, there is a large consignment of wood. I have to…steal some to keep us alive…. If you refuse to help me, I am sorry, but I shall have to do away with you."

Added to this continuous nervous strain were the increasing physical disabilities caused by hunger and cold. All pipes, in all houses, were burst…in order to obtain water, we had to melt snow. For some time, it had been impossible to get any soap. Here, I may mention, that Sophie and I were the only people in our house who were free from lice…. Our scanty amount of fuel had to be carefully conserved, to enable us to cook our one meal a day. This generally consisted of a potato with possibly a scrap of horseflesh. We had to sleep in our clothes. The bed clothes were a grimy black because there was no possibility of ever washing and drying them.

I often cried, literally cried, of hunger knowing that I should give Sophie my share of the grit which was called bread…. It was then that I learnt the habit of smoking a cigarette instead of taking food.

It [is] impossible to describe the horror…when orders were suddenly issued for whole districts to be searched during the night. The only warning we got was when the electric lights in our quarter of town were suddenly switched on, about eleven-thirty…. I used to watch the soldiers when our house was being searched, wondering anxiously if ten-year-old Sophie would remember what to say when rudely shaken up out of her sleep and asked what her name was.

# APPENDIX TWO

Letter of Fedor Schotte to his adopted son Fritz and his wife Rhoda. Translated from the German by Leo Saal.

St. Petersburg
February 17, 1919

My dear children:

At last there is an opportunity to write to you. The Swedish Consul, Mr. Heilborn, came back to town and will leave again as soon as it is possible; he will take this letter. There is nothing encouraging to tell you but I'll try to convey to you the essential events. Last October I happened to be at the Hotel d'Angleterre when I got the news that our firewood has been requisitioned. I went with Albrecht and Herman to see the Commissar. The Consulate protested and Herman brought the letter to the Commissariat concerned. They told him that the wood was not registered but we had proof that it was. In the Commissariat there were two youngsters who asked us to show the paid bill. I told them that the wood was bought two years ago and that today the prices are much higher. I asked for 40,000 rubles for damages, but I was told that "in such a case the wood is requisitioned."

You have certainly heard about the attack on the Consulate, but I want to give you a few details. When diplomatic relations were severed between Germany and Russia, members of the Consulate wanted, of course, to leave immediately. But they couldn't get their passes because of some holiday. On Sunday, November 11th, Xenia, our old servant, came running. "The Bolsheviks are here." I went out. The lobby was full of the Consulate's belongings, luggage, etc. There were also people who still had some business with the Consulate, the soldiers who guard the Consulate, people who wanted to leave with the Consulate officers and employees. There were soldiers in Russian uniforms carrying weapons and some bandits in civilian clothes who called themselves internationalists. There was screaming and cursing; the Swedish Consul wanted to intercede but it was all in vain. The people from the consulate had to give the keys to their rooms and we all were locked into rooms 40, 41, and 43. We heard some demonstrations were going on outside.

In the evening, the officers and employees were taken away. For 7 days they were imprisoned. After 4 days I got my keys back but all my papers were searched. After the people from the Consulate were freed, they stayed 2 more days with us. At first I wanted to leave with them too. But Xenia raised hell. First we decided that Albrecht and Martha would stay and I would leave, but then I decided to remain too.

After the Consulate left, all the employees had to register. Albrecht registered as head of the supply desk, Martha in charge of the linens, I as administrator. Then a committee of 5 persons was organized on orders from Moscow. There was a fake vote. We were told that all employees should leave the building; they didn't want any witnesses to the robbery. A man by the name of Perz, one of the few educated people, gave us a speech: "After long years of fighting imperialism and capitalism their powers are finally defeated. The difference between master and slave has disappeared for all time. We have achieved the ideals of humanity — freedom, equality, and brotherhood. This is inscribed on our banners and those who are against it deserve the bullet." This man Perz, it is said, was a political agitator at the French front. He was sentenced to 15 years imprisonment there but he escaped.

The committee was completely under the direction of Gorokhowaya. (Gorokhowaya Street No. 2 was headquarters of the CHEKA — the extraordinary commission, forerunner of GPU, NKVD, KGB.) In charge was Filter; Perz was secretary; there also was a man from Moscow called Bruch. Mennecke switched to their side as soon as the Consulate left. He is a despicable character.

On November 21 we were told "Schotte will not get food any more." This I was told by the young man who used to sit at the register. Finally on January 10 Mr. Neddermeyer provided five ration cards for us. On December 3 we were informed by letter that the German Revolutionary Workers' and Soldiers' Council had decided that all former agreements with the Consulate-General were void and I was asked to leave the building. So were Albrecht Holl and Martha. I protested, of course, and said that I had no means, that I had been in prison during the war, and that it is inhumane to throw a 65 year old man out of his own house; that it couldn't be the job of the Soldiers' Council to prosecute Germans. I was called to a meeting with the Council's head. He told me that they didn't want to persecute me and that I could move into the Hotel d'Angleterre. He accused me of keeping in touch with the former Consulate-General. This conversation took place in the presence of a new Council President, a man named Brieske, who came from Moscow to replace Filter. Brieske himself is a simple man, probably a craftsman. Filter, it was said, went to Berlin.

On December 4th, the housekeeper from the Hotel d'Angleterre came to see me and said that Comrade Mennecke had ordered that the linen be requisitioned. I said that the linen had been laundered in November and not paid for, that the employees had received no pay. It didn't make any difference. I had to pay 300 rubles for the bill myself. I submitted my bill for November. "This must be first looked into," I was told.

On January 3rd I was told that the Soldiers' Council will move to the Moyka and that the employees can be dismissed. Shortly thereafter the trucks came and started to move everything — and this continues to this day. It's hard to say how many things they have stolen from us, and I can say only that the building is not fit for a future German office. Happily I was able to secure our personal belongings and your apartment has not been touched.

There was a race by the various Commissars to take over the Hotel d'Angleterre. First came people from the People's Supply Commissariat, then from the Political and Propaganda Commissariat; then a delegation from the Commission on the Evacuation of POWs and, finally, the Commissar for Food Supply. The latter came with an order and armed soldiers. I told him that this was German property and showed him the papers of the German Consulate-General and also of the Swedish Consul. "It doesn't matter," was his answer. "And don't talk so much. If you do not comply, I will use force." I relented.

Most of the delegates who used to live here were dirty and uppity women. The POWs had occupied the third floor since November. The propaganda people were also supposed to pay but I haven't seen a penny yet. The commissars occupied the best rooms after they had already made a mess at the Hotel de Paris. Most of the employees were fired. The rent, they said, they would cash in themselves and they also took the 5,600 rubles which were in the till.

There was no wood to heat the building and I went out to find people who would deliver wood. I found five men with sleighs on November 17th and the next day the wood was delivered to the Hotel d'Angleterre. They delivered it on the 18th and 19th and asked for pay. But the hotel was taken away on the 19th, so I went to the various commissars to protest. But all those bandits had one answer: You hired the people, you have to pay them. I spent three days on the issue, but eventually I had to pay the bill myself: 4,200 rubles. One night the new inhabitants went into the cellar with newly-made master keys. That became known and some of the commissars were removed and are to be tried but I don't believe that this will be the case. The new people who came were just mad that they didn't get any of the loot.

Some of the radiators are already broken. The employees don't get any pay and yet they are afraid to complain. At the time the Hotel d'Angleterre was requisitioned, Mr. Rakow from Moscow appeared here . He said that he was an important man — Lenin, Zinovyev, Trotsky and Radek were all his friends. "Moscow thinks that things are not going right here; that things should be pursued more energetically." Two days later he left, returning again after six weeks. He said the Russian Government had appropriated one million rubles to support the Soldiers' Council and the German POWs. "The 40,000 POWs still in Russia had to be taken care of." He said he had to travel to Berlin now. Probably he has to show them how to make revolutions.

Uncle Richard was denounced as a speculator and imprisoned at the Shpalernaya, but after four weeks they told him he could go home. He said the people in prison were all decent persons but the food was abominable. Lieschen worked for the comrades until February 1, but now she is out of work. Olga couldn't get employment because of her name; the poor girl must take care of the whole family. On December 30 we were at Herman Saal's for a baptism; then on January 1 we went to Saal seniors where the engagement of Vera to Herr Schmiedeberg was celebrated. The parents had learned about this engagement earlier the same day. Saal Sr. was not able to continue the Eilers' business. There were too many difficulties and disappointments and he has closed the business. His wife couldn't stand the difficulties and has closed her business too. Herman now works as a comptroller of the Workers' and Peasants' Inspection. Mrs. Else is feeling all right, at least she is always in good spirits. The Blumenfelds, however, are in bad shape; he earns very little and has lots of troubles. Guenther complains; Stenge is in poor shape but is employed by the Bolsheviks; Aliman was told to leave town; I have seen Grimm — he says he needs 25,000 rubles a month to survive. Smelt died of starvation.

The Bolsheviks need money and therefore a special revolutionary tax is to be levied on Petersburg, and the comrades thought of us too. I should pay 50,000 rubles, you are charged 75,000, and Uncle Richard 356,000. I have protested and said that I have no money.

"Don't you have an account?" I was asked.

"No," I said.

"On what basis have you been assessed?"

"This I would like to know myself."

The situation here is terrible. A pound of bread costs up to 25 rubles and so do millet and barley. A pound of butter and sugar 85 rubles, pork 55, horsemeat 20 rubles, potatoes, onions, and cabbage 8 rubles and so on.

There is no wood for heating and the Bolsheviks have requisitioned 200 wooden houses to be torn down for fuel. Besides the problem of food, people live in constant fear that their apartments will be requisitioned and the furniture taken away. In the streets one sees many sleighs laden with furniture of all kinds, sometimes beautiful things; officially it is not permitted to buy or sell things; in most stores the contents have been requisitioned and, anyhow, most of them are closed. The streets are empty; Petersburg is a sad place. How it looks in the evenings is hard to describe: there are no lights and one barely sees anyone, only those who must be there, and they try to take detours through the main streets. Nobody dares to use side streets at night.

I am particularly sorry about the Blumenfelds. They are such nice people. But old father Anspach is particularly affected by the famine. You will remember the words I said in Kamyshlov. I said then that I had an unexplained fear of returning to Petersburg. And this fear was justified. I am now an old man but I can still survive with what I have. From the Hotel d'Angleterre I have some money from the sale of the remaining wine and other small items.

[The letter concludes with Schotte's hope for a better time to come, for the return of his children, and with greetings to relatives in East Prussia where the addressees resided. Fedor Schotte was arrested soon after he wrote this letter. He died in a Moscow prison and Albrecht Holl went to Moscow to attend to his burial.]

## Appendix Three

Statement by Ira Saal, sister of Leo Saal, written on July 21, 1988, in Germany. Translated from the German by Leo Saal.

I lived in Leningrad where I was born in 1918. Since 1937, I was a student at the first medical institute in Leningrad. In the spring of 1941, I was in residency in a hospital not far from Leningrad (west of Leningrad) where my mother also lived at this time. This was after she came back from exile.

On June 22, the Second World War began for us. It was on that date that the Soviet Union was first attacked. I had to return to the city, to Leningrad, because I was on my last semester, and due to the events we were supposed to continue our studies immediately. Summer vacations were cancelled.

In September our studies were interrupted since the city was under attack by air as well as by artillery. We were not able to take the last medical exams and therefore did not receive our diplomas. We were sent to the city hospitals or to the front to do our work.

I was assigned to a hospital in which half of the patients were wounded soldiers and the other half were civilians. I was permitted to live at home and was not drafted as a military doctor.

My best friend, however, who had already finished her studies, worked as a surgeon with the military service. (She had already been drafted.) She had a small child at home and, therefore, she was also permitted to live at home. She asked me to move to her place in order better to take care of her child, since my duties were often by night. We were four women and one small child together; the two other women were members of the family of my friend. We all were still young, between 20 and 24 years old. When we had air raids or artillery raids, and the other members of this our "family" were either at work or trying to buy whatever one could get (this was in July, August and September), I was usually with the three-year-old at home. Sometimes I went with her to the air raid shelter.

The famine began in September. However, at this time one could still go to the suburban areas of the city and gather some potatoes and cabbage, and this helped us a lot. But the real hardship began in October.

No food was distributed except for 500, 300 or 200 grams of bread. But even this was soon reduced to 400, 250 and 125 grams a day. This was the ration until February-March 1942, as far as I remember. If it had been bread, it would have been better, but it was a mixture of flour with all kinds of other stuff, in most cases sawdust. This was, of course, not really known to us, but later on we learned about it when there were exhibits after the war about the conditions that existed in Leningrad.

People died of famine right in the street. Sometimes when we came from work they were there lying dead — sometimes for several days until they were picked up and buried.

Often one could see a woman or a man pulling a sled with a dead body. Women usually were more capable of dealing with famine than men. Often one could encounter corpses simply covered with something because the relatives were not in the position or had not the strength to carry them to the cemetery. The air raids and the artillery attacks often caused fires and the buildings usually burned down since there was no water and no people who had the ability to extinguish those fires.

It was also a very cold winter. Temperatures often reached minus 40° Celsius. Our little group had lots of luck and this kept us alive. Our male friends and husbands sometimes came from the front line for one or two days. The front line was in the outer suburbs and they got leave or they had something to do in the city proper. When they came, they brought something with them. Sometimes it was their dry rations; sometimes other soldiers gave them some of their rations, and in turn would receive some when they visited their own families. So every soldier helped the other out on such occasions. There was an officer of high rank among our acquaintances who helped us off and on. His family had been evacuated from the city.

Bread was distributed for the next day — for two days actually. Many people took their two-day ration and ate it at once and then remained hungry for two days after that. This was, of course, very bad. In our little group we arranged to eat always a little bit three times a day. The bread was divided for everyone in equal parts and the child received a little bit of butter and sugar when it was distributed. We always kept a little from the morning ration and in the evening we ate our bread ration with hot water. Sometimes one had also a little bit of tea. Water was boiled in a samovar. The samovar was heated with pine cones. There was no lumber available. Actually whatever was available was used to heat the rooms. Most of the wooden structures and houses were torn down during this time, and I don't think there were many wooden houses left in Leningrad after the war. For dinner we had a thin soup which consisted of water, some flour, and some salt. This we ate without bread. But we had three meals a day.

We had a bath every week, although it was really difficult to carry the water. One had to carry it on a sled from the river. We heated our premises every day but of course it was cold, and there were many days of minus 20° down to minus 40° Celsius during those winter days. For heating we also used furniture. This was our daily life until the end of March. By that time the encirclement was interrupted in the area of Tikhvin, and an evacuation of some of the inhabitants of Leningrad could begin. It took place by trucks over the Ladoga ice, and then from there to Tikhvin, and from Tikhvin one would take the train.

In the opposite direction, some supplies now came into the city. Food, of course, over the ice by trucks and later on by boats. Sometimes this supply line was interrupted by bombing or by artillery fire. But the worst was over. Life was getting a bit better. Bread rations in Leningrad were increased and some groceries became available. However, spring brought new difficulties, new dangers. This was mainly tuberculosis. Death was prevalent particularly among the young people. They died of this illness in a short time. Every day corpses were brought out of the apartments where students lived. There was also the danger of other epidemics since the city was very dirty and there were neither the people nor the strength to do much cleaning.

I left the city on April 5, 1942. I can still remember this day very well. My good friends helped me put whatever I possessed on a sled and pull it through the wet snow towards the so-called railroad station. In order to make it easier my belongings were packed in two sacks.

It was nighttime when I started my way to the station. I arrived there in the morning. It was on the high bank of the river where I threw my things down, and slid down the embankment towards the trucks which were waiting there. Some soldier helped me to put my sacks on the truck. I had a few cigarettes to give him for that. We started towards Lake Ladoga, which was still frozen, and then to the so-called "Big Earth."

Here I would like to say that no reporting, no book — even a very well-written book — no film, nothing, can really describe the situation of the embattled city to give the right impression. One had to see the faces, the frost-bitten faces, and the figures dressed — or simply covered — by everything they could put on themselves. They could barely move or moved like very old people. And then there were the the covered-up corpses lying on the streets or propped up against the walls. One had to see this with one's own eyes.

It took us a month by train to reach the North Caucasus. It was not an easy trip either. Once we had crossed Lake Ladoga, we boarded a train, not one with passenger cars, but the usual freight cars. Before boarding the train, the people who lived around the station brought us some food. They had not experienced too bad a winter. I was stupid enough to drink a glass — or rather a jar — of milk which had not been boiled, and I became very ill. I was put down on my belongings in a corner of the freight car, and, frankly, I did not think that I would get well again. Many people died on this trip south, mostly people who could not ration their intake of food, and got sick just as I did.

Also, before I had left the city, I had developed sores on my hands; the skin had split and there were open wounds but they were not infected. I had bandaged my hands before I left. By the time we were approaching Stalingrad, I decided to renew my bandages on one of the stops. When I took off the bandages, I saw that the wounds were dried out and had begun to heal. Thus, I became aware that, despite all the loss of energy, and despite the sickness of my stomach and my intestines, there was enough strength in me to hope for a recuperation.

My appearance, however, must have been rather scary. I looked pretty wasted. When we reached the North Caucasus, there was a railroad station called Povorino. I still remember its name today. Next to the station, as was often the case, were people with food — a kind of market. They tried to exchange the food for thread and textiles, or whatever there was. I walked slowly with my three spools of thread, and saw a man with two small loaves of bread. I asked him whether he wanted to exchange them for the thread. He agreed. Then came two other women. The one who looked a little bit better asked for the bread, and said that the woman who accompanied her would otherwise soon die of hunger and weakness. The man looked at me and said, "This one will not last long either." This was when I understood how badly I must have looked. Certainly we did not know how we looked. Nobody had any mirrors.

On the way, I had made friends with a younger girl, a girl who was not that badly off. She had recuperated quite well because she had a big supply of men's clothing which she had exchanged along the way. We became friendly and decided to stay together. Her boyfriend, like mine, had been at the front and her mother had died in Leningrad of hunger.

Finally we arrived at the place where we disembarked. It was a big village in the area of Krasnodar, 30 kilometers from the Sea of Azov and the city of Yeysk. We had to stay there and were assigned a place to live. The two of us got a room with a woman whose husband was at the front and who had no children. Eventually she moved in with her sister and we had the house to ourselves.

The first days I was still very weak so Anya (the girl with whom I lived) went out and exchanged things and bought food, and I stayed at home and cooked. Slowly I gained strength. After one and a half months I thought that I could look for work. One morning when I was having breakfast a man came on horseback and asked for me. He said I had to be ready with my belongings in one hour. And he posted a soldier with a rifle in front of our door and departed.

One hour later a horsedrawn wagon came and loaded whatever I had and we went to the railroad station. My belongings consisted of only a few groceries, and not much else. Of course I had no money. As I established later on, Anya had also stolen some of my things but at this time I did not notice it. This, then, was my trip from the North Caucasus to Kazakhstan. I think we were about three weeks on the way there. Once a day we received some food when we stopped at some station. We also got our daily bread ration, 300 or 400 grams a day.

In the beginning of July we arrived at a big village, 120 kilometers away from Karaganda. In a few days, we had to go to work in the fields. Up to now, the only food we had was what we could exchange for things. Thus I did not have much clothing left when we arrived there. I had not had too many things to begin with. Once we started our work in the fields, we got fed. But we worked about 10 kilometers away from the village where our things were left. During the transport I developed some kind of skin disease and could not sleep at night. My stomach was not in a good shape either. I made it a week working in the fields, but then I did not feel strong enough, and ran away. The heavy work and being unable to sleep made me really quite weak.

During this stay in the village I had met a woman who was a medical doctor. I told her about my difficulties with my intestines and she gave me some medication. She could not help me otherwise, but she gave me the idea to write to Karaganda to the medical authorities. She herself was at this time on inspection of the region since she was the head doctor of the local hospital. She asked me a lot about Leningrad since she had good friends there. She was from Moscow and was of Ukrainian origin. Her husband was of German descent, and this was the reason why she also had been sent here to Karaganda.

So, as I said, I left the field work, and walked to the village where we had our belongings. There was a medical office, and I went there to get some kind of medication for my skin.... As I entered, I heard somebody say, "There she is, there she is..." and I saw two good-looking women. One of them was the doctor I had met. Her name was Nina. The other woman was chief of the health authority office for this region.

They thought they could arrange for me to work temporarily in the laboratory of the hospital where Nina worked. And they also gave me medication. I stayed in this hospital for about a week, and then was transferred to my new place of work. I worked there for about two years, first as a laboratory technician, and later as a medical doctor. During those years I had all kinds of experiences, both good and bad.

The main thing was that I found good friends there. Nina, the doctor whom I mentioned, became a good friend; she is still a good friend and is now 80 years old. Another good friend was Greta. She was from Germany, from the area near Königsberg, now Kaliningrad. She was, I guess, a member of the Communist Party and had fled to the Soviet Union.

She eventually lost her husband and her two sons, but she was a very courageous and dependable woman. Sadly, she was not well; she had tuberculosis. In 1955, she returned to East Germany, where she died in 1959. I lived with her from the end of the war until she left. She was really a very good friend of mine and I have only good memories of her and our times together.

There were also a lot of hard times. At one time, I was supposed to be drafted into the so-called labor army, and we had tried very hard to avoid this happening. The fact that I worked in the medical field was helpful. Also, during those years, I was severely ill with typhoid fever. In Kazakhstan, the winters are very cold; minus 40° Celsius is quite usual. Our clothing was, of course, insufficient. I also suffered from a nerve inflammation in my lower back which I was unable to cure, and I suffer from it still. But, overall, those two years were not the worst ones. It was war, and nobody had an easy time of it.

After two years, I was transferred to Karaganda where they badly needed medical personnel and I worked in a laboratory.

Until my retirement, I changed my place of work only once, when I was transferred to a children's hospital.

In 1956 I was set free (released from exile), i.e., I could travel again and went for a visit to Leningrad. I also went to Alma-Ata to look for my father's grave but did not find it. Beginning in 1957, I tried to get permission to visit my mother in Germany, but each time my application was rejected. I made five applications up until the time she died in 1965. After 1977 and the Helsinki Agreement, I was given permission to go to Germany for a visit.

In 1948 my son Lev was born. His father was Russian; he had been adopted by a German family of the Volga region and had grown up there. In his passport he was listed as German and had therefore also been exiled to Kazakhstan. Our marriage did not last, partly because we were not permitted to live together. So my son Lev was my responsibility. Eventually he also went to medical school and since 1974 has been working as a medical doctor.

After my retirement I did part-time work in a sanitorium for children. Eventually I was able to exchange my Karaganda residence for one in the city where my son lives and where he had married in 1976. His wife is Russian and is a highway engineer. They have two children: Gherman, born in 1979, and Tatiana, born in 1985.

In July 1988 I went to Germany again for a visit with my cousins. It was also a great joy for me to meet my two nieces from the United States, Irene and Christine.

This I wrote down at the request of my relatives on July 21, 1988.

# Appendix Four

*John L. Stoddard's Lectures. Complete in Ten Volumes.* Volume Six. Boston: Balch Brothers Co., 1898, pp. 312-316.

There is an institution in Moscow which no traveler should fail to visit. It is the Foundling Hospital, into which about thirteen thousand infants are admitted annually. It is said that no cities in the world surpass those of Russia in the comforts provided for outcast children. The Government grants, yearly, a million dollars to this hospital alone; yet there is another nearly as large as this in St. Petersburg. In many cities of Europe, when a child is brought to such an asylum, a bell is rung and the door turns upon a pivot so as to present to the applicant a little table. Upon this the infant is laid. The door then continues its revolution, and the child is wheeled gently within the walls of the hospital never again, perhaps, to be seen by its parents. In this institution, however, there is no such secrecy; for it receives even the children of poor parents, who find it difficult to support them and who give them to the State. No other questions are ever asked than these: "Has the child been baptized?" If so, "By what name?" The infant is then registered on the books of the institution, with a regular number, and a receipt for it is given to the parents of the infant, who may visit and even claim the child at any time within ten years. If I thought I could make a success of it, I would attempt a description of what I saw in this vast hospital. The simple arts of washing and dressing babies are here brought as near to perfection as it is possible for me, at least, to imagine. Suffice it to say, the little foundlings are bathed in copper tubs lined with thick flannel, and then are dressed on soft pillows, instead of on the bony knees or sharp crinoline of the nurses. Yet, notwithstanding these luxuries, at the time of my visit most of the infants cried more unmusically than I ever heard babies cry before; but perhaps it was because they screamed in Russian.

## APPENDIX FIVE

Misha's Story. Excerpts from a taped conversation in 1990 between Misha Vogt and Leo Saal. Translated by Leo Saal.

The night the war started — June 22, 1941 — I had just finished writing my dissertation. It was the time of the "white nights" and I had been up most of the night; it was sunrise when I wrote the last sentence and lay down on the couch. The window was open and I wondered about the constant noise of airplanes, but then fell asleep. When I woke up I went to the other room to tell my wife that my big opus was finished. But she looked at me strangely.

"Misha — it's war!"

I put away my dissertation and left for the Polytechnical Institute. It was Sunday but lots of people were there and, one by one, they were summoned to the Party Committee. When my turn came I was asked to volunteer for the Red Army and explained that I was a reserve officer, that my military specialty in audio measurement was accounted for in the mobilization plan.

On July 7 I was called up and assigned to artillery regiment No. 193 in Toksovo near the Finnish border. But a few days later we were transferred back to Leningrad. There I was assigned to an anti-tank battery. The cannons were brought from military schools and the trucks arrived from collective farms.

I was able to go home and say goodbye to my wife. We parted on Nevskiy Prospekt; I didn't want my wife to come to the barracks which were surrounded by a crowd of crying women. My unit left for Gatchina where we met officers who had come back from the front. They told us that the front was not where the papers reported it to be.

"But you'll see for yourselves."

We took up positions between Luga and Kingisepp in a small forest with an earth bunker. Kirov Military School trainees had taken up a position nearby at a small river.

On August 8 the Germans attacked. Our battery switched positions several times and came under fire. Luckily the shells fell either short or long. But our battery chief got struck by a bullet straight through his heart.

When the Germans broke through, our battery moved from one encirclement to another. We remained without supplies in a small forest. I decided to get out; alone I thought I might make it. A *politruk* — political leader of a small military unit — from an infantry regiment joined me. It was August 13; we had not seen the army kitchen since August 6 and were without food and water.

We came under machine-gun fire, found a hole, lay down flat, and slept. In the morning we were covered with shot-off branches from the bushes above us. The *politruk* decided to surrender and we set out towards the road on which the German columns advanced. Some German soldiers jumped out of a car with pistols drawn. The first German took off the *politruk's* cap and tore off the red star.

"I'll do it myself," I told him in German.

"What else do you have?" the soldier asked.

"400 rubles and binoculars."

"Fine, we can give them to Lieutenant Vogt."

"You don't have to do that — I *am* Lieutenant Vogt," I answered.

Now the German shouted: "He speaks German!" They took me into their car; the *politruk* was told to climb on a tank and I didn't see him again.

The other Lieutenant Vogt could not be found and I was brought, minus binoculars, to a church in Jablonitsa, a POW assembly point.

The next day a German interrogations officer arrived. "Are you a *politruk?*" he asked.

I said no. The officer told me to take off my cap. I had cut my hair short before being called up. "All right," the officer said, "*politruks* have long hair." I said that he couldn't go by that. "I cut my hair because war is a dirty business; one never knows when there is an opportunity to wash one's hair."

"We have orders that *politruks* are to be shot. Are you a deserter?"

"I am an officer and now a prisoner of war."

"Too bad. But for you the war has ended anyway and soon the whole damn business will be over."

"You think so?"

"We count on 12 more weeks."

"You'll be lucky if it's over in a year."

"No, no," the officer replied. "We are not equipped for a winter war." To this I had no answer.

The next morning we were loaded on trucks and driven to Lake Samro where we could bathe. Then we marched on foot to Strugi Krasnyye, were packed into railroad cars, and ended up in Vilna. On the way we didn't get any food — and worse — nothing to drink either.

In Vilna we marched through the entire city. People were standing around shouting at us. "There you have your Bolsheviks! They sure left you in the lurch, didn't they?"

We were marched to Slushkov, an old castle with a moat. Peter the Great had stayed there; later it was a prison, then military barracks, and now it was a small POW camp with only about 5,000 men. For a long time a very thin soup was the only food we got. Since I spoke German I was assigned to the POW hospital which occupied two big halls separate from general quarters. Two Russian doctors, the male nurses, and I had a room for ourselves. Most of the sick prisoners in the halls had dysentery and were in bad shape. Very little could be done for them; not even blankets were available. They died like flies. At 7 p.m. the camp was locked up; those who died during the night were brought into the room where the

wounded were treated during the day. When the German corporal arrived in the morning the dead were carried away and
stacked like wood in the old blacksmith's shop.

I played cards with the doctors while the nurses brought in
the dead bodies. When I arrived in September the food was
atrocious; once I counted 13 peas in the watery soup. Often
there was no bread. Sometimes we got boiled potatoes but
they were not even washed.

It was my responsibility to count the dead; sometimes
there were 60 a day. Once while making rounds I found a
dead body covered with a shirt in a far corner. This was unusual; they always lay there naked. I lifted the shirt and
found out why: cannibalism. I told the men to carry the body
out right away and cover it with another body before anything was found out. In the blacksmith's shop where the bodies were stacked later there were rats, plenty of them, so it did
not matter there.

Each week the bodies from the smithy were loaded on a
wagon and pulled by POWs to a burial ground. Once, when
a wheel broke and bodies fell off, one of the dead spoke. He
was brought back to the doctors; I never knew what happened to him after that.

The Germans in charge of the camp were second reserve
soldiers, old men under the command of a private who told
me: "The more of them die, the better. We can't feed them all
anyway. When typhoid strikes, there will be many more
dead." And so it was.

When typhoid did break out Germans were no longer permitted to enter the camp and I had to report the daily counts
of the dead myself to the German staff.

In October a commission came from Rosenberg's East
Ministry to talk with POWs who had German names. When
I was called in I was stopped approaching the door.

"Do you have lice?" they asked.

"I certainly do."

"Then stay where you are."

The men on the commission were civilians and some spoke very good Russian. Could I prove that I was German?

I said that I might have a cousin in Berlin who could confirm it and he was living in Wilmersdorf when I had written to him in 1920 after the death of my father. A member of the commission told me not to worry; they would find my cousin. Anyway I was a *Volksdeutscher*. One step up on the ladder from being an *Untermensch*, I thought. *Untermenschen* was Nazi lingo for persons of "inferior race," i.e., subhuman.

In December 1941 I was called to the German staff. There was a letter from my cousin confirming what I had told the commission and asking what I needed. Since Soviet POWs had no correspondence privileges, the letter was read to me and I was told to write an answer which they would forward for me.

At that time a Ukrainian camp police of former POWs was organized. They were issued captured uniforms — Belgian, British and French. I was to be their interpreter which would mean a better life for me. But I collapsed, ill with typhoid fever.

I was brought on a sleigh to a Vilna hospital just outside of town, undressed, shaved all over, and put in a bathtub filled with warm water and given soap and a brush. Then, draped in a bed sheet, I was brought to a room where I could lay down on a cot while two men asked me questions. Female nurses came with a stretcher, covered me with blankets, and carried me through a snowy wood. When the wind blew off my covers the nurses put me down in the snow, retrieved the blankets, and covered me again.

Finally I came to a barrack where it was warm; there were beds, even sheets and blankets, and about 40 men with typhoid fever. The nurses were Polish girls; one brought me hot tea. Then I got a terrible headache and didn't know what happened to me during the days which followed. The two camp doctors were also brought in later with typhoid fever. Up to that time there had been no delousing in camp; the delousing station came later. I spent about a month in the hospital and got so weak I couldn't speak normally. I had to learn to speak and walk all over again. But I survived.

By the time I returned to camp there was a new administration, among them an older World War I officer, a captain in the Abwehr, who assigned me to conduct debriefings. The Abwehr staff had other interpreters but they spoke only Polish and even their German was not very good. From then on I worked for Captain Rimsha from the Königsberg *Abwehrstelle* (ASt), the local intelligence station, who sent in the assignments; I sent him back his reports.

One day my captain came in wearing a new medal. "Vogt," he said, "you have earned this one for me." We both laughed. By this time I lived pretty well. I got bread and cigarettes to give prisoners during the debriefings and profited from it too. The real power in camp was the camp police, mostly Ukrainians and pretty rough fellows. They could now fill their bellies from meager POW rations and ran around with sticks; their usual answer to questions from POWs was to hit them with their sticks. The police and kitchen personnel governed camp life; German soldiers kept hands off. The major in charge of the camp, an Austrian, liked geese and had them prepared in the camp's kitchen under German guard.

In February 1942 Lieutenant Colonel Messner took over. He was a decent man and established some order. The number of deaths steadily decreased; in about two months the dying stopped. Messner ordered vegetable gardens established; produce went to the camp kitchen. He also organized workshops. With him I visited the Vileyka Camp not far from Vilna, a big camp with about 150,000 POWs where the death rate had reached 1,000 a day. How many were buried there in the big cemetery no one knew. There was only one cross that had been put up at the request of a POW.

Late in 1942 I accompanied Colonel Messner to Olita where a Ukrainian cavalry unit was being organized. The policy of the big stick reigned there too. Two generals who came to Olita on inspection asked me whether the unit could be trusted to secure railroads.

"Would many of them defect, do you think?," they asked.

"It depends on how much the sticks are used," I answered.

Back in Vilna POWs were beginning to be transferred to Germany for work in industry. After Stalingrad, officers of Vlasov's ROA arrived and Russian newspapers were distributed. ROA officers had visited the camp earlier in 1942 but they were not allowed to do any recruiting then. Now two ROA recruitment officers stayed permanently in camp.

In the summer of 1943 I got four weeks leave. My Berlin cousin was a foreign service officer and had written to the general in charge of POW camps. I was granted leave on condition that I didn't wear either a Soviet or German uniform and was given purchase orders for a civilian suit and shoes. On July 20, 1943, I arrived in Berlin. The curious thing about it was that thirty years earlier to the day — July 20, 1913 — I had come to Berlin with my parents.

My cousin arranged for me to meet an officer from Staff Walli who asked me if I would work for them. I agreed and was brought first to Suleyovek, then to Staff Walli, and now I am here.

# Bibliography

Bitov, Andrey. *Pushkin House.* Farrar, Straus and Giroux, 1987.

Brodsky, Joseph. *Less Than One: Selected Essays.* Farrar, Straus and Giroux, 1986.

Crossman, Richard, ed. *The God That Failed.* New York: Bantam Books, 1965.

Gehlen, Reinhard. *Der Dienst: Erinnerungen 1942-1971.* Mainz-Wiesbaden: Hase & Koehler Verlag, 1971.

Gilbert, Martin. *The Second World War: A Complete History.* New York: Henry Holt & Co., 1989.

Graber, Gerry S. *Stauffenberg.* New York: Ballantine Books Inc., 1973.

Hilger, Gustav and Alfred G. Meyer. *The Incompatible Allies: A Memoir-History of German-Soviet Relations 1918-1941.* New York: The Macmillan Co., 1953.

Hubbard, Leonard E. *Soviet Labour and Industry.* Macmillan and Co., Ltd., 1942.

Ivinskaya, Olga. *A Captive of Time: My Years with Pasternak.* New York: Doubleday & Co., 1978.

*Izvestia.* Issue No. 78, 1965.

*John L. Stoddard's Lectures. Complete in Ten Volumes.* Volume Six. Boston: Balch Brothers Co., 1898.

Keegan, John. *The Second World War.* New York: Viking Penguin, 1990.

Kennan, George F. *Memoirs, 1925-1950.* Boston: Little, Brown and Co., 1967.

——————————. *Russia and the West Under Lenin and Stalin.* New York: Little, Brown & Co., 1960.

Klemperer, Klemens v. *German Resistance Against Hitler: The Search for Allies Abroad, 1938-1945.* Oxford: Clarendon Press, 1992.

Koestler, Arthur. *The God That Failed.* New York: Bantam Books, 1965.

Laqueur, Walter. *Thursday's Child Has Far To Go.* New York: Charles Scribner's Sons, 1992.

Lehndorff, Hans Graf v. *Ostpreussisches Tagebuch: Aufzeichnungen Eines Arztes aus den Jahren 1945-1947.* Munich: Biederstein Verlag, 1961.

Mandelstam, Nadezhda. *Hope Against Hope.* New York: Atheneum, 1970.

Mandelstam, Osip. *The Noise of Time: The Prose of Osip Mandelstam.* San Francisco: North Point Press, 1986.

*Osteuropa.* Sonderdruck. Deutsche Verlags-Anstalt Stuttgart, 1990.

Mazière, Christian de la. *Ashes of Honour.* London: Wyndham Publications Ltd., 1976.

Pasternak, Boris. *Doctor Zhivago.* London: Wm. Collins Sons & Co. Ltd., 1958.

Pushkin, Alexander. *Eugene Onegin.* London: Penguin Books, 1979.

Reed, John. *Ten Days That Shook the World.* New York: Modern Library, 1960.

Reese, Mary Ellen. *General Reinhard Gehlen: The CIA Connection.* Virginia: George Mason University Press, 1990.

Rilke, Rainer Maria. *The Lay of the Love and Death of Cornet Christopher Rilke.* New York: W.W. Norton & Co., Inc., 1959.

Solzhenitsyn, Aleksandr I. *The Gulag Archipelago 1918-1945: An Experiment in Literary Investigation.* New York: Harper & Row, 1974.

——————————. *One Day in the Life of Ivan Denisovich.* New York: Time Inc., 1963.

——————————. *August 1914.* New York: Farrar, Straus and Giroux, 1972.

Sinyavsky, Andrei (Abram Tertz). *Goodnight!* New York: Viking Penguin, 1989.

Stendhal (Marie Henri Beyle). *The Private Diaries of Stendhal.* Robert Sage, ed. and translator. New York: W.W. Norton & Co., 1954.

Sudoplatov, Pavel. *Special Tasks: The Memoirs of an Unwanted Witness — a Soviet Spymaster.* New York: Little, Brown & Co., 1994.

Vassiltchikov, Marie. *Berlin Diaries, 1940-1945.* New York: Vintage Books, 1985.

Walter, Jacob. *The Diary of a Napoleonic Foot Soldier.* New York: Doubleday, 1991.

Weiss, Peter. *Trotsky in Exile.* New York: Atheneum, 1973.

Werth, Alexander. *Russia at War: 1941-1945.* New York: Avon Books, 1964.

Wonlar-Larsky, Nadine. *The Russia That I Loved.* Haywards Heath: Elsie MacSwinney, 1937.